182

ENVIRONMENTAL IMPACT ASSESSMENT

Environmental impact assessment

Edited by
T. O'RIORDAN
R. D. HEY
School of Environmental Sciences,
University of East Anglia

SAXON  HOUSE

Published by
SAXON HOUSE, D.C. Heath Ltd.
Westmead, Farnborough, Hants., England

ISBN 0 347 01141 1
Library of Congress Catalog Card Number 76–12045

Printed in Great Britain by Robert MacLehose & Co. Ltd.
Printers to the University of Glasgow

Contents

List of tables

List of figures

Preface

The idea of comprehensive assessments of the wider (and less easily measured) environmental impacts of proposed policies, governmental regulatory activity and particular development proposals originated with the US National Environmental Policy Act of 1969, especially s. 102(2)(C). NEPA was drafted as an administrative statute in the sense that it requires federal agencies to 'take into account' the wider and longer term consequences of their proposed actions. Following the passage of NEPA on New Year's Day 1970, first a number of American states and subsequently various European nations became interested in transferring some of the principles of NEPA to suit their own political cultures and planning procedures.

Since 1947 the British Government has accepted the view that any development proposal, of whatever scale, must be considered from the viewpoint of the wider public interest. Private ownership in this country is always tempered by social obligations and public duties. In one of its policy notes, the Department of the Environment makes this point plain with respect to modifying applications for planning permission: 'The material question is not whether owners and occupiers of neighbouring properties would suffer financial or other loss, but whether the proposal would affect the locality generally and lead to a change in its character which would be contrary to the public interest.' [1]

So for nearly thirty years, British planning policy has incorporated some notion of environmental assessment. But in practice this has not always been particularly well done, as indicated by the steady increase of public dissatisfaction with existing development control procedures and decisions, a dissatisfaction manifested either by pressure group protest or by impatience with the long delays prior to final decisions on planning applications.

In September 1973 the Secretary of State for the Environment asked George Dobry QC to investigate the development control system and to report. Following extensive consultation with interested parties, he duly presented his findings in two publications. [2] In both he made it clear that he was in favour of much greater public disclosure of the social and environmental consequences of development proposals than is the present case, and advocated the idea of environmental impact assessment for selected cases, partly to ensure that the developer was aware of the wider implications and partly to assist planners, the public, and their elected representatives to make more sensible decisions. As a guide to developers when preparing such assessments, Dobry recommended that they have regard to the effect on six aspects of large scale proposals, namely, traffic, roads and public transportation; ground and surface water drainage; publicly provided services; appearance of the surrounding area; employment; and noise and air pollution. In addition, he suggested that possible environmental hazards and other induced effects be studied, along with some investigation of the merits and disadvantages of alternative sites. All this information, he argued, should be reviewed by interested groups in special 'pre-enquiry' conferences to provide substantive but informal exchanges of views before the proper public enquiry was convened.

In August 1974 the Environment Secretary appointed a two man study team from the Department of the Environment to investigate this matter more thoroughly. [3] Their terms of reference were to consider the desirability of introducing a system of impact analysis in the UK and to suggest how this might be incorporated into the existing development control system. In addition, they were asked to consider the circumstances and kinds of proposals to which EIA should apply and the nature of the appropriate methodology for producing such assessments. In July 1975 the team published an interim report [4] in which they advocated the principle of EIA, but recommended that it only be applied by statute to large scale development proposals associated with complex environmental impacts. The preparation of EIAs would be the responsibility of the developer under the guidance of the local planning authority. The team also suggested that in preparing structure plans the local planning departments collect and assess relevant environmental information which should be of assistance when specific EIAs are considered. Local planning authorities would be expected to work closely with the developers in determining the nature and content of EIA.

All this aroused much interest in the British planning community, so the Department of Environment, through its Planning and Transport Research Advisory Council, decided to hold a symposium on environmental evaluation in September 1975. [5] A large number of papers discussing various methodological aspects of EIA were presented to the symposium, including a public statement by the DoE study team. [6] This does not complete the list of DoE initiatives into EIA, for the Department is currently sponsoring two studies of appropriate methodologies for EIA: one to devise an interdisciplinary framework for environment assessment in structure planning which is being conducted by the Institute of Operations Research at Coventry, the other to develop similar guidelines for large scale development proposals contracted to Brian Clark at the University of Aberdeen.

The IOR study is still in progress, but the Aberdeen study is now complete and part of it appears in Chapter 8. The latter was established largely on the initiative of Mr W. D. Lyddon of the Scottish Development Department, who was keen to ensure that local authorities were furnished with comprehensive guidelines to help them review the second and third order effects of oil-related developments on the Scottish coastline, and to ask the right kinds of questions of the developers from the very beginning. [7]

The DoE response to the whole matter of EIA is not yet known. Clearly during a period of tremendous political pressure to minimise increases in public spending and any additions to central government and local authority staff, there are powerful arguments for delaying the introduction of a mandatory scheme to cover all development control. In his comments on the Dobry report, [8] the Environment Secretary rejected many of the proposals on the grounds of additional costs and lack of administrative expertise. It seems unlikely therefore that he will treat the final report of his study team any more favourably.

This book contains the papers and discussion of a seminar, generously sponsored by the Ford Foundation and convened and chaired by Lord Zuckerman, which was designed to look at some additional aspects of EIA that had not received adequate debate in the DoE initiatives described above. The aim was to bring together a diverse group of people of widely differing views to look at how EIA should fit into the broad process of policy making and decision taking in this country in its twin role as a nation of long traditions and as a new member of the European Economic Community. The spirited debate that ensued raised some interesting questions concerning private and public morality in taking decisions, the proper role of scientists and scientific evidence, the degree to which the general public should be involved and informed, the part played by the law in assisting the public to protect their environmental quality, and above all the relationship between environmental impact assessment, political policy making and the longer term interests of future generations. We hope that the discourse which follows will assist the interested reader to make up his own mind about the desirability of environmental impact assessment, both as a procedure in itself, and as a component of government policy.

In the preparation of this volume we gratefully acknowledge the assistance of Mr L. W. Bear, for producing the excellent transcript of the original discussion, Mrs Gil Booth, for promptly and efficiently dealing with our typing requirements both before and after the seminar, and Mr David Mew, for drawing some of the diagrams.

T. O'Riordan and R. D. Hey
January 1976

Notes

[1] 'Development Control Policy Note', Department of the Environment, London 1969, para. 4.

[2] G. Dobry, *Review of the Development Control System*, interim report, January 1974, final report, February 1975, HMSO, London.

[3] The study team consisted of Mr J. Catlow and Mr C. G. Thirlwell, both employees of the Department of the Environment.

[4] J. Catlow and C. G. Thirlwell, 'Environmental impact analysis study: interim report', Department of the Environment, London, July 1975.

[5] DoE Planning and Transport Research Advisory Council symposium on environmental evaluation, Canterbury, Kent, 25–27 September 1975. See also R. Johnson, 'Environmental impact assessment is on the way', *New Scientist*, 6 November 1975, pp.323–5.

[6] J. Catlow and C. G. Thirlwell, 'Environmental impact assessment', paper to the symposium on environmental evaluation. See note [5].

[7] Scottish Development Department, *Planning Inquiries*, Circular 44/1975, Edinburgh 1975.

[8] Statement by the Secretary of State for the Environment on the report by Mr George Dobry QC on the Review of the Development Control System, HMSO, London, November 1975.

PART I

Introduction

1 Background to environmental impact assessment

LORD ASHBY, FRS

There are various factors which lead to the idea of environmental impact assessment, and a number of reasons why such assessment is considered desirable. The phrase 'environmental impact assessment' comes from s. 102(2)(C) of the National Environmental Policy Act 1969 (NEPA). A proposal to adopt a practice to serve similar ends, i.e. to include an environmental impact analysis in the procedure under the Town and Country Planning Acts, is now being studied by a working group in the Department of the Environment. [1]

The idea of assessing environmental impact and making plans to deal with it may be said to have begun with Noah's Ark and to have a long tradition in the history of prophecy. The recent innovation is that prophets now try to base assessment on scientific evidence rather than on superstition. But it is only recently that this kind of prophecy has been taken seriously. It is less than two decades ago that a distinguished economist felt bound to write: 'Peering into the future is a popular and agreeable pastime which, so long as it is not taken seriously, is comparatively innocuous. But the claim that there is, or can be, a "science of prediction" might easily do more harm than good.' [2] Some rudiments of environmental impact assessment (EIA) are implicit even in early examples of environmental legislation. Thus, Napoleon in 1810 issued a decree which divided noxious occupations into categories: those which must be far removed from habitations, those which may be permitted on the outskirts of towns, and those which can be tolerated even close to habitations, 'having regard to the importance of the work, to the nature and configuration of the soil, and to the importance of the surrounding dwellings.' The characteristic of the modern EIA is that it extrapolates from present scientific knowledge to assess the probable consequences of some human intervention in nature. But although EIA uses the techniques of science, it differs from ordinary scientific enquiry, because it is dealing with events which have not yet occurred, may not

3

occur, and whose chance of occurrence may be changed by the very statement that they may occur. That is why EIA is not just an exercise in probability theory, and hence why it is wise to remain sceptical about the efficacy of EIA, because it does not yet have any sound theoretical basis.

Two social trends lie at the root of the present enthusiasm for EIA. They are:

1   The trend since the early nineteenth century from the politics of interest towards the politics of values. This was evident first in laws to protect human minorities (slaves, children, etc.), and recently in laws to protect the environment generally (in the Town and Country Planning Acts) and other living things, for what appear to be altruistic reasons (as evident in the Conservation of Wild Creatures Bill now in Parliament).

2   The growing belief among people, though most of them cannot rationalise this, that they cannot disengage themselves from the ecological effects of their activities. The symbiotic relationship between man and nature, which is the message of Darwinism, is now permeating social values; not directly, of course, but through a succession of episodes about the environment, publicised by pressure groups and dramatised by the mass media, which demonstrate that human activities can upset equilibria, not only in the local environment but in the global environment. Examples of this are: (a) the accumulation of carbon dioxide (as monitored in Hawaii and the Antarctic) at the rate of about 0·7 ppm per year — an increase of 10 per cent since 1890 due to the combustion of fossil fuels; [3] (b) the evidence for long term accumulations of mercury from the analysis of bird feathers in museums, and of lead from the analysis of mosses in herbaria; [4] and (c) the worldwide distribution of DDT and PVCs. And recently there is the well publicised scare about the possible effects of flurocarbons in aerosols on ozone in the stratosphere. [5] Whether the scare is justified or not is an open question, but there is no doubt that the residence time of aerosol residues is very long. So it is now conceivable that human activities might provoke large and irreversible changes in the biosphere.

EIA, although not under that name, already plays a part in many planning decisions in Britain. For example, in the 1960s the Central Electricity Generating Board was obliged to build a new power station, not on the optimum site for the economics of the power station, but on another site where the annual costs of producing power are at least (at the present value of money) £500,000 more than they would have been on the optimum site. That was the outcome of a planning enquiry at which evidence from the conservationists won the appeal. [6] But to prepare an EIA is not yet an obligatory part of the planning process, either for the siting of works or for the production of new chemicals and materials, unless they are to be used in food or drugs. If EIA had been obligatory, we might have been saved the troubles caused by anionic surface acting agents in hard detergents, and the siting of a carbon-black factory close to human habitation in South Wales. [7]

The question, therefore, is whether EIA should be mandatory in Britain for any activities likely to endanger the environment, as it is already for projects in the United States in which the Federal Government is concerned. Before it is assumed that impact statements similar to those demanded in the USA are desirable in Britain, we have to ask how successful they are in America. Some say that NEPA is an environmental *Magna Carta*; others that it is an interference with free enterprise, and an obstacle to innovation.

The American experience

NEPA was the outcome of a complex network of happenings. First there was a strong tradition for conservation, fostered by groups like the Sierra Club (founded 1892) and the National Audubon Society (1905). More recently there were zealots with a mission (like Rachel Carson) and administrators with vision (like Steward Udall). There were well publicised examples of the lack of foresight in using new technology, which acted as flashpoints to set off a chain reaction in public opinion. In November 1959, for instance, some Wisconsin cranberries were removed from the market because it was found that they had been sprayed with a chemical believed to be carcinogenic. It was this event which stimulated a report from the Science Advisory Committee to President Kennedy in 1963. The politicians then realised that the public conscience was ahead of them, so they lost no time in catching up and taking a lead. There was, for instance, a White House conference on conservation in 1962; and the wave of enthusiasm about public participation in great issues (such as civil rights, medicare and environment) led to powerful and effective lobbies, and ultimately to Henry M. Jackson's Bill S1075 in February 1969.

Following the enactment of NEPA on 1 January 1970, there was a phase of over-reaction to real and imagined environmental hazards. A notorious example was the precipitate legislation in half a dozen states to eliminate the use of phosphates in detergents by early 1973, on the assurance from the manufacturers that sodium nitrilotriacetate (NTA) was a satisfactory substitute. However, it was disclosed that NTA is a chelating agent which could bring heavy metals into solution in drinking water, and that it could lead to the formation of nitrosamines, some of which cause cancer. This episode ended by a directive from the Surgeon General of the United States in September 1971, forbidding the use of NTA in detergents. The phase of over-reaction was followed by a backlash, but the environmental movement in America has now settled down to a steady state and is doing impressive work to protect the environment. After five years it is possible, though still premature, to assess the value of EIA. [8]

In the five years 1970–74 the number of environmental impact statements filed with the Council on Environmental Quality was 6,077. They covered mainly public works: roads, airports, power stations, nature reserves; but they included also statements for pesticides, waste disposal, mining and even weather modification. [9] EIA in America has certain weaknesses. It covers only projects with which the Federal Government has some concern, although twenty-four states now have mini-NEPAs of their own. It works commonly by court action (there have been over 400 law suits) rather than through negotiation and where necessary public ministerial enquiry as in Britain. [10] It obliges developers under s. 102(2)(C) to provide such detailed information that beneficial projects may be held up, yet there is doubt about the credibility of some of the data demanded. Even so, in one law suit (Environmental Defense Fund v. Corps of Engineers) it was decreed that the EIS must discuss 'all known *possible* environmental consequences'. [11]

But EIA in America has scored some successes. It has insisted on public disclosure and this has acted as a powerful educational force to keep up public interest. It has drawn the courts into giving citizens the right to sue even when the threat to the environment does not touch them personally. It has (and this is its most important achievement) compelled planners to take very much greater precautions than they would otherwise have done. Thus, it was recently reported that over forty projects of the Corps of Engineers were held up or banned because the EIS was inadequate. The citizen support for this national movement to protect the environment is evident from the response to two recent bond issues to finance conservation: one in New York for $1·15 billion, and one in Florida for $250 million. [12]

Some provisos about EIA

The second question to be considered is: Is EIA desirable? Obviously any operation which diminishes uncertainty about the future is desirable. So my answer to this question is 'yes', but it is a strictly provisional 'yes'.

The first and most emphatic proviso is that EIA should not be over ambitious. The present is littered with dismal failures of predictions made in the past about the present; indeed, the few successful prophecies have been made by novelists rather than by scientists. Predictability of events plotted against future time follows a sort of inverse square law, and unforeseeable discontinuities are liable to throw out the most sanguine extrapolations. So it is preferable that all EIAs should be labelled 'on the packet' with the reminder that not only are they probabilities, but they are probabilities to which no standard deviation of reliability can be attached.

Second, it is necessary to distinguish the hierarchy of categories of EIAs. The most modest, and therefore the most credible, refer to the first order effects of local projects. If a coalite works is sited on the south-west corner of a town in England, the inhabitants will be more likely to suffer from smoke than if it is sited in an adjoining valley to the north-east side of the town. This might seem obvious, but there are coalite works in Yorkshire which have been mis-sited in just this way. The assessment of simple second order effects for local projects is also credible; for example, the sewage disposal problem which may arise from the housing which would follow from the employment brought by a large new industry. This is happening already on the east coast of Scotland.

It is when one comes to the third order effects and to the application of EIA to nationwide and international problems that the assessment becomes not only more important but more difficult. One example of a third order effect comes from the Aswan Dam on the Nile. It was not foreseen that in the still waters above the dam the snails which carry bilharzia would multiply, causing a serious spread of the disease. Nor was it foreseen that one effect of the dam would be to stop the annual discharge of nutrients into the Mediterranean, with the result that the phyto-plankton population would be starved. This in turn has diminished the sardine fisheries disastrously: the annual catch has fallen from about 18,000 tons to 500 tons.

When the EIA is dealing with a product, such as a new pesticide, which may be exported all over the world, there is a perplexing conflict between the potential benefit of the product and therefore the need to get it manufactured without delay, and the innumerable second and third order effects which might follow its manufacture, and which, if they are all followed up (including the long term effects of low concentrations), would paralyse innovation altogether. Polyvinylchlorides (PVCs) provide a

7

recent example. They have been on the market since 1929. They have great social benefits; for instance,, they must have saved innumerable outbreaks of fire, because one of their virtues is that they do not ignite except at very high temperatures, and are therefore valuable for cooling and insulating electrical equipment. [13]

It was not until 1966 that it was discovered that PVCs get into the food chain and accumulate in fatty tissues in fishes and predatory birds, and that they are now widespread (and will remain so for years) in the biosphere, and can certainly be considered as having damaged the environment. Would any reasonable EIA in 1929 have disclosed this? And even if it had, would public opinion at the time have prompted politicians to restrict its use? And how do you balance lives saved through a diminished fire risk against increased mortality among peregrine falcons? Unfortunately there seems to be no way at present of predicting the dangerous properties of a new chemical from its molecular composition. The Royal Commission on Environmental Pollution did propose that research should be done on the kinds of molecular structure which might have to be regarded as under suspicion and which would therefore need more thorough EIA than *prima facie* harmless substances. Chemicals which are non-biodegradable, or chelating, or fat soluble, would naturally fall under suspicion and might have to be treated as guilty until shown (they could never be *proved*) to be innocent. [14] Nothing dramatic is likely to come from this research, but ultimately it might give useful leads which will enable EIA for new chemicals to be more practicable than at present.

A third proviso is that if EIA is introduced into the planning procedure, it will be applied at a very early stage before options and alternatives are narrowed. If it is applied late in the process, or as an afterthought (as it was for the CEGB power station mentioned earlier) it wastes money and ruffles tempers. Also it is hoped that EIA, if introduced, will not swamp the planning procedure to the detriment of other considerations. The environment is important, but so are industry and employment, and the benefits which some new enterprises bring to society. In a recent review of American policy on air pollution control, Arthur Stern reviews twenty years of federal air pollution control in the United States. One of the things which those in charge of policy 'did wrong' he says, was '. . . to legislate and regulate in such a manner that . . . land use planning has become subsidiary to air pollution control regulations rather than to have air pollution but one of several factors requiring consideration in determining the optimum use of . . . land.' [15]

Some dangers of EIA

A decision to introduce mandatory EIA would raise some important socio-political issues. One of them will be dealt with briefly to illustrate the need for impact assessments of EIA itself. Except in preparation for war, nations do not seem to be capable of adapting their policies in anticipation of an environmental hazard; only in response to it after it has become apparent. This is partly because the hazard is not certain to eventuate, and the average citizen likes to put faith in his good luck, but also because there is a strange and little understood gap between what people believe and how they behave about their belief. Unless we understand this gap and learn how to bridge it, EIA in a democratic country may become little more than a paper exercise; politicians will not be able to restrain pressure for short term benefits at the expense of the long term welfare of the environment.

Here is an illustration of this point. It needs no further impact assessment to know that a common consequence of heavy cigarette smoking is lung cancer (perhaps up to 30,000 deaths a year) and that a common consequence of road traffic in Britain under the present regulations for automobile safety is 7,000 deaths and about 350,000 injuries each year. But these daily environmental hazards elicit no homeostatic response from British society. Cigarettes can still be advertised freely and the nation reaps a tax from the £1,000 million spent on them. Automobile designers can put their efforts into cosmetic styling rather than into safety design. Yet (and this is why the phenomenon is so strange) the same man who regularly pushes up the carboxyhaemoglobin level of his blood to 6 per cent by smoking four or five cigarettes in the evening may advocate draconian measures to cut down the carbon monoxide emissions from car exhausts, although even in a busy street there is rarely enough carbon monoxide to have as much effect on his carboxyhaemoglobin level as the four or five cigarettes have.

What this suggests is the need for research on the subjective risk—benefit attitudes which the public have toward environmental hazards. These attitudes are a function of three main variables: (a) the frequency with which a hazard, or a nuisance, or a disamenity is likely to occur; (b) the number of people who are *simultaneously* affected by the event; and (c) the propinquity of the event. Thus 7,000 people killed over a year is not regarded as a problem calling for urgent national enquiry. But 70 people killed at one moment in a plane crash or a railway accident, provided it is in one's own area, is a terrible tragedy, calling for a public inquiry, the assignment of blame if possible, and legislation to minimise a repetition of the event. Yet the risk of death in an air crash is 0·29 per 100 million passenger miles; and the risk of death in a train accident in Britain is less than 0·1 per 100 million passenger miles. [16]

This apparent digression has a moral for the introduction of EIA; namely, the necessity to educate the public to evaluate the assessments in the rational way that scientists evaluate them. The US Environmental Policy Act lays down that environmental impact statements shall be made available to the public. This disclosure is essential; but accompanying this disclosure there must be education. It is evident from the examples given that subjective risk—benefit attitudes are not rational, yet risk—benefit attitudes constitute the public response, and hence the political response, to environmental impact assessments. If we do not recruit the public participation into the action to be taken when we have got an EIA, we may run into another political peril.

It was Dicey who warned his readers against the collectivist danger that a government might overrule the wish of the people for the good of the people. If EIA, especially with emphasis on its second order effects, is made mandatory for the planning process, we may find that planners are deliberately, albeit with the best of intentions, changing the *norms* of society without reference to Parliament, in ways in which a judge could not change the *laws* of society. This may or may not be a good thing, but it would be dangerous if public opinion were not carried along with the activities of the planners. In other words, it will be essential to have parliamentary scrutiny and surveillance of the institutions entrusted with assessment. Of course the most satisfactory solution to this last problem is for the wish of the people to coincide with the good of the people. We may never reach this utopian state, but the road towards it is through education in the scientific attitude; and the assessment of environmental impacts will depend on the capacity of politicians and the public to evaluate probabilities in a rational way.

Discussion

Because environmental impact assessment is a relatively unfamiliar concept in Britain, and since there is already a fairly sophisticated, and somewhat envied, planning machinery in the UK, a number of participants were doubtful that the American experience could be transferred to British institutions and accustomed practices. *Biggs* (Confederation of British Industries), for example, pointed out that as a result of the recent reorganisation of local government and the water authorities, plus the advent of recent legislation in the area of industrial health and safety [17] and pollution control, [18] it would be inadvisable to establish a new body which might undermine the promising progress to date, despite the fact that most of these organisations and much of this legislation deal with events that are short term in nature. He added that the CBI would be unhappy if local councils were to be granted new and mandatory powers which might undermine the existing largely successful practices of consultation and voluntary compliance in the licensing and enforcement of pollution control. The present system, in his view, already embodies many of the principles of EIA and works well. [19]

Train (Cremer and Warner) endorsed these views, stressing that the strengths of British legislative procedures lie in their ability to find a reasonable balance between the various views of interest groups by means of consultation and the weighing of evidence. There is always the potential danger that EIA would upset this balance, particularly where public issues of a non-technological nature are involved.

Davis (Anglian Water Authority) was anxious to clarify the distinction between prediction and assessment. The fact that a problem could be anticipated did not preclude it from occurring. Far too frequently, he maintained, authorities are forced to act after an event because it is extremely difficult to justify the expenditure of money on some of the wider aspects of a decision before it is made. Thus water authorities have to remind local councils of the expenditures necessary for sewage treatment plants before they authorise a new housing scheme. In fact he was very doubtful if the water authorities had the finances or the statutory powers to undertake EIAs, particularly at the regional level. The principal duties of the authorities are to provide a satisfactory water service and safeguard the public health; in his view, these presumably override all other considerations. In any case, the regional water authorities are saddled with a debt of well over £3,000 million, so EIA might well prove to be a luxury they could not afford.

The question of the appropriate scope of the EIA aroused much interest. *Lord Zuckerman* was concerned that the amount of scientific material simply in the realm of technological assessment was astoundingly vast and often controversial, while the complicated procedures for reviewing the environmental effects of new products all but stopped their manufacture. Was there any end to this? *Shaw* (Norfolk County Council) was concerned that EIA could become too narrowly focused on physical and ecological repercussions when the major spheres of interest for planners were social and economic, especially when talking about the wider effects of planning decisions. He also remarked that it would be

11

inadvisable to concentrate EIA on large scale capital projects, because these are few and far between. The major problems that planners have to face at present are the incremental cumulative effects of small scale change, both on the landscape and on populations. He felt that there was a tremendous need for some form of systematic monitoring mechanism to analyse these aggregative effects, but remained sceptical that EIA as presently proposed would do the job.

Lord Zuckerman took up the point about the difficulties of assessing environmental impact. He noted that the carbon-black plant was built soon after the war when there was a dire need for the product. At that time there were no protests about the plant; only when society becomes more affluent (or more influenced by media coverage) does it react to certain environmental effects that were once tolerated. *Davis* was concerned about the way in which information is presented to the public. Sometimes a decision may be delayed if too much information is released, as this can add to the existing confusion.

Both *Lord Ashby* and *Meyers* (US Environmental Protection Agency) disagreed with this view. The public is quite capable of understanding issues if they are properly informed — the problem is to arouse their interest in matters that may not, on the face of it, appear terribly important. Regular liaison between local authorities and the press regarding the nature of the problems they face and the proposals they are contemplating would be of great help. Meyers was a strong advocate of public disclosure. He felt that EIA should be published as a document that any intelligent person should be able to understand, and hence respond to, via his political representatives. In fact the openness aspect of EIA is now so popular in the States that people are thinking about inflation impact statements and economic impact statements (both looking at second and third order effects on the economy in general) to justify expenditures before decisions are made.

Meyers also commented that NEPA covers more than federal financing; it applies to federal licensing, permit granting and the allocation of grants and contracts. Because private industry requires federal authorisation for so many things (licensing of nuclear power plants, permits for effluent disposal), much of its activities are subject to environmental impact statements. These generally refer to aspects of decisions that are not normally assessed. Technical information that is relevant to project design and construction will obviously be well detailed, but that is essential to the completion of the project. The wider ramifications on the surrounding environment and people, however, are not generally of such interest to the developer. NEPA simply makes sure that this kind of information is gathered at the most important time – the conceptual design stage.

But despite reservations about the power of the courts, Meyers emphasised that the courts only ensured that the procedural requirements of NEPA were followed and that the impact statements were as complete as possible. The American EIS does not force a decision; it merely helps to ensure that a project is designed and constructed in a manner that reflects environmental considerations (e.g. the trans-Alaskan pipeline). It does not and cannot expect that there will be no residual damage. So long as there are other good reasons for a decision, one can proceed. Thus EIA is merely part of the process of political judgement.

Hookway (Countryside Commission) questioned Lord Ashby on his remarks about planners altering societal norms, since they should remain accountable to local politicians and to Parliament. *Lord Ashby* replied that it is part of the British tradition to grant environmental protection officers, including planners and pollution control personnel, the discretion and authority to make political decisions. When the Alkali Inspectorate inspect a factory, they take into account not simply its polluting emissions, but the state of the firm, its finances, the morale of the employees and the general effect of causing it to spend money on abatement – and all this is quite independent of the degree of abatement expected of a more efficient and profitable factory nearby. The British custom is pragmatic and humanitarian, and decisions tend to be made on the merits of the case in question. [20] European practice, on the other hand, is more uniform – similar treatment for all. Because British tradition leaves many environmental decisions to civil servants, it could be dangerous if EIA legislation granted these people *de facto* political powers without the necessary parliamentary surveillance.

Notes

[1]   See J. Catlow and C. G. Thirlwell, op.cit.

[2]   J. Jewkes, D. Sawers and R. Stillerman, *The Sources of Invention*, Macmillan, London 1958, p.225.

[3]   F. S. Johnson, 'The oxygen and carbon dioxide balance in the earth's atmosphere' in F. S. Singer (ed.), *Global Effects of Environmental Pollution*, Dordrecht, Holland 1970, pp.4–11.

[4]   B. Lundholm, 'Interactions between oceans and terrestrial systems' in F. S. Singer, op.cit., pp.194–201.

[5]   See for example the review in *New Scientist*, 2 October 1975, pp.7–18.

[6]   See R. Gregory, *The Price of Amenity,* Macmillan, London 1971, p.114.

[7]   See J. Bugler, *Polluting Britain: A Report,* Penguin Books, London 1972, pp.3–8.

[8]   See the various *Annual Reports* of the Council on Environmental Quality published by the Government Printing Office, Washington D.C., e.g. 1972, pp.221–60; 1973, pp.234–51; 1974, pp.371–421. Also E. S. Mills and F. S. Peterson, 'Environmental quality: the first five years', *American Economic Review*, vol. 65, 1975, pp.259–68.

[9]   Council on Environmental Quality, *Fourth Annual Report*, Government Printing Office, Washington D.C. 1973, p.237.

[10]   Ibid., p.237.

[11]   Council on Environmental Quality, *Third Annual Report*, Government Printing Office, Washington D.C. 1972, p.242 (italics added).

[12]   Ibid., p.251.

[13]   Evidence of the fire suppression qualities of PVC can be gained from their fire risk ratings for insurance purposes compared to other liquids. If petrol has a rating of 100, kerosene would have one of 40, mineral oil 20 and PVCs 3. See the report of the Interdepartmental Task Force, 'Polychlorinated biphenyls and the environment', Government Printing Office, Washington D.C. 1972, p.12.

[14]   Royal Commission on Environmental Pollution (Sir Eric Ashby, Chairman), *Second Report: Three Issues in Industrial Pollution*, Cmnd 4894, HMSO, London 1972. See also *Proceedings of the Royal Society*, vol. B.185, 1974, pp.125–224.

[15]   A. C. Stern, 'Air pollution control: a perspective', *Journal of the Air Pollution Control Association*, vol. 25, 1975, pp.681–4.

[16]   C. Sinclair, 'The incorporation of health and welfare risks into technological forecasting', *Research Policy*, vol. 1, 1971, pp.31–58.

[17]   Health and Safety at Work Act, 1974.

[18]   Control of Pollution Act, 1974.

[19]   The nature of the relationship between waste discharges and the pollution control inspectorate is a controversial matter. See J. Tinker, 'Britain's environment: nanny knows best', *New Scientist*, 9 March 1972, pp.530–4, and 'The Midlands dirty dozen', *New Scientist*, 6 March 1975, pp.551–3. Also J. Bugler, op.cit., especially pp.3–31, 111–29, and the Fifth Report of the Royal Commission on Environmental Pollution, *Air Pollution Control: An Integrated Approach.* HMSO, London 1976.

[20]   The Royal Commission on Environmental Pollution, see note [19], endorses the view that pollution control should be based on the merits of each case and the nature of local circumstances. The Alkali

Inspectorate are charged with ensuring that industry uses the 'best practicable means' (BPM) to reduce noxious emissions. Referring to noise, the Control of Pollution Act 1974 states that 'practicable' means 'reasonably practicable having regard among other things to local conditions and circumstances, to the current state of technical knowledge and to the financial implications.'

PART II

Current experience

2 Assessment of the environmental impact of nuclear power [1]

G. H. KINCHIN

Environmental impact of such a diverse undertaking as nuclear power has many aspects. To some people the main environmental impact of a reactor or factory may be that the view is spoiled, and this could be a justified complaint for those who live within visual range, perhaps less justifiable in other cases. To other people the main impact may be in the pay packet, for an employment-giving factory may be a most welcome addition to the environment of man. Still others think of the environment as untouched nature in danger of pollution by waste substances and waste heat discharged into it. Others may see a threat in the potential for accidental release of radio-iodine from thermal reactors and of plutonium from fast reactors and fuel processing plants. The questions one may ask include, 'How may all these, and doubtless other, aspects of the environmental impact problem be taken fully into account in an ideal system?' or – depending on one's temperament and one's avocation – 'How in practice, now and in the future, can environmental impact problems be dealt with in the United Kingdom?'.

First, some idea will be given of the nuclear power programme, before considering its impact. In 1974, nuclear power contributed about 12 per cent of the total electricity generated in the United Kingdom (3·6 per cent of UK total energy requirements). Nuclear stations so far are used as base load stations, the older, less efficient of the fossil-fuelled stations being stood down during off-peak periods, so that at present only some 7 per cent of installed electrical power is nuclear. Estimates of the future rate of increase of installed electrical power depend on assumptions made about trends in the economy and the success of energy conservation. A current illustrative programme for the United Kingdom predicts an increase in installed electrical capacity from the present level of 70 GW(e) to about 100 GW(e) in 1985, and about 200 GW(e) in the year 2000. On the basis of this programme the contribution of installed nuclear power is predicted to rise as shown in Table 2.1.

Table 2.1

Predicted increase in installed electrical capacity,
conventional and nuclear, to the year 2000

Year	Total installed power GW(e)	Nuclear installed power GW(e)	Nuclear installed power (per cent of total)
1975	70	5	7
1985	100	15	15
2000	200	100	50

The earliest nuclear power stations in the UK installed in about 1960 had a capacity for a two or four reactor station in the range 100–500 MW(e). Present day two reactor stations have an installed design capacity around 1,300 MW(e) and frequently four reactors can be accommodated on one site. So perhaps 30–40 such nuclear reactor sites, or their equivalent, are likely to be in operation by the year 2000.

Most uranium ores in use today contain 0·1–0·3 per cent by weight of uranium, and the limited nature of world supplies of this grade of ore will become increasingly apparent between now and the year 2000. However, the utilisation of uranium for producing electricity could be increased about 50-fold, and the coming shortage of uranium could be circumvented, if fast reactors could be brought into service during the intervening period. Opinions vary about the contribution that these fast breeder reactors will be able to make to installed nuclear capacity by the end of the century, but the most optimistic forecast predicts it will be about one third. (While thermal neutron reactors 'burn' the U 235 isotope and a small amount of Pu 239 created by neutron capture in U 238, fast neutron reactors 'burn' plutonium 239 and matters can be arranged so that the fast reactor creates or 'breeds' more Pu 239 from U 238 than it 'burns'. The overall effect broadly is to increase reserves of uranium from a usable 0·7 per cent uranium – i.e., the U 235 isotope – to something of the order of 60 per cent uranium; that is why there is intense interest in fast breeder reactors for the future.

At present there are no deposits of uranium ore in the United Kingdom which it would be economical to mine. All our requirements so far have been imported, and the mining and milling of uranium ore has been carried on abroad. This state of affairs is unlikely to change in the foreseeable future. The fuel requirements of all UK operating reactors are at present satisfied by the equivalent of just over 1,000 tonnes of imported uranium ore concentrates. Several processes lie between the arrival of ore concentrate at our ports and the delivery of finished new fuel to the reactor. These and other processes are essential components of the nuclear complex, carried on in factories, and therefore, in principle, part cause of the environmental impact of the 'nuclear fuel cycle' or 'nuclear power complex'.

In the United Kingdom the initial chemical treatment of uranium and its formation into metal rods or uranium dioxide pellets and their enclosure in metal sleeves or cans, is carried out in a factory at Springfields between Preston and Blackpool in Lancashire. Isotopic enrichment of U 235 in uranium is produced by gaseous diffusion of uranium hexafluoride in a factory at Capenhurst, near Chester. The Springfields and Capenhurst factories are owned and operated by British Nuclear Fuels Ltd (BNFL). The third fuel factory owned and operated by BNFL is at Windscale, near Whitehaven on the Cumbrian coast. At this site, among other operations, uranium and plutonium are separated chemically from the spent fuel received from nuclear reactor sites, and the fission product activity is separated and concentrated in solution and stored. This summary of the nuclear complex, still in part in a developmental stage, should include the research and development stations of the United Kingdom Atomic Energy Authority (UKAEA). The main seat of basic nuclear research is AERE at Harwell, just south of Oxford. The research establishment, AEE Winfrith in Dorset, contains, as well as research laboratories, the prototype steam generating heavy water reactor (SGHWR), at 100 MW(e) a sizeable power producer in its own right. The UKAEA establishment at DERE Dounreay contains the Dounreay fast reactor which has been in operation for a decade, partly as a power producer, but mainly as a testbed for fast reactor fuel. The latter is the type of fuel used in the core of the much larger prototype fast reactor, also at Dounreay and designed to produce 250 MW(e). Dounreay also houses chemical reprocessing and other plants.

Principles and practice of siting

The United Kingdom is so densely populated, so much of its countryside is protected as 'green belt' country, area of outstanding natural beauty or national park, and the engineering requirements (foundations, availability of cooling water etc.) of nuclear power plants are sufficiently restrictive, that the electricity generating boards and government ministries and agencies have to think very hard, consider many aspects and consult many people, before a site for a nuclear plant is chosen.

It may be that the United States, having a far greater land area per head of population and different governmental processes, has arrived at a similar state of affairs later by a different route. Until the late 1960s, reactor site licences in the USA were issued by the Licensing and Regulatory Division of the United States Atomic Energy Commission on the basis of an exclusion radius and the distance to the nearest population centre, which were calculated according to certain rules reflecting the assumed risk that an accident might release noble gas fission products and radio-iodine into the atmosphere. Then the Calvert Cliffs' legal decision [2] over a certain site on the eastern coast changed all that, by insisting that other aspects of the environmental impact should be considered — not only the radioactive impact, but thermal and other non-radioactive considerations. Also, with the passage of the National Environmental Policy Act (NEPA) of 1969, power plant site selection procedures underwent extensive change, and decisions which historically had been made by electric utility managers were henceforth placed in the public arena. As a result, the scope and emphasis placed on site selection studies have been greatly expanded. The electric utility in the USA is now required to consider not only the desired site, but all other feasible sites within the geographical area covered by its operations; and for each site the many relevant environmental factors have to be considered. The utilities and their consultants have in many cases brought into use formal semi-mathematical criteria for listing and sorting the relative merits of sites, and even mathematical decision theory has been advocated by some organisations as a tool for deciding between sites each of which has many attributes. The following lists of topics taken from a recent paper from the planning organisation of a group of utilities serving the Pacific North West indicates the breadth of the study required.

Site development criteria

    (a)   Water supply — its availability, portability, etc;
    (b)   Waste heat dissipation — once-through or cooling towers, etc;
    (c)   Meteorology — inversion frequency, wind direction rose, etc;
    (d)   Site area — for the plant and for the exclusion zone;
    (e)   Land acquisition — availability, zoning restrictions, etc;
    (f)   Topography — economics of location, flood hazards, etc;
    (g)   Geology — foundations, sources of building materials, etc;
    (h)   Seismology — earthquake safety;
    (i)   Other catastrophic phenomena — storms, floods, landslides, etc;

(j)   Access – i.e., for major reactor components;

(k)   Transmission – load loss, etc.

Some of the topics mentioned above were involved in an initial rough cut process, and may occur again in what follows.

Environmental criteria

(a)   Water quality – effect of cooling water on aquatic ecosystems;

(b)   Population – numbers of people at various distances from reactor;

(c)   Land use – i.e., wilderness, recreation area, scenic beauty, etc;

(d)   Public safety and acceptance.

Economic criteria

(a)   Cost of engineered safeguards compensating for a less than optimum site;

(b)   Cost of cooling water supply, pipelines, pumping;

(c)   Land acquisition costs;

(d)   Site preparation costs;

(e)   Foundation costs;

(f)   Materials transportation costs;

(g)   Transmission costs.

In a country as large as the United States, the number of apparently possible sites is so great that initial sifting techniques are usually employed so that detailed statements about all sites are not in fact required, many sites being rejected because of obvious points of unsuitability. For example, a regional site survey for thermal (fossil or nuclear) plant sites made recently in the State of Ohio, involved a systematic survey of the whole state in order to identify candidate regions. There were 107 such regions of 64 square miles each which were identified primarily on the basis of hydrology and demography, and the best 51 of these were selected for further study. This further study, assisted by numerical scoring methods to evaluate the combined merit of attributes such as those mentioned above led to the selection of just three sites. Once the options were obtained on one of the top candidate sites, the field investigations began. Thus recommendations on purchase of the sites could be made with a high degree of confidence.

At this point one tends to reflect that there is nothing essentially very new in all this. We have heard or read it all before in the nuclear power industry in England. The United Kingdom's legal and governmental structure may be different but the end result is much the same — all the above factors are considered and where the responsible minister feels it necessary a public enquiry is held. In all cases, licences and authorisations have to be issued by the relevant government department or ministry. Similar arrangements exist in most other European countries.

Of course, long before this stage is reached, the Electricity Board will have considered its future requirement of power stations and the regions where power is required. Because no river in England or Wales has a sufficient dry weather flow for the direct cooling of a major power station, coastal sites are sought or recourse has to be had to cooling towers. The great weight of the reactor usually imposes limitations even though foundation designs have evolved to cover a variety of subsoil conditions.

Major restraints on development are occasioned by presence of: (a) national parks; (b) areas of outstanding natural beauty; (c) areas of high landscape value; (d) green belts, approved by the Minister or under consideration; (e) land over, say, 800 ft above sea level; (f) forest parks; (g) national nature reserves; and (h) built-up, urbanised areas. With reference to item (h) population numbers and distribution to a distance of many miles around the site have to fall within curves laid down by the Nuclear Installations Inspectorate. These help to identify the population distribution minima desirable for reasons of population safety in the event of an accident. Topography, local communications, population mobility and other special features have to be evaluated for their probable effect on any emergency measures necessary if an accident occurred. Taking all these factors into account greatly restricts the choice for new reactor sites. Having identified a possible site, the Board is then obliged, under the Electricity Acts, to obtain the consent of the appropriate minister. Such consent is only given following receipt of the views of the local planning authority and opportunity is given for other organisations and the general public to register objections. If the local planning authority objects or if the minister considers that other objections are sufficient to warrant it, a public inquiry is held at which the Board has to produce evidence to justify its proposal and is subject to cross examination by objectors. The minister comes to a decision after considering a report from the inspectors who conducted the enquiry. It was under these arrangements, to take one example, that a proposed nuclear power site at Connor's Quay, Flintshire, which the Electricity Board considered technically suitable, was rejected after a public inquiry had been held in 1971. About that time the minister refused consent for a nuclear power station at Stourport on the River Severn. On the other hand, ten reactor sites are in use by the CEGB in England and Wales and one by the SSEB in Scotland; these are in addition to the nuclear sites operated by the UKAEA and BNFL.

Discharges of radioactivity to the environment

Gaseous

External radiation is the main hazard. At present, discharges to atmosphere from power reactors and reprocessing plants contribute about one-tenth the total UK population exposure from nuclear power waste operations. In gas cooled reactors continuous filtration and monitoring of carbon dioxide cooling gas ensures that occasional controlled releases to atmosphere (blowdown) and any natural leakage from the pressure circuit contain only small amounts of particulate and gaseous activity. For reactors with steel pressure vessels, cooling air is forced between the pressure vessel and the concrete biological shield, and argon a natural constituent of the air becomes activated by neutrons to form the short lived argon—41 which is discharged to atmosphere. The air is filtered before discharge to remove any radioactive particles taken up.

In heavy water reactors, control of tritium releases to safe levels is necessary.

The main discharges to atmosphere from fuel reprocessing plants are long lived gases, particularly krypton—85 and tritium, released after dissolution of fuel. Radionuclides of shorter half life such as iodine—131 decay to insignificant levels during the cooling period before reprocessing. The longer lived iodine isotope, iodine—129, although of no radiological importance at present will have to be considered as a long term source of population exposure.

Liquid

In coming to a decision on how much can be permitted to be discharged, an assessment is made of all the complex routes or pathways by which the discharged material may come into contact with man. The pathway which would result in the highest exposure to the public is determined, and the estimated ability of the environment to accept the waste safely is based on this pathway combined with the internationally accepted dose limits. This involves scientific studies of the dietary, occupational and domestic habits, age structure and recreational activities of the relevant population. Foodstuffs considered include milk, laver bread made from seaweed collected on the coast near Windscale, oysters near Bradwell in Essex, crabs and lobsters near Winfrith in Dorset, and trout from the lake at Trawsfynydd in Wales. Drinking water derived from the River Thames is sampled. In some cases external radiation is considered, e.g. from sludge on fishermen's nets near Dounreay in Scotland or sediment on the sea shore.

From Magnox power stations the main liquid radioactive effluents discharged to the aqueous environment are the neutralised regenerant liquors from the ion exchange plants associated with the irradiated fuel storage ponds, and the tritiated liquors from the carbon dioxide coolant gas driers. The very large initial dilution achieved by mixing with discharged condenser cooling water as it leaves the station ensures that even before it reaches the environment, the average concentration of radioactivity in this water is below permitted drinking water levels.

The greatest amounts of radioactivity discharged to the aqueous environment in the UK come from irradiated fuel reprocessing plants; discharges of large volumes of low level effluent are made to coastal waters at Windscale and Dounreay. These discharges contain longer lived fission products and heavy elements and include water from fuel element cooling ponds, evaporator distillates, gas scrubbing liquors and laundry wastes as well as the least active effluents from the solvent extraction process.

Discharges of low level liquid effluent are made from research establishments in the South of England to the River Thames and to coastal waters.

Solid

All highly active wastes are stored pending decisions on the desirability of further treatment, improved storage or ultimate disposal. Controlled burial of low level solid waste is authorised at the BNFL site at Drigg in Cumbria, the Authority site at Dounreay and at a quarry in Lancashire. The authorisations specify the types of radioactive material and specific activities in waste. Some miscellaneous waste, of low activity but not meeting the criteria for burial, is disposed of after concreting in sealed drums by dumping in specified areas of the Atlantic deeps; the operation is approved by the Ministry of Agriculture, Fisheries and Food and in recent years has been carried out under the auspices of the Nuclear Energy Agency of OECD. Because of the low levels of activity and the large environmental capacity no marine monitoring programme has been required.

Transport operations

Transport of radioactive materials including new and irradiated nuclear fuel is carried out under government regulations and within the framework of standards recommended by the International Atomic Energy Agency. Proper packaging and adherence to conditions of carriage ensure that radiation exposure of transport operators and public is negligible compared with exposure from other sources in the industry.

Thermal effects

In the UK nuclear power stations are, with one exception, located on the coast, where ample supplies of cooling water are available. Optimisation of the positions of the intake and outfall of the cooling system have been based on studies of mass water movements and rates of mixing leading to estimates of the spread and recirculation of heated discharges. The biological and chemical consequences of discharging warm water have been extensively studied by the generating boards and ecological research over many years has confirmed that there are virtually no adverse thermal effects from power stations, including the particularly sensitive oyster fisheries in the vicinity of the Bradwell nuclear station.

Indeed, the warm water discharges are of positive benefit to the growing interest in commercial fish farming; the White Fish Authority's fish farming project on a site adjoining the nuclear power station at Hunterston is particularly worthy of note.

Statutory control

Having indicated some of the possible environmental effects, it would be wrong to leave the topic without at least a summary of the extensive statutory controls which apply to the effects of possible significance. The principal statutory instruments which control the environmental aspects of nuclear power are the Radioactive Substances Acts of 1948 and 1960, the Nuclear Installation Acts of 1965 and 1969, and various regulations relating to the transport of radioactive materials. Under the Radioactive Substances Act the disposal and storage of radioactive wastes is governed by the Secretary of State for the Environment and the Minister of Agriculture, Fisheries and Food (in Scotland by the Scottish Development Department). The Act requires registration of persons storing or using radioactive materials and makes it an offence either to dispose of non-exempted wastes without authorisation or to exceed an authorisation. The authorising departments consult with local authorities, and follow principles laid down in a Government White Paper of 1959. These limit radiation exposure of individuals from waste disposal to the dose limits recommended by the International Commission on Radiological Protection (ICRP), and impose an average limit of 1 rad per 30 years for the total population of the country. Furthermore one is required to do what is reasonably practicable, having regard to cost, convenience and the national importance of the subject, to reduce doses far below these limits.

The Health and Safety Executive (created in 1975 under the Health and Safety at Work Act) is responsible for the licensing of nuclear sites under the provisions of the Nuclear Installations Acts, but the Secretary of State for Energy (in England and Wales) or the Secretary of State for Scotland retain an overall responsibility for nuclear safety. Detailed licensing procedures and inspection under the licence are carried out by the Health and Safety Executive's Nuclear Installations Inspectorate. Regulations covering transport of radioactive materials have also been made under relevant Acts of Parliament.

Radioactive discharges from the major nuclear sites of the UKAEA, BNFL and the electricity generating boards are controlled by authorisations issued by government departments — in England and Wales jointly by the Department of the Environment and the Ministry of Agriculture, Fisheries and Food, and in Scotland by the Scottish Development Department. Studies of the pathways by which discharged material can come into contact with man give an upper limit for the proposed discharge, but the authorisation is normally limited to a lower amount depending on the demonstrable need for the discharge and on the best practicable means for reducing it. For discharges of liquid effluent to sea or to fresh water, the authorisation specifies the limits of radioactivity permitted, usually as total activity with further restrictions for specific radionuclides or groups of radionuclides. For airborne releases the authorisation requires the best practicable means for reducing the discharge. For each discharge of liquid or airborne effluent the authorisation requires that samples be taken at discharge points and in the environment in order to confirm that specified limits are being observed and that exposure to the public is being kept at acceptable levels. The departments also carry out independent environmental monitoring checks.

Radiation exposure to the population in their environment

Two groups of people must be considered when assessing the radiological impact of waste discharges:

(a)   Individuals or small groups in the population, usually (but not always) local to the nuclear site who, because of potential somatic risks, are limited to one tenth of the dose permitted by ICRP for those occupationally exposed; and

(b)   the population at large for whom genetic considerations limit permissible average exposure to a lower level.

Authorisations limiting the discharge of radioactive materials to the environment have ensured that no member of the public has been exposed to levels exceeding the relevant individual ICRP dose limits. Indeed, published assessments made independently of the industry by authorising government departments show that from only three discharges − to sea from Windscale (7 per cent), and Dounreay (4 per cent) and to the lake from Trawsfynydd (6 per cent) − have exposures of individuals or groups in 1972−73 exceeded 1 per cent of the dose limit. The latest report of the Ministry of Agriculture, Fisheries and Food on radioactivity in surface and coastal waters (for 1972−73) concludes that, as a consequence of the stringent standards set, not only are the exacting requirements of the ICRP recommendations met but, in all disposals, radiation exposure to the public is well within the prescribed dose limits and in many instances is very much less.

The estimated present average radiation dose to the UK population as a whole from all forms of waste discharged from worldwide nuclear power programmes including that of the UK (see Table 2.2) is less than a hundredth part of the limit of 1 rem/30 years imposed in the UK, and not much more than a thousandth part of the average background level from natural sources. Indeed, it is similar to that which would be added if the population of a single provincial English city were moved from England to Wales where the natural background level is higher.

Present and future environmental impact of nuclear power

Table 2.2 shows the relative contributions to the present genetically significant radiation exposure to the UK population.

Looking ahead to the predicted expansion of the nuclear power industry, it is anticipated that, even if there were no changes in the

Table 2.2

Relative contributions to the present genetically significant
radiation exposure to the UK population

Source	Annual genetically significant dose	
	(mrad y^{-1})	%
Natural background	87	83·7
Man made environmental		
Fall out	2·2	2·1
Nuclear power (waste)	0·1	0·1
Miscellaneous sources	0·3	0·3
Medical irradiation	14	13·5
Occupational exposure		
Nuclear industry	0·15	0·15
Other occupational groups	0·25	0·25

Based on material published by National Radiological Protection Board
and the Ministry of Agriculture, Fisheries and Food.

principles or procedures for dealing with waste discharges, by the end of
the century average exposure to the UK population (predicted to be $\approx 10^4$
man rems) would still be less than 1 per cent of the level recommended in
the 1959 White Paper on the Control of Radioactive Substances, and not
much more than 0·1 per cent of the natural background level. Although
technology already exists to reduce the levels of some discharges and
current research is aimed at solving some of the outstanding problems,
adoption of new control procedures must depend on an analysis of the
cost and benefit of so doing. In taking such decisions, and bearing in mind
that effort and money for reducing very small risks cannot be unlimited,
certain things must not be overlooked. One is that it would not make
sense for the introduction of new processes, with the aim of reducing
population exposure, to be at the expense of an increase in the exposure
of those working in the industry for whom both the average individual
exposure and the collective dose is already far higher than for the rest of
the population. Another is that, as in any country a proportion of the
population exposure comes from plant in other countries, there is an
incentive to consider international or regional controls rather than purely
national ones.

Discussion

In view of recent press publicity concerning proposals by British Nuclear Fuels Ltd to reprocess the nuclear wastes of Japanese power stations, *Woolf* (Lawyers Ecology Group) was concerned that the whole business was contingent upon a technology of post-processed waste vitrification that was still to be developed. Clearly there had been no environmental impact assessment, for it was still possible that the British nuclear industry could be saddling itself with something that might permanently damage the environment. *Kinchin* (Atomic Energy Authority) replied that vitrification was merely a more convenient method of storage, and that adequate (although admittedly not totally desirable) arrangements for storing wastes in liquid form already exist. The issue, he felt, was more one of economy than safety, for the double walled tanks with cooling coils which hold the waste at present are expensive to construct and maintain. (He later maintained, however, that this cost is relatively small compared to the total costs of the plant.)

Johnson (Commission of the European Communities) was more concerned about generic issues associated with nuclear plants generally, not individual cases. The public inquiry does not cover broad matters of policy such as the desirability of nuclear generation, or the criteria for site selection, so the public has only the opportunity to comment within a limited frame of reference. Thus the really important political questions and associated technical considerations are not properly debated. EIA would not necessarily redress this weakness. *Meyers* (US Environmental Protection Agency) commented that in a sense the American EIS does cover some of this ground, since the US Environmental Protection Agency works with the Nuclear Regulatory Commission to develop a broad policy in relation to such matters as overall safety and transportation. This results in a series of umbrella briefs which do not affect the siting of particular plants, so the EIA is confined to the merits of each specific case. He was quite satisfied that there was an orderly method to the NEPA requirements, even though many citizen groups remain dissatisfied with the rate of progress.

Kinchin was anxious to emphasise that, to a degree, environmental assessment already takes place in the UK. For example, where waste disposal from a nuclear installation could produce an adverse effect (where there were oysters in the vicinity for instance), there would be a detailed investigation. But he agreed that the broader generic issues were not subject to special study and were properly the prerogative of Parliament. *Searle* (Earth Resources Research) thought that in this particular instance Parliament had not performed this vital function properly, for there has been virtually no opportunity for MPs to review the British nuclear programme.

The policy of siting plants far from centres of population concerned *Brooks* (Liverpool), partly because this meant that power stations were often situated in high amenity areas, and partly because he felt that insufficient consideration might have been given to the beneficial value of the waste heat from such stations. Because this waste heat is dissipated fairly rapidly over distance, proximity to urban sites would be of considerable economic advantage. This is already occurring in Sweden, but when he had suggested that it might be feasible around the Dee estuary, the local newspaper refused to publish his views for fear of alarming the public. The point is not merely that there are no proper procedures for assessing siting policy, but also that there are still no clear criteria as to what is an acceptable hazard, which the public should or could be persuaded to accept. While the safety record of the nuclear industry in the UK has been remarkably good, the experience of human error in the US suggests that one must take the hazard of human incompetence into account. He found the Connor's Quay issue rather curious, since within fifteen miles of the proposed side were some 1·5 million people. Clearly the criteria for determining desirable minima of adjacent population were not properly worked out. He believed that the reason for the denial of planning permission was due to the likelihood of a substantial increase of settlement in the vicinity of the plant resulting from the possible establishment of a new town and adjacent industrial development.

Brooks was also anxious to stress the dangers of another kind of hazard which he felt should also be subject to proper public scrutiny, namely, the sabotage of a nuclear plant or the diversion of nuclear waste materials by groups seeking political advantage. If urban terrorism were to worsen, then the tasks of siting nuclear plants adjacent to built-up areas could be much more serious than they are presently assessed. Clearly the development of the nuclear industry will involve matters of military security which we may not yet have adequately contemplated. On this point, he was supported by *Searle*, who felt that questions of highjacking and policing should be included in EIA. It was clear, he believed, that the risks were fairly significant because insurance agencies have not been able to devise a suitable risk assessment procedure upon which to base their premiums.

In reply *Kinchin* doubted whether sabotage was a serious possibility, since, unless the saboteur was extremely knowledgeable about reactor design and operation and knew how to short out the complicated

32

protective mechanisms, he would require a quantity of explosive that would be far more effective elsewhere. Nevertheless the industry certainly had to take this matter into account, though this was not generally a factor influencing site selection.

With respect to the question of risk, he accepted that there were no generally agreed criteria. The US study of reactor safety [3] did not produce a standard, nor did it comment on whether the safety level of nuclear reactors was the right level or not; it merely ascertained that the risk of 100 generating stations was many orders of magnitude less than the risks from man made or natural hazards. But he acknowledged that this is a highly controversial question. Certainly no-one knows yet how to balance the dangers from infrequent large accidents against the costs of frequent smaller ones. Nevertheless, one cannot quantify the degree of risk on the basis of insurance premiums. To begin with there is usually limited liability in such cases, and, in any event, governments usually provide special protection. [4] As to the matter of siting, he believed that it really made little difference where a plant was located in the event of a really serious accident; the problem was to reduce the probability of such an event occurring.

Notes

[1] The author wishes to thank Dr J. R. Beattie, ASRD, and Dr B. A. J. Lister, AERE Harwell, for their substantial contributions to this chapter.

[2] The Calvert Cliffs' decision was handed down in 1971 by Justice Wright of the Washington DC Circuit Court in response to a petition by the Calvert Cliffs' Coordinating Committee noting that the Atomic Energy Commission had not fulfilled the requirements of NEPA when licensing nuclear power stations. In summary, Justice Wright ruled that the AEC was required to write a 'detailed statement' of all environmental issues irrespective of whether it was requested by an interested party. He also commented that regulatory agencies themselves must balance this information against other non-environmental considerations and not leave this to the courts or to Congress. In addition, he required all agencies to produce their own EISs regardless of their special competence; i.e. they could not 'contract out' certain parts of an EIS to another agency, though other agencies may review such statements in public. See T. Stribling, 'Natural Environmental Policy Act interpreted as requiring strict procedural compliance of federal agencies', *Natural Resources Journal*,

vol. 12, no. 1, January 1972, pp.116–24.

[3]   This report, known as the Rasmussen Report, was published by the US Nuclear Regulatory Commission under the title *Reactor Safety Study, An Assessment of Accident Risks in US Commercial Nuclear Power Plants*, WASH-1400, Washington, October 1975. It was subject to heated criticism, but the authors remain firm in their conclusion that the chances of death due to nuclear reactor failure are less than 1 in 5 billion, cf. 1 in 100,000 and 1 in 4,000 from death by air travel and motor travel respectively.

The whole matter of nuclear safety is the subject of a special proposition that will be put to the voters of California in June 1976. Regardless of the outcome, the proposition will raise public awareness of the nuclear safeguards issue and influence future policy. See R. L. Grossman, 'The California nuclear safeguards proposition', *Environmental Policy and Law*, vol. 1, no. 3, December 1975, pp.141–4.

3 EEC guidelines for environmental impact assessment

D. HAMMER [1]

The title of this chapter should not lead to the assumption that the European Community has already set up guidelines for the introduction of environmental impact assessment procedures in its member states, although it is seriously considering this possibility.

The Council of Ministers of the Community has stated – in its decision establishing a Community Action Programme for the Environment (taken on 22 November 1973) – that 'the best environmental policy consists in préventing the creation of pollution or nuisances at source, rather than subsequently trying to counteract their effects', and that 'effects on the environment should be taken into account at the earliest possible stage in all the technical planning and decision-making process'. In the same decision the Council also adopted the objective of ensuring 'that more account is taken of environmental aspects in town planning and land use', and requested that an evaluation be made of the 'effects on the quality of life and on the natural environment of any measure that is adopted or contemplated at national or Community level and which is liable to affect these factors'.

One of the most adequate ways to implement these principles and objectives in practice would be the simultaneous introduction of uniform environmental impact assessment procedures in the member states of the Community. EIA would integrate the environmental dimension into decision making processes on local, regional, national and Community level, and would contribute to the solution of transfrontier environmental problems. This might help to avoid the distortion caused by competitive situations in the Community which could arise if EIA was only adopted in some of the member states and not in others, or if approach and procedures were significantly different from one country to another. Of course, besides the beneficial effects which are to be expected from the introduction of EIA, there would be some associated costs of preparations and delay which would have to be borne by private industry or public agencies, i.e. finally the tax payer.

To the author's knowledge, at least four member states are currently exploring the possibility of introducing their own EIA procedures so it is possible that significant differences in approach may eventually arise. The Council is aware of this; its declaration also states that 'major aspects of environmental policy in individual countries must no longer be planned and implemented in isolation. National programmes in these fields should be coordinated and national policies should be harmonised within the Community'.

On the basis of all these declarations and environmental policy principles adopted by the Council of Ministers, the Commission considered that environmental impact assessment procedures should be introduced in the Community and be based on common evaluation criteria which should be drawn up and adopted under the second environment programme. The Commission made a declaration to this effect at the last Council of Ministers meeting on environmental problems which was held in Luxembourg on 16 October 1975. This suggestion was generally well received by the environment ministers of member states, so that the Commission now feels encouraged to elaborate more precise proposals.

Environmental impact assessment in member states

West Germany

West Germany is the only country where environmental impact assessments are systematically undertaken at present. Even there the government decision is of a very recent date: 25 August 1975, so clearly no practical experience could have been gained so far. At the outset, a standard system of environmental impact assessment was envisaged, through legislation covering major actions at all levels of government. This intention has finally been abandoned, partly because of difficulties encountered with the federal system of government, but also because of opposition to the use of such legislation by different federal ministries. In August 1975 the federal government issued administrative instructions containing guidelines for the examination of all federal actions in the context of existing environmental policy. The Länder have already expressed their intention to introduce similar procedures which would be

36

applicable to state actions.

France

In France, the Ministry of the Quality of Life has been promoting a draft bill and decree relating to the protection of the environment which was enacted in late 1975. Article 2 of the draft bill (dated April 1975) simply provides that works and planning projects which are undertaken by a public agency or which require a licence or other form of authorisation must observe environmental requirements.

An earlier version of this same clause (dated July 1974) was much more outspoken. Moreover, the earlier draft bill was accompanied by a draft decree which went into further details concerning the content of the environmental impact assessment and made certain organisational proposals to ensure that the assessments were properly undertaken.

The amendments to the draft bill and the withdrawal of the draft decree seems to be due to opposition from other ministries. They considered that legislation on these matters was probably not necessary and that the required changes could best be achieved through amendments to the appropriate dossier of instructions for the approval of particular works and projects, thus avoiding the risk of double standards.

Netherlands

In the Netherlands the Advisory Council on the Environment favours the introduction of EIA both as an integral part of the procedure for granting licences and as part of the physical planning process. The competent Ministers of Health and Environmental Hygiene and of Economic Affairs have not yet determined their view, but it is believed that the Ministry of Health and Environmental Hygiene is broadly sympathetic to the introduction of some form of EIA. For practical reasons, however, it may give priority to the incorporation of EIA procedures into those licensing systems within its competence, rather than initiate general legislation for the application of such procedures to all government actions.

United Kingdom

The situation in the UK has already been discussed. Studies undertaken by different government departments have recommended the introduction of some form of environmental impact assessment procedure.

With regard to the remaining Community member countries, the general situation can be summarised as follows:

1 Each of the member states is taking an active interest in EIA and is broadly amenable to adopting a more systematic approach to environmental impact assessment and its integration within certain of their planning and decision processes. However, none has yet finalised the detailed form of such an arrangement, with the single exception of Germany.

2 Support for the introduction of EIA is understandably strongest in the environment ministries. Certain other ministries have expressed reservations over particular aspects of EIA procedures and the method of their implementation. It is therefore likely that EIAs will be, at least in their initial stages, restricted to more specific actions which fall within the competence of the environment ministries.

3 If these intentions are carried through, then in the absence of Community action there will be significant differences between member states as to the nature, authority and performance (notably in the provision for agency and public consultation) of EIA and hence in its political and practical effectiveness.

The Commission therefore felt that it would be appropriate to formulate a position on a possible Community-wide system of EIA. The Community would, of course, have to try to eliminate, or at least reduce, the concern of certain national ministries, and conceive a system that would be sufficiently flexible to be incorporated in existing decision making and planning processes in the different member states, yet specific enough as to organisational guidelines and provisions to ensure effective performance.

Possible Community legislation in member states

For the reasons expressed already, the Commission considers that EIA should be introduced simultaneously in all the member states. The best legal instrument to do this would be a Community directive which is binding as to principle, but leaves to the national authorities the choice of form and methods.

In the author's view, the Community directive would need to contain provisions and guidelines relating to the following seven areas:

Field of application

The field of application of environmental impact statements in member states should be defined more narrowly and precisely than in the American system, although still with sufficient flexibility in interpretation to allow for differing circumstances and institutions between member states. Two important areas of application can be identified:

Project assessment Projects refer to specific schemes likely to have a significant effect on the human environment. They might relate to new industrial developments, road or other infrastructure schemes and housing area redevelopment. The authorisation procedures relating to these new developments would include licensing, building permit and/or development control schemes, special public enquiry procedures relating to public authority infrastructure schemes and legislation directly authorising specific major new developments.

A full environmental impact statement should not be required for all projects. Therefore guidelines should be prepared covering possible exemptions having regard to the nature of the activities associated with the project, its size and location.

Plan and programme assessment Plans and programmes cover groups of projects and include national plans relating to the development of major economic sectors (e.g. energy, transport, agriculture) and regional and local plans of an economic or land use nature. The environmental impact assessment of plans and programmes should be regarded as complementary to the assessment of individual projects though with a different emphasis and form. Given the greater complexity of environmental assessments of plans and programmes, the Community procedures should be confined to project assessment at first and only subsequently to plan and programme assessments.

Other possible areas At present the author does not believe that procedures for approving Research and Development projects and new products should be selected for the early application of EIA procedures. In both cases there should be further study of the adequacy and possible areas of improvement of existing methods of assessment before these are applied to such cases.

Content of environmental impact statements

A major issue is whether the EIA should be confined to the environmental impact of a proposed action or whether it should be a complete economic, social and environmental decision making document. The latter is sometimes advocated in the US. A general view on all the implications –

economic and social as well as environmental — would certainly provide the most solid basis for political decision making. Although this may be attempted in particular countries, the difficulties of introducing such a scheme on Community level would be insurmountable.

Environmental assessment of individual projects should therefore be mainly restricted to such matters as pollution impacts and visual intrusion impacts, and should only include natural resource depletion effects where the local depletion of a resource (e.g. water) is a significant concern. Assessments of plans and programmes could pay further attention to depletion effects as well as undertake a more strategic assessment of pollution and visual intrusion impacts.

Screening procedures should be used to restrict detailed analysis to those environmental impacts likely to be the most significant. This could be specified in accompanying guidelines to the directive. The quantification of all significant impacts should be attempted where this can be meaningfully undertaken, although the statement should indicate both the basis of the calculations and the reliability of the measures derived.

In view of the considerable work involved in making thorough analyses of the impact of alternative courses of action, the requirement to review alternative actions in the EIA should be waived where the applicant can demonstrate that acceptable remedial measures could be applied to the proposed action. A requirement to publish a final version of an EIA (incorporating the view of other agencies and the general public) should be waived where existing provisions in the relevant decision or planning process adequately serve the same purpose.

Although against developing EIA into a complete economic, social and environmental decision making document, nevertheless the author would suggest that a summary of the relative economic and social costs of the proposed action should be made available publicly either in a separate document or as part of the EIA itself.

Methods of assessment

General guidance on assessment methods should be attached to the directive, and this should be elaborated by subsequent publication of more detailed instructions. Already assessment methodologies for individual projects are relatively well developed and it is desirable that the 'best practice' existing in the Community should be brought together in the form of a project assessment manual. However, assessment methods for plans and programmes are less well developed and further work should be undertaken to remedy their major deficiencies before EIA is formally extended to this area.

Structure of Community EIA system

Organisational provisions in the directive or its accompanying guidelines should cover the following: (a) the departments or agencies in the member states authorised to exercise any discretion in selecting the actions to which the EIA procedures should apply; (b) requirements relating to a minimum period between the completion of particular stages in the EIA procedure and the completion of the decision making process for the proposed action; (c) the parties or agencies responsible for preparing the draft (or drafts) of the EIA; (d) the required content of the EIA and methods for determining its adequacy; (e) requirements for agency and public comment on EIA; and (f) requirements for the post-auditing of individual actions and for general reviews of the operation of EIA.

Financing of Community EIA system

Consideration should be given to the desirability and practicability of making an EIA system self financing. This could be done through a system of fees, payable by those seeking authorisation for their projects, and set at a level designed to cover the financial costs borne by the authorities which undertake the EIA.

Role of the European Commission

The European Commission should undertake the following responsibilities in relation to the implementation of an EIS system in member states: (a) monitoring the progress of implementation of EIA procedures in member states; (b) participating in the EIA consultation process for prescribed types of proposed actions; and (c) elaborating the EIA guidelines.

Preliminary and transitional arrangements

In order to assist the smooth introduction of a Community EIA system, provisions should be made for (a) the length of notice that member states should be given to prepare for the implementation of such a system; (b) the arrangements during the transitional period, including arrangements for the introduction of an EIA system in stages; and (c) the preparatory arrangements which should be implemented before the date when the EIA system first comes into operation.

Such a directive to member states should be supplemented by provisions for the application of an EIA procedure to a range of actions undertaken by the Community itself. Council and Commission should therefore agree on a model EIA procedure for application to their own planning and decision making processes. The model procedure should contain provisions and guidelines relating to the same seven areas as outlined above, and therefore should be seen as a parallel directive at Community level to that already discussed. This does not mean that the content of the two procedures would have to be identical. Although there are certain parallels between the categories of action and decision making and planning processes in the member states and the Community, there are also significant differences. In particular, Community actions invariably involve member states as intermediaries for their implementation and, for certain actions, the member states may possess considerable discretion as to the detailed form of the action taken. The precise nature of this Community–member state relationship, in respect to different categories of Community action, must therefore be established prior to determining the appropriate model procedure, its structure and the responsibilities of the appropriate authorities.

Discussion

This chapter raises an interesting paradox. How can the European Commission reconcile a policy of protecting environmental amenity on the one hand, whilst safeguarding competitiveness of trade on the other, yet demand that all member nations meet certain guidelines for EIA? Surely these guidelines will have to be flexible enough to take into account the enormous variations of assimilative capacity that will be found from one region to another, and the differing national policies with respect to environmental protection. *Lord Ashby* recalled that the 1973 Declaration of the European Communities stressed this very point, and to illustrate his case he cited the need to recognise that motor car exhaust regulations need not be the same in the north of Scotland, where there was insufficient solar energy to produce photochemical smog, as, say, in Sicily. On the other hand, there were areas where some degree of international regulation was necessary, as for example, the export of atmospheric pollutants from the UK to Scandinavia.

Hammer (Commission of the European Communities) stressed that the Commission's guidelines would only fix the procedural aspects of EIA. They would determine *what* has to be examined and in which way, but not fix levels for admissible pollution or nuisances in individual cases. The Commission's guidelines would also provide sufficient flexibility to incorporate procedures already existing in member states. As to the matter of different degrees of emission control from motor cars, he remarked that since cars are traded or driven across national borders, it does not make practical or economic sense to vary the levels of emission control very much, regardless of differing environmental capacities to absorb pollutants, since to make cars of different product design would essentially impose barriers to trade.

Davis (Anglian Water Authority) disagreed with this and pointed out that many European countries had inferior standards of environmental cleanliness compared with the UK. He was also doubtful that EIA could be implemented successfully in the EEC, and that it would prove advantageous to national decision making. *Brooks* (Liverpool) pointed out that the objective of a competitive situation was not to eliminate the advantages gained from the inequalities in environmental assimilation (which were God given), but to exploit these to maximum economic advantage. Thus there was a great danger that the concept of harmonisation advocated by the European Commission might lead to the lowering of quite proper economic advantages. Surely the objective of EIA in the EEC is to maximise economic efficiency within the confines of politically acceptable environmental standards. He was also concerned by Hammer's remarks that new products and processes for research and development should not be subject to EIA until assessment methods are improved upon. Did this mean that EIA would only be applied to existing technologies?

In reply *Hammer* commented that EIA should not be ruled out for new R and D products, but there were problems. For example, in the case of new chemical products it would be necessary to know all possible effects, but this would in turn require analysis of constituent elements that might mean the disclosure of industrial secrets. As for the wider issues of harmonisation and competitive advantage, he pointed out that all member states have agreed in principle to the idea of EIA and that there is a general consensus that the competitive situation is fairly balanced, given differing wage rates, taxation levels and environmental conditions, so any action taken by one country might upset this. In this regard, he cautioned those who displayed a degree of British chauvinism that the UK would have to accept the fact that as a member of the EEC a certain degree of cooperation with mutually acceptable policies will be expected. As for the matter of objectives, he believed that we cannot wait until everything is scientifically proven before taking action. So there is a need to adopt less than perfect measures which are sufficiently flexible to be altered as scientific advances improve the quality of evidence available.

Note

[1]   The views expressed here are entirely those of the author and do not necessarily reflect the views of the European Commission or the European Economic Community.

4 US experience with national environmental impact legislation

S. MEYERS

When the National Environmental Policy Act (NEPA) became law on 1 January 1970, it was hailed by optimistic environmentalists as the most significant domestic legislation of the twentieth century, but discounted by the sceptics as an act establishing well meaning goals but lacking adequate procedures to assure implementation. The record over the past five years has proved these sceptics to be wrong. There are five issues to be considered: the nature of NEPA, its role, its limitations, its impact to date, and its likely effect in the future.

What is NEPA?

NEPA is a federal law. In a sense, it amends all other federal laws because it applies an environmental mandate to a wide range of federal programmes.

Section 101 of the Act states the intent:

> The Congress, recognizing the profound impact of man's activity on the interrelationships of all components of the natural environment ... declares that it is the continuing policy of the Federal Government to use all practicable means and measures ... to create and maintain conditions under which man and nature can exist in productive harmony, and fulfill the social, economic and other requirements of present and future generations of Americans.

NEPA applies to Federal Government actions. These include direct federal projects, and developments that are supported by the Federal Government through grants, loans, licences, permits or other actions. [1] NEPA also applies to federal legislative proposals to Congress and to federal regulations. Thus, in one way or another, NEPA affects many programmes that touch all aspects of American life.

What does NEPA do?

NEPA created the Council on Environmental Quality to advise the President on environmental matters and generally to oversee compliance by federal agencies with the Act. [2] It requires federal agencies to consider the environment, along with traditional economic and technical factors, before taking major actions. It asks agencies to examine their laws and regulations to identify requirements that prevent accomplishing environmental objectives and to take actions to correct these deficiencies. Finally, it creates the environmental impact statement (EIS) requirement (s. 102(2)(C)): whenever a federal agency proposes to take a major action having a significant effect on the quality of the human environment, it must prepare a detailed statement of the environmental effects and make this statement available to the President, the Congress, and the American public.

The law does not define what is a major action or a significant effect, but it does have five requirements which must be addressed in an EIS: (a) the environmental impact of the proposed action; (b) any adverse environmental effects which cannot be avoided should the proposal be implemented; (c) alternatives to the proposed action; (d) the relationship between local short term uses of man's environment and maintenance and enhancement of long term productivity; and (e) any irreversible and irretrievable commitments of resources which would be involved in the proposed action should it be implemented.

The Council on Environmental Quality has published implementing guidelines advising agencies on preparing EISs, and there have been a number of court interpretations. Some additional requirements are as follows:

> 1   Environmental analysis should be built into the early planning process, when there is flexibility to consider alternatives. In a recent court case it was stated: 'The EIS should be prepared late enough in the development process to contain meaningful information, but . . . early enough so that whatever information is contained can practically serve as input into the decision making process. In any event, a draft statement must be prepared at least 90 days before the agency takes the action'.

2 The analysis that is required is a systematic, interdisciplinary one. Ideally, the action must be viewed in as broad a context as is practicable: for example, not only primary but secondary effects must be studied. If there are related actions, or other significant developments in the vicinity, the agency should look at cumulative effects.

3 The effects to be analysed include not only pollution but also effects on fish and wildlife, on vegetation and other natural areas, on groundwater recharge — on all significant aspects of the quality of the natural environment. Also, NEPA requires analysis of social environmental effects, such as impact on community living patterns, and significant displacement or inducement of population.

4 Federal agencies should make a concerned effort to identify alternatives that would mitigate adverse effects. One alternative that must be evaluated is 'no action'. [3] The courts have said that the evaluation of alternatives must be as broad as reasonable, even going beyond the mission or authorities of the sponsoring agency.

5 The public must be informed. The most common method is obtaining comments on a draft EIS. The final EIS, which must be filed with CEQ at least thirty days before the action, must disclose the comments and respond to them. Other methods of public involvement, such as hearings and advisory committees, have also been encouraged by the EIS process, even though NEPA does not require these methods as a matter of law.

What does NEPA not do?

Federal agencies have the responsibility to identify for themselves the projects that need EISs and, after complying with the EIS process, an agency will decide what course of action to take, subject as usual to congressional mandate and direction of the President. NEPA does not give CEQ or EPA or any agency the power to stop a federal project of another agency. The Act is self policing and agencies must build their own environmental staffs and expertise.

After the agency has fulfilled the procedural requirements, it can still go ahead with the action even if the EIS shows it will have an adverse environmental effect. It is hoped that the agency will be able to implement the measures identified through the EIS evaluation to reduce the harmful effects as much as possible.

Citizens and groups have the right to sue a federal agency to comply with NEPA if they believe the agency has failed to write an EIS on a major project significantly affecting the environment or if an EIS that has been prepared is inadequate under the law. To date there have been over 250 litigations under NEPA, while the CEQ has issued two sets of guidelines to assist agencies when preparing EISs.

What have been the results of NEPA?

After an initially slow start, federal agencies have created NEPA staffs and built up their environmental expertise. All major agencies have NEPA regulations containing criteria and procedures for determining 'major' and 'significant' actions. As a screening mechanism, most agencies conduct environmental assessments of many more actions than eventually require EISs.

Several thousand EISs have been issued. The largest category is transportation − highways and airports. Other categories of projects on which EISs have been prepared are: water resource projects (impoundments, channels and other developments); nuclear power plants; mining, timber harvesting, recreation and other activities on federal lands; urban renewal projects; military projects; sewage treatment plants; and oil and gas production on the outer continental shelf. On energy developments (other than individual nuclear power plants and oil and gas lease sales), major EISs have been prepared on prototype oil shale leasing, geothermal resource leasing and coal leasing programmes, and on the programme for developing the liquid metal fast breeder reactor. There have been some EISs prepared on other research and development efforts; generally NEPA is applied at the pilot scheme stage. There has been an effort to prepare programmatic EISs which analyse the broad policies and regulations under which major federal programmes operate. These broad EISs provide a background against which individual actions in those programmes are subsequently assessed and facilitate development of project specific EISs. [4]

Many federal agencies have transferred the principal responsibility for data collection and environmental assessment to state and local governments or the private sector, when the federal action is funding or approval of a state or local project. For example, the Nuclear Regulatory Commission requires power company applicants for nuclear power plant licences to submit a full environmental report. This has had the effect of spreading the mandate to meet NEPA requirements throughout all sectors of the economy. Among other things, this course of events has created a

48

good deal of business for environmental consultants and greatly encouraged the interdisciplinary study of many kinds of development problems.

In a sense, this interdisciplinary approach has been a means for different federal and state programmes to find a common ground on which to analyse developments that involve several kinds of official action. However, while there has been steady progress in this direction, this integrative process still has a long way to go.

In addition, many states have adopted laws similar to NEPA for state actions. So far twenty-four states and the Commonwealth of Puerto Rico have enacted such a statute and a number of other states are considering similar legislation. [5]

The EIS process has served as a strong avenue for citizen involvement in federal agency decision making. There have been many citizen suits concerning a variety of federal projects and programmes and compliance with NEPA, and some actions have been halted by the courts while the sponsoring federal agencies comply with the EIS requirements.

Some projects which have posed substantial environmental issues have been stopped altogether or substantially altered for the better as a result of NEPA assessments. For example, the US Army Corps of Engineers dropped plans for a pier to conduct ocean research off Assateague Island National Seashore after analysing the adverse effects on the park and available alternatives. The Department of the Interior decided not to authorise substantial enlargement of an existing airport in Grand Teton National Park to serve jets after its draft EIS and the comments on it showed that a jet airport would substantially impair enjoyment of the park. As an example of action that was improved by the NEPA process, the trans-Alaskan pipeline design and construction should have substantially less impact on the environment as a result of needed improvements identified in the EIS.

Perhaps more important, underlying the EISs that are prepared are thousands of environmental assessments of potential actions that screen out many unsatisfactory projects. Also implementation of NEPA has encouraged improvements in agency planning processes, in technical standards for design and operation of projects, and in regulations for controlling the environmental effects of many types of activities – from urban building design to mining on federal lands.

A very controversial aspect of NEPA, and a very significant aspect in terms of democratic governing processes, has been the full disclosure potential of the law. For some kinds of programmes, disclosing who receives the benefits and who pays the cost can lead to substantial

c

pressure for changes in the decision making process.

Finally, EISs have been blamed for stopping some needed projects and for contributing to inflationary delays and modifications that further added to project costs.

However, there have been some shortcomings in agency implementation of NEPA. For example, to begin with many agencies did not prepare fully adequate EISs, particularly in terms of analysing alternatives. Often this was because the EIS was prepared after the action had been substantially decided and flexibility to respond to environmental concerns was lacking or would result in expensive changes. In part, this problem was inevitable because NEPA had no 'grandfather' clause exempting projects that were partially underway to ready to go. [7] Thus agencies had to apply NEPA requirements to ongoing programmes that had adverse environmental consequences, with resulting delays and expense if changes to protect the environment were made, or agencies prepared superficial EISs that in effect justified business as usual. After several years of implementing NEPA, this problem has been considerably reduced and we are seeing more meaningful application of NEPA principles to early planning processes.

Two of the most difficult aspects of projects to analyse are their secondary and cumulative effects. Methodologies for accomplishing such analyses, and institutions for implementing the findings, are still rudimentary in many cases. Another methodological difficulty is assessing priorities and hierarchies of effects. EISs often catalogue many types of effects without analysing their meaning or relative significance and trade off values.

So far most EISs have concentrated on the physical environmental effects. NEPA addresses the quality of the human environment which includes the social as well as physical environments, but analysis of social effects has not been a major aspect of NEPA implementation, particularly as a factor which triggers preparation of the EIS. However, once the decision is made that an EIS is needed, some social impacts are discussed in the statement such as displacement of populations and disruption of school districts and neighbourhoods.

The courts are still struggling with the question of the *procedural* versus the *substantive* effect of NEPA: that is, whether NEPA requires an agency to fulfil the environmental analysis and disclosure requirements, or whether it also requires the agency to forgo an action which is shown to have unavoidable adverse consequences for the environment. So far the courts have indicated that compliance with NEPA is essentially limited to procedural requirements, unless an agency decision was clearly arbitrary

50

and capricious in providing insufficient weight to environmental values. [6]

What is the assessment for the future?

NEPA is viewed by many as a highly significant and effective environmental law that is revolutionising federal decision making. As indicated, others have regarded the law as a tool for obstruction, a procedural roadblock for both good and bad projects, and a giant paperwork machine.

The absence of a 'grandfather' clause [7] in the application of NEPA, and the effects this has had on certain federal programmes and the quality of EISs, has continued to be a problem for some agencies. However, as NEPA has been integrated into basic agency planning requirements, this problem is being eased considerably. Most agencies have made substantial progress in applying NEPA to their programmes and in improving the quality and timeliness of their environmental analyses. There is a strong need to continue this process of integration into the basic decision making and analytical framework of federal agencies.

NEPA provides a case-by-case approach to environmental issues. While application of the Act to specific projects has also had the effect of improving planning processes, it still does not fill the need for improved policy and institutions to deal with nationwide environmental problems. NEPA has, however, highlighted many of these problems and encouraged agencies to improve their programmes within current institutional limitations, and the flexibility of the law makes it applicable in areas where more substantive standards or controls would not be feasible.

In order to keep NEPA effective, there is a need for continued good will on the part of federal agencies to ameliorate criticism of those constituents whose projects may have been affected by the EIS requirements, and a need for quality administration and efficient, open resolution of conflicts to avoid unnecessary obstruction of needed programmes.

NEPA has represented, and helped to lead, a trend in more open government—requiring agencies to explain to the public what they are doing, for whom, and at what cost. For the most part, this has had a very healthy effect on the quality of decision making. One can only hope that the right balance can be struck between agencies' need to act and the open consideration and balancing of competing demands, which will protect the long term integrity of this important law. There will remain, of course, the conflicts to be resolved about how much society is willing to pay or to forgo in order to protect environmental quality for future generations. But while we are looking at the costs, it may be well to note that NEPA can help to identify and weed out projects that are likely to be expensive mistakes.

NEPA implementation is becoming a way of life in federal agencies of the US; it is being adopted increasingly by state and local governments as a useful tool for better government, and is an invaluable mechanism for programme self evaluation and improvement and environmental protection.

Discussion

Meyers (US Environmental Protection Agency) stressed the point that NEPA is an administrative Act which relates to agency procedures; it cannot and does not stop projects from going ahead, although it can and does ensure that at least the project or regulatory activity is executed with full knowledge of the environmental consequences and frequently with sufficient modifications to safeguard environmental quality. Thus the current delay in the surface mining of coal in the Rocky Mountain States was not due to NEPA but to the lack of proper safeguarding legislation and the inadequacy of local water supplies vital to the extraction of the coal. But unless Congress specifically authorises to the contrary, the provisions of NEPA cannot be bypassed no matter how great the urgency or the need. [8] However, a project may go ahead even if there is a court case pending, unless the court issues a temporary restraining order and follows this up with a permanent injunction. [9]

The scope of NEPA aroused much interest. *Meyers* repeated that the EIS is not mandatory for non-federal projects or procedures in states which do not have their own NEPA equivalent. But in fact a surprising number of projects are covered by its provisions, since most privately or state-sponsored projects require some regulatory permission by a federal agency. For example, under the 1972 Federal Water Pollution Control Act, the EPA must license all discharge applications via a system of permits, and the issue of a permit is subject to an EIS. This would affect nuclear power stations and new housing developments. And by virtue of the 1970 Clean Air Act, the EPA is required to review all federal projects whether under NEPA or other agency regulations. If it finds any adverse effect on public health, welfare or environmental quality, it can make this public and send it to the Council on Environmental Quality which receives all EISs. Although this particular statement is advisory, it can be used to political and legal advantage since it is both publicly accessible and factual.

While *Davis* (Anglian Water Authority) accepted that it was relatively easy to define air and water quality standards, he was doubtful whether NEPA really upgraded the powers of enforcement. Did the American EIS result in an improvement in environmental quality or was it merely concerned with the effects of future development? *Meyers* replied that one of the principal advantages of the EIS was to keep the federal agencies honest in their operations and accountable to the public. All comments on a draft EIS must be made public, so an agency proceeds knowing that the community is aware of the environmental risks. Thus agencies are now more accountable to a wider public interest than the clandestine constituencies with which they were previously associated.

The procedure for obtaining permission to proceed with a project was raised by *Train* (Cremer and Warner). *Meyers* replied that a draft impact statement had to be filed with the CEQ for sixty days during which time anyone could read it and make comments. Sometimes the proposer would alter the project during this stage under threat of legal action if he were to proceed; sometimes he would modify his scheme as a result of the public debate or agency advice. Thirty days after the final impact statement is deposited with the CEQ, the developer is free to proceed. Usually there is no follow-up after project commencement, but the EPA does monitor performance in cases where the proposal was originally considered environmentally unsatisfactory or where they stipulated that, in granting a permit, emission standards must be progressively improved.

In the matter of who prepares and pays for the EIS, *Meyers* remarked that this was the responsibility of the agency involved, but because it would have to obtain and verify relevant information from the proposer of the project (say a nuclear installation or an oil refinery), they would require at least two years to prepare the statement. The CEQ, EPA and other agencies, in consultation with state departments and private industry, have prepared guidelines to assist their employees in gathering information, and in preparing and reviewing statements. Such guidelines are available to all interested parties and cover a wide range of projects.

NEPA does require that alternatives to the proposed development are reviewed, but usually there are limits to how far this can go. Economic considerations normally determine and hence narrow the scope for reasonable alternatives (e.g. nuclear power as opposed to alternative fuel sources), but in the case of major federal projects certain options must be considered. For example, the Corps of Engineers, who wish to continue the construction of the Cross—Florida Barge Canal, have been asked to look at the environmental consequences of railways and/or roads as alternatives to the canal.

Lord Zuckerman asked whether NEPA could be bypassed on the grounds of military security. As far as *Meyers* was aware, the Act did not specify any exclusionary terms but the Pentagon could, if it wished, withdraw from the scheme, though it has chosen not to do so for most of its activities. Under the 1967 Freedom of Information Act, Congress had declared the principle that all information was public knowledge unless it could be shown that full disclosure would be detrimental to the national interest or commercial viability.

Notes

[1]   A controversy has developed as to whether NEPA applies to the work of the federal regulatory agencies such as the Environmental Protection Agency and the Interstate Commerce Commission as well as the activities of the traditional 'resource' agencies, e.g. the Corps of Engineers or the Forest Service. In enacting the 1972 amendments to the Federal Water Pollution Control Act, Congress specifically exempted EPA regulatory activities from environmental impact reviews, except for grants for new waste treatment works and permits for new sources of effluent. Although this ruling has been upheld by the courts, EPA has voluntarily decided to prepare EISs subject to full public review, when determining national environmental quality standards as guidelines for air and water pollution control, and other regulatory guidelines.

[2]   The Council comprises three members, appointed by the President, and a small full time research staff. It is simply not equipped to handle the thousand or so impact statements prepared each year, so usually requests that the initiating agencies monitor their own material.

[3]   In the legislative history of NEPA, Congress made it clear that s. 102(2)(C)(iii) meant 'alternative ways of accomplishing the objectives of the proposed action and the results of not accomplishing the proposed action'. Subsequent court rulings have interpreted this to mean that there should be consideration in good faith of the merits of abandoning a proposed project in all impact statements.

[4]   Probably the most ambitious to date is the review of the fast breeder nuclear reactor programme. See also T. B. Cochran, *The Liquid Metal Fast Breeder Reactor: An Environmental and Economic Critique*, Resources for the Future, Washington 1974.

[5]   For a good review, see the *Fifth Annual Report* of the Council on Environmental Quality, Government Printing Office, Washington 1974, pp.401–9.

[6]   Nevertheless, various court rulings have emphasised that agencies have an obligation to take environmental values into account at every 'distinctive and comprehensive stage of the process beyond the staff's evaluation and recommendation'. So agencies are required to balance environmental evidence against all other considerations when making final decisions.

[7]   The 'grandfather' clause exempts any activities or procedures which are legally permitted under prior legislation. In the case of NEPA, all federal activities were subject to its provisions from the day of enactment, 1 January 1970; this included projects already authorised, but not constructed.

[8]   Under the Trans-Alaskan Pipeline Authorization Act of 1973, Congress exempted the trans-Alaskan pipeline from any additional environmental impact assessment on the grounds that an adequate EIS had been prepared and the project was in the national interest.

[9]   The trans-Alaskan pipeline was stopped for forty-four months from March 1970 to November 1973 before it was finally authorised by Congress.

PART III

The role of the law

5 Protection of the environment under current English law

A. D. WOOLF

There is no English law which specifically protects the environment. It is part of the contrast between the basic common law unwritten constitution of this country and the written constitution of the United States, that in the US one can produce a three page document which is The Law to protect the environment. This is not to say there are no laws dealing with environmental conservation in the UK, for there are many which aim to repair environmental wrongs and seek to restrain acts that would affect the environment. But none is as comprehensive as NEPA.

Our relevant law falls into two categories. First, the statutory laws, the Clean Air Acts, the Water Acts, the Public Health Acts, the Countryside Acts — a whole series of different statutes, culminating in the two recent important Acts, the Control of Pollution Act and the Health and Safety at Work, Etc. Act — which set out a whole series of more or less precise statutory duties. They set up agencies, usually inspectorates of one sort or another, to enforce them, and give those agencies powers and occasionally, but not traditionally, duties. Alongside these are a vast range and type of civil and common law actions which are less familiar to the ordinary citizen concerned for the environment, and will therefore be considered more closely than the statutory provisions.

The law of tort

Under the law of tort, there are a number of different types of action which the citizen can bring to protect his environment. First, there is the action in private nuisance, which affects the possession or enjoyment of land. This, however, can only be brought by the occupier of land, and its effectiveness has been further hampered in the environmental sense by the nineteenth-century judgement that what is a nuisance in Belgravia is not necessarily a nuisance in Bermondsey. [1] Environmental quality is a function of prevailing standards. You might be able to restrain the introduction of a tanning factory in Belgravia, but would have to put up with it if you lived in Bermondsey, where you would be more likely to encounter it.

Secondly, there is public nuisance, which is both a civil and a criminal offence, but is hardly seen in the law reports since it is usually more difficult to obtain proper legal remedy and frequently requires the intervention of the Attorney General. However, there was a case before the Court of Appeal recently which said that if a gentleman who phoned a bomb hoax had in fact disturbed the comfort of an appreciable number of citizens, he would have been guilty of the offence of public nuisance, and possible applications for environmental purposes spring readily to mind. [2]

The private citizen can use public nuisance in two ways: he can bring a private prosecution or, if he suffers damage greater than that suffered by any member of the public, he can sue for damages and for an injunction. In a case decided as recently as 30 May 1857 in the Court of Criminal Appeal it was stated that:

> the law of the country would surely be very defective if life and property could be exposed to danger by the act of another with impunity. The well-founded apprehension of danger which would alarm men of steady nerves and reasonable courage passing through the streets in which houses stand on adjoining houses is enough to show that something has been done which the law ought to prevent by pronouncing it to be a misdemeanour. [3]

Maybe this can be criticised as old law, but it is still very much alive, and possibly some enterprising citizen will one day look to it.

Third, something akin to public nuisance is the rule of strict liability, enunciated in the case of Rylands and Fletcher, decided a little more recently, about 100 years ago. The judgement, which is still good law, states:

> The true rule of law is that the person who for his own purposes brings on his land and collects and keeps there anything likely to do mischief if it escapes must keep it in at his own peril and if he does not do so he is *prima facie* answerable for all the damage which is the natural consequence of its escape. The person whose habitation is made unhealthy by the fumes and noise and vapours of his neighbour's alkali works is damaged without any fault of his own and it seems but reasonable and just that the neighbour should be obliged

60

to make good the damage which ensues. [4]

Fourth, there is the action in negligence, which assumes that every man, every citizen, every corporation and every agency, has a duty to carry out his or its activities with reasonable care to ensure that those activities avoid the infliction of unnecessary harm. Negligence actions have been most widely used in cases of personal injuries due to road traffic accidents or arising out of employment. The reasons why negligence actions have been litigated in those fields more than in any other are primarily institutional in nature. In road traffic there is compulsory insurance. In the employment situation there is the overwhelming presence and interest of trade unions which will take up cases for their members. But it is interesting that in the environmental field attempts to explore the value of these types of action are almost unheard of. That they could be used and could be of great value is apparent from various slightly odd cases, two of which are of fairly recent vintage.

One was a case brought by a lady against Bognor Regis Borough Council when her house, which she had purchased from a builder who had gone bankrupt, started to fall apart. She said the foundations were inadequate. They had been statutorily inspected by the local authority building inspector, and she claimed that the inspector owed her a duty of care in the way in which he carried out his responsibilities, and hence that, had he exercised due care, he ought not to have passed the foundations as adequate. She claimed therefore that the council should pay her the damage she had suffered. The Court of Appeal concurred and awarded her damages. [5]

The second case was even more unusual. Three Borstal officers had been sent to Brownsea Island off the coast of Dorset to supervise a working party of Borstal trainees under their care. At the end of the day's work, the three officers all chose to go to sleep at the same time. The inevitable consequence was that some of the trainees attempted to escape to the mainland in a boat which they purloined with greater skill than they navigated it. The Dorset Yacht Club sued the Home Office for damage suffered in the ensuing collision by one of their vessels, and the House of Lords ruled that the officers owed a duty of care to anyone who might be injured by the escape of the trainees who were under their care and control. [6] So the negligence action, in the hands of an imaginative lawyer, can go into some quite remarkable fields; and could become a powerful good to any public servants who neglect their duty to protect the public interest — including its environment.

Protection against illegal executive action

The prerogative writs of *prohibition mandamus* and *certiorari* are available to the citizen who, affected by an arbitrary or capricious administrative act, can apply to the courts either to prohibit it or to change it. The citizen can bring private prosecutions, as imaginatively demonstrated by Raymond Blackburn in his campaign against pornography. The citizen can also bring many types of action in the name of the Attorney General. He has a right to call upon the Attorney General to take action to defend the public interest if he can show that a sufficiently general section of the public interest is affected. However, there is practically no record of any of these types of action being taken except in the most limited fields.

Planning law

The citizen's right to object to planning developments is *prima facie* quite good. The citizen's right to have anything done, however, is limited to making objections and inviting the minister to call in an application for a public enquiry. If the minister does not wish to do so, the citizen has no rights. If a public enquiry is held, the inspector's advice to the minister at the end of it has no force. The minister is free to take his decision in complete opposition to his own inspector if he wishes to do so. Yet the activity and resources of environmental groups in the legal field has been overwhelmingly concentrated on the public inquiry forum, perhaps because it is almost the only one in which legal representation will usually be dispensed with.

Limitations to citizen initiated legal intervention

Why has there been so little action by the citizens' groups with all these legal weapons at their disposal? There seem to be three major deterrents to action in this country. The first, so far as the courts are concerned, is that you cannot sue, you cannot seek an injunction (and usually this is what environmental groups want) unless you have a sufficient personal interest in the subject of the action to entitle you to a remedy. Now, just how wide standing to sue is in this country no one has yet explored. [7] There have been various pronouncements of the courts which seem to be extremely restrictive. There have been suggestions in some cases that the courts might entertain a wider category of interests as giving standing to sue, but it is a hurdle that several have failed to leap over in various cases. For example, in his pornography action against the Metropolitan Police, Raymond Blackburn got a settlement before court judgement, but had he gone to court, there are strong indications that he would have lacked standing.

The second deterrent is money, for taking an action to court is extremely expensive. We do have a legal aid system which could perhaps be pressed into service rather more than has been attempted to further the interest of groups seeking to defend the environment, but the scope for its use seems extremely limited. Since legal aid is means tested, groups would have to use their poorest members as litigants in order to qualify. But even this approach could fail, for a legal aid committee must take into account the wealth of others who share the same interest as the applicant; in almost every case where an environmental interest is to be defended by a group of citizens, the legal aid committee might say, 'You can pool your resources; you have a very wealthy peer whose name appears as sponsor on your notepaper; you do not qualify for legal aid'.

Undoubtedly the main obstacle to citizen initiated legal action in the environmental field in the UK is the financial consequence of losing the action. For, unlike the case in the US, where successful litigants pay their own legal fees, the losing party in Britain must bear all the costs of the action — both his and those of the other party. Certainly this is a factor influencing the proliferation of legal activity in the US, for if a group wants to challenge an environmental issue they can do so almost with impunity if there are lawyers willing to take the case. There is much to be said against the US system. Inevitably there will be injustice if the successful defendant who has been embroiled in litigation against his will succeeds, yet still has to pay all his own costs, but our system makes the liability to costs an appalling deterrent. Let us suppose that you wish to take out an injunction against a government department or a wealthy corporation such as Rio Tinto Zinc. You might win, but you cannot stop the procedure there. The case then goes to appeal — all the way to the House of Lords if necessary. You cannot stop it at any stage, except by surrender. So you have caught a tiger by the tail, and very few people are prepared to take this sort of risk particularly in order to defend the public interest.

Thirdly, there is the problem of proving a case. If you want to take an action to prevent something which is going to damage the environment, the onus is on you to show proof throughout. The problem of obtaining reliable and incontrovertable information is great enough; but the costs of acquiring that material may be prohibitive when there is a substantial issue.

Public officials and public accountability

By and large, it would seem impracticable for the citizen to take action through the courts to prevent threatened assaults on the environment. If so, we are left with the paternalistic approach of putting the protection of the environment in the hands of certain public authorities with powers and duties to take action in the public interest. In theory, this would seem to be perfectly satisfactory, but in practice, the record is not good. For example, the Factory Inspectorate is responsible for supervising health and safety in Britain's factories. It faces all kinds of appalling problems, but it is small, and it is, or has been, seriously undermanned and underfinanced. It has Acts to enforce with which no one complies. The factory inspectors would not expect to go through any place of work in the country and find that the Acts are fully complied with, so the inspector who wants to prosecute has to prepare his own papers, present his own case and spend a day in court. The fines will probably be so insignificant from the point of view of the enterprise which he is prosecuting, that he gets discouraged, and, in order to achieve anything, is almost forced into a somewhat cosy relationship with industry. He tries to educate and persuade those who are willing to be educated and persuaded, while reconciling himself to the view that the recalcitrant really are beyond the reach of the law.

Let us consider the case of asbestos, which was condemned as an extremely hazardous substance by the Merryweather and Price Report in 1930. At the same time, the International Labour Office said that, since the asbestos industry was in its infancy, control procedures must be introduced at once before it became a general hazard. So in 1931 regulations were introduced in this country which were quite capable, if enforced, of controlling that hazard. The industry could have accepted them, although asbestos would have been a more expensive product and would have been confined to uses where it was vital. The fact that there was no attempt to enforce those regulations became distressingly clear when it was found that a factory in Bermondsey was killing off its entire work force and pouring out asbestos dust into a nearby council housing estate. Eventually, when an action for damages was pending and one requirement of those 1931 regulations was insisted upon, the factory was closed down.

The history that emerged was of inspectors longing over the years to do something about it, but coming up against the familiar wall of bureaucratic inertia. However, it was also discovered that the inspectorate sympathised too much with industry, that it did not see its role, whatever the law might say, as shutting down factories, and that it was not willing to prosecute one offender if it could be shown that another, similar, one had not been prosecuted. So the whole approach of the law failed. [8]

Recently the legislation for safety and health in factories has been recast. In the environmental field, s. 5 of the Health and Safety at Work, Etc., Act 1974 makes it the duty of any person having control of premises to use the best practicable means for preventing the emission into the atmosphere of noxious or offensive substances. Having established the Health and Safety Commission, s. 11 actually lays down that: 'It shall be the duty of the Commission to assist and encourage persons concerned with matters relevant to any of the purposes of this part of the Act to further those purposes.' If this were in the United States the Health and Safety Commission would be flooded with prerogative writs, but citizen action of this sort in the UK would be unlikely for the reasons already given.

Nevertheless, citizen action is necessary in environmental matters for many reasons, but in particular because those responsible for promoting projects (whether in the public or private sector) that are liable to change the environment are mostly concerned with their profitability and little bothered with the consequent undesirable effects. They will not voluntarily undertake a study to see what impact the project will have on the environment, and it requires the force of law, as the Americans have demonstrated, before appropriate action will be taken. These considerations are missed for a range of reasons, but basically because the decision makers are not required by any procedure to ask the right questions, and the more decision making is a closed process, the less the decisions are exposed to the public gaze, to criticism and informed public intervention, the greater are the chances that vital areas will be completely overlooked.

Environmental impact assessment could be an important part of the answer, provided, first, that it is democratic — which means that it is open and public and that it is implemented at the early stage of planning before options are closed, when public intervention is most effective — and, second, that it should be comprehensive. Mr Hammer suggests that EIA should be limited, at least initially, to issues of pollution and visual impact. It is apparent from the US experience that the range of environmental impacts of any large scale development goes far beyond that, and such a limitation could not be justified. It appears that the DoE study team [9] is limited by its terms of reference to questions of land use planning. While EIA would improve the decision making process in land use planning and would ensure that relevant considerations and fully informed evidence was available to decision makers, it seems that this limitation is justifiable only as an interim measure during a comparatively short period for the development of the necessary interdisciplinary skills. But do not imagine that simply feeding EIA into the land use planning system and leaving out of the requirement all the other decisions and actions which cumulatively affect the environment will in itself achieve very much. It will have to be developed very specifically to decisions to grant or refuse licences. It will have to be developed in relation to the Health and Safety at Work Act, especially as the duty to render materials and articles safe for use at work is widened to a more general duty in regard to consumer health and safety in product production. And especially it will need to involve the citizens and the concerned groups of citizens which, in the environmental field, have proliferated at such a rate over the past few years as in itself to show that the public is not satisfied with the degree of environmental protection offered by the law and the government at present. Ultimately, however, to make EIA properly effective, it will be necessary to provide those groups with the sinews of war and unambiguous rights to intervene.

Discussion

Undoubtedly an important function of the law is to arbitrate rights and wrongs. But what happens when two apparently legitimate rights are irreconcilable? *Lord Zuckerman* raised this point with the illustration of two people, one of whom believed his environmental wellbeing was enhanced by disposal spoil tips, while the other felt that his amenity was degraded. *Woolf* (Lawyers Ecology Group) replied to the general point that the law is designed to handle such conflicts by weighing the balance of expert evidence, and by using the rather refined tools of onus and standard of proof. Basically the law says that any action is lawful unless it is forbidden. As to the specific point of amenity, however, the law really says very little. Very probably neither person would have legal standing to dispute their case. So despite the widespread belief that the law ensures that all interests are adequately protected and represented, when it comes to environmental wellbeing for the public at large, the law is sadly deficient. *Shaw* (Norfolk County Council) commented in this connection that in his opinion people should not have a right to a view, [10] although they should have a right to a minimum level of environmental quality.

Shaw's main concern, however, was the status of law with respect to the actions of public and private bodies. While superficially the law treats both groups similarly, in practice the public authorities are given more room for manoeuvre. This is particularly the case for those organisations responsible for policing themselves by virtue of their powers to grant planning permission. *Woolf* replied that the Lawyers Ecology Group was formed partly in response to this particular question since many environmental groups complain that public bodies are not subject to the same rules of development control when applying for planning permission as are private citizens. The only insurance against malpractice is citizen intervention, which generally is denied in such instances. Hence the value of EIA as a partial (and hopefully) interim remedy while citizens' environmental rights are clarified.

It is difficult, however, to draft legislation to avoid either broad but bland declarations or restrictive regulations that might well impede all activity. *Woolf* noted that generally UK legislative declarations are too broad (or certainly lack the action forcing provisions of NEPA), because it is customary to grant public officials wide scope for discretionary judgement. For example, s. 11 of the 1968 Countryside Act asks every minister, government department and public body to have regard for the desirability of conserving the natural beauty and amenity of the countryside, but there can never be any proof that such a duty has actually influenced a decision. However, there was no reason, he believed, why Parliament could not have been more specific; having legislated such a laudable objective, it should have ensured that its intentions were carried through in practice.

A third point of discussion centred around the question of anticipating action, very much a feature of EIA. *Train* (Cremer and Warner) pointed out that most common law actions are *post hoc* and almost require evidence of a mischief before put into effect. Generally, the statutory legislation follows this failing, although he noted that the recent Control of Pollution and Health and Safety at Work Acts do require some consideration of environmental implications at the planning and design stages. *Davis* (Anglian Water Authority) corrected this by pointing out that various pollution prevention acts granted to the old river boards and river authorities the responsibility to review all applications for waste discharge and to require that they met certain conditions, although admittedly this was usually done on a cooperative basis with the licensee and the planning authorities.

Davis, however, was more concerned that the cost of new environmental regulations had not been properly assessed, and that EIA might add further to these costs without guaranteeing a satisfactory return. He advocated a more cautious, 'wait and see' approach to this whole matter. *Woolf* responded that EIA was simply a mechanism for elaborating a variety of considerations (including such cost implications) that otherwise would probably be ignored, and since the public is not adequately able to protect its own environmental rights under present law, EIA is a necessary procedure to force public officials to do this job for them.

Notes

[1]　St. Helens Smelting Co. v. Tipping (1865) 11 H.L. Cas. 642.
[2]　R. v. Madden, *The Times*, Law Report, 1 July 1975.
[3]　Reg. v. Lister and Biggs, (1857), Cox vol. 7, p.342.
[4]　1868 L.R. 3 H.L., 330.
[5]　Dutton v. Bognor Regis UDC, (1972) 1 A.E.R., p.462.
[6]　Dorset Yacht Co. Ltd. v. Home Office, (1970) 2 A.E.R., p.294.
[7]　For a helpful discussion, see the excellent analysis by Sir Leslie Scarman in his *English Law: The New Dimension*, Stevens, London 1974, especially pp.51−60; and J. E. Trice, 'The problem of *locus standi* in planning law', *Journal of Planning and Environmental Law*, vol. 1, 1973, pp.580−7.
[8]　A recent report highlights the dangers of regulatory permissiveness on the part of the former Factory Inspectorate. According to a report of the Ombudsman published on 30 March 1976, the Factory Inspectorate failed to ensure that workers in an asbestos manufacturing plant at Acre Mill in Yorkshire were adequately protected from the lethal dust. During the period 1949−70 when they visited the site, 40 employees died and over 200 relatives contracted the cancerous disease, asbestosis.
[9]　See the paper presented by J. Catlow and C. E. Thirlwell to the Department of Environment symposium on environmental evaluation, Canterbury, Kent, 25 September 1975.
[10]　Under the common law of nuisance the right to a view is not normally protected, though rights to other aspects of environmental amenity are safeguarded.

PART IV

Methodology

6 Impact prediction in the physical environment

R. D. HEY

The accuracy with which we can assess physical impacts is dependent on our understanding of how the natural environment functions. Given perfect understanding it should be possible to predict exactly the direction, degree and rate of change of the physical environment as it responds to a given stimulus. As our knowledge is often less than perfect, the accuracy of any prediction will be reduced.

To review the various methods that are available to assess physical impacts reference will be made to the study of alluvial channel response to river regulation.

Response of alluvial channels to river regulation

River regulation, including inter-basis water transfers, has been advocated as a means of equalising water supplies and demands in England and Wales up to the year 2001. [1] Consequently the natural flow of many rivers will be modified. As river channels have adjusted their shape and capacity to the natural flow régime any modification to this pattern could cause erosion and deposition and adjustment to the new climate of flows. [2]

The accuracy of impact prediction, direction, degree and rate of change is dependent on our level of understanding of river channel processes; in particular why and how a river adjusts its shape and size in response to a given range of flows.

Conceptual models

In the absence of any information on channel adjustment mechanisms it would be necessary to rely on engineering experience in order to estimate the possible consequences of river regulation. The susceptibility of natural channels to erosion and deposition will obviously depend on the degree of regulation and the size and character of the river being regulated. Slight discharge adjustment downstream from a dam site is only likely to be of local significance. In comparison inter-basin transfers through river intakes/outfalls may have considerable impact especially if abstractions from, and releases to, a small tributary are used to maintain river levels on the trunk stream. Provided regulation does not alter the frequency of overbank flooding, because it is recognised that flood events are responsible for major channel changes, it is usually assumed that there will be no significant impact. This rationale suggests that increased flood frequencies will cause erosion and reduced frequencies deposition.

Although this intuitive approach predicts the direction of change there is no assessment of the degree or rate of change. In order to remedy this omission it is necessary to obtain greater insight into channel adjustment mechanisms. Statistical models offer a first step in this direction.

Statistical models

Provided causal relationships can be established between the variables that define the river system a model can be developed which will define the direction and degree of change with a certain level of probability.

The river system can be defined by the variables describing the geometry of the channel and the valley, those describing the flow of water and sediment, and those defining the material through which the stream flows. Using partial correlation procedures field data can be analysed to show the interrelationship between every pair of variables. The coefficients produced in this way not only measure the strength of the relationship between the variables but also indicate whether the relationship is direct or inverse. After removing statistically insignificant relationships, the remaining variables can be used to identify the dependent (effects) and independent (causal) variables. Although statistical methods define the necessary variables the establishment of causal relationships is an inductive process based on the original conceptual model. This indicates that rivers adjust their average bankfull dimensions to the discharge, sediment load, bed and bank material size characteristics and the valley slope. A flow diagram incorporating the results of the statistical analysis can be produced to illustrate this relationship (Fig. 6.1).

Although rivers experience a range of flows engineers have suggested that they adjust their average overall shape to a single dominant flow which would give the same gross shapes and dimensions as the natural sequence of events. [3],[4],[5] Field and experimental observations indicate that this is the flow at, or about, the bankfull stage. [6],[7]

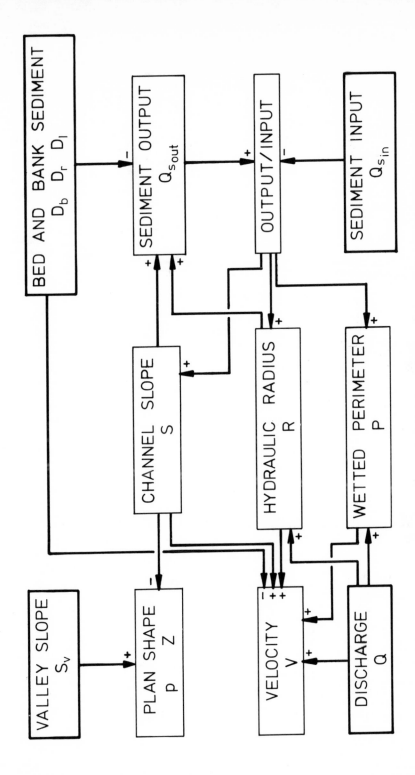

Fig. 6.1 Conceptual model of causal relationships operating in river systems. (The + ve sign denotes direct relationship, – ve sign inverse relationship; independent variables in corner boxes.)

73

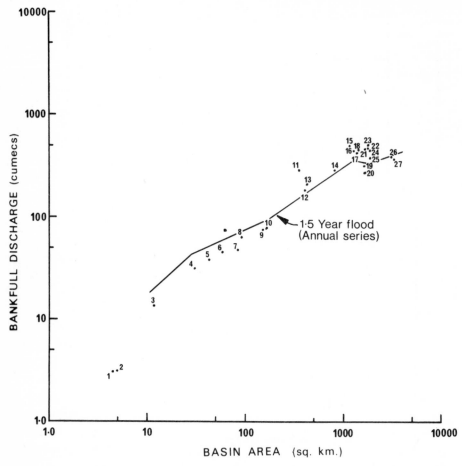

Fig. 6.2 Bankfull discharge in relation to the 1·5 year Flood (annual series), River Wye

Statistical evidence concurs with this because bankfull flow explains a greater part of the variance in the dependent variables than any other discharge value.

Before the effect of river regulation can be established the bankfull/ dominant discharge must be related to some measurable characteristic of the flow régime. For stable gravel bed rivers this has proved to be the 1·5 year flood (annual series) (Fig. 6.2). If this is altered by regulation the channel will eventually adjust its dimensions and the flow diagram (Fig. 6.1) will qualitatively indicate how the channel will react. An increase in the 1·5 year flood will cause erosion and channel enlargement and vice versa if it is reduced.

Statistical methods can also be used to predict the new equilibrium geometry of the channel. By subjecting field data to multiple regression analysis equations can be derived which link the dependent with the independent variables. [7] Like all statistical models these equations are probabilistic and the accuracy with which they can predict the new hydraulic geometry will depend on the degree of correlation between the dependent and independent variables. In addition the model will only apply within the limits of the observed data. To produce a more general model it will be necessary to obtain data from a wider variety of river environments in order to reduce the covariance between the independent variables.

The greatest drawback with statistical models is their inability to cope with dynamic situations. Identification of causal relationships immediately discounts the possibility of any interaction between the independent variables. With river regulation schemes the new equilibrium condition can only be predicted if the flow régime is the only independent variable affected by regulation. In the real world upstream and downstream feedback mechanisms continually operate in such a way that change in one variable will immediately affect all the others. Unless it is possible to define this interrelationship any assessment of channel response based solely on change in flow régime will be grossly in error.

To resolve this problem further information is required about the operation of channel processes and feedback mechanisms. This will enable the development of a deterministic and dynamic process—response model which will allow the simulation of channel adjustment both in time and space.

Simulation models

Simulation modelling techniques offer the most sophisticated approach to

75

the assessment of physical impacts. Provided all the necessary information regarding the operative processes and feedback mechanisms is available this method allows the continuous modelling of these processes in a quantitative and deterministic way.

Initially it is necessary to understand why bankfull flow is the dominant or channel forming flow. Wolman and Miller [8] in their study of the magnitude and frequency of sediment transport processes rationalised this problem. Their research showed that the frequency of occurrence of the flow doing most transport and the bankfull discharge were identical and this explains why bankfull flow appears to be the dominant or channel forming discharge. The magnitude and frequency of the flow doing most work is dependent on the flow régime and the nature of the sediment transport processes (Fig. 6.3). For stable gravel bed rivers this is the 1·5 year flood (annual series) whilst for sand bed channels the return period of bankfull flow is lower. [9]

Any change in either the flow régime or the sediment input load will immediately cause erosion or deposition. Positive feedback mechanisms will initially dominate because at a section changes increase the channels propensity to transport sediment during erosion and reduces its potential during deposition. Negative feedback mechanisms eventually become dominant, due to the upstream extension of erosional or depositional activity, and this establishes a new equilibrium condition. Degradation ceases when headward erosion, resulting from drawdown effects, increases the sediment input; whilst aggradational activity ceases when upstream deposition, resulting from back water effects, decreases the sediment input. During periods of instability the bankfull channel dimensions adjust to the flow doing most erosion or deposition; when eroding the capacity of the channel increases and the return period is reduced and vice versa when depositing. The flow variability is also influenced by these systematic changes in channel capacity. Depositional activity reduces channel capacity, increases flood attenuation and reduces the flow variability; whilst erosion increases flow variability. [9]

Clearly this identifies the dynamic nature of natural systems because all the variables interrelate and it is impossible to identify cause and effect. Not only can discharge affect the channel but feedback mechanisms enable the channel to influence the discharge variability. In order to obtain an accurate assessment of channel response to river regulation it is necessary to define the physical laws controlling channel processes and feedback mechanisms.

Channels respond to the input conditions through the operation of the governing or process equations. These equations define why and how a

76

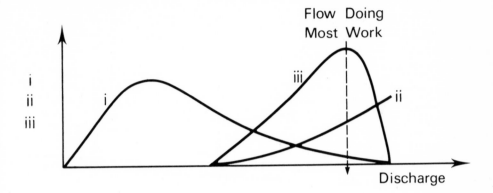

Coarse suspended and bed load

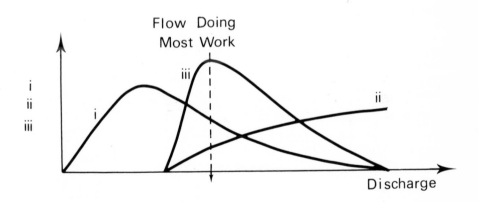

Fine suspended and wash load

Key: (i) Frequency
      (ii) Instantaneous sediment discharge
      (iii) Collective sediment discharge

Fig. 6.3   Definition of flow doing most work

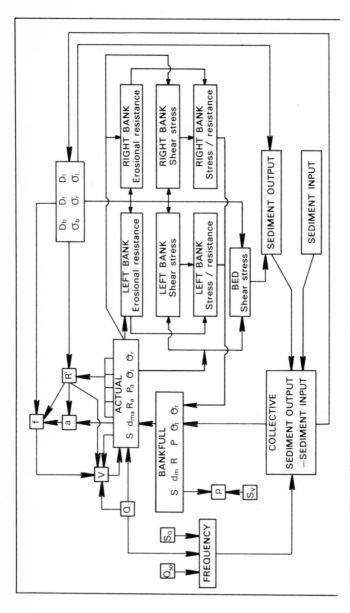

Fig. 6.4 Adjustment of bankfull geometry of gravel bed rivers to all the governing equations (Definitions: Q discharge, Q_{50} median daily discharge, S_Q standard deviation of daily discharge values, V velocity, S channel slope, d_m maximum bankfull flow depth, R_a bankfull hydraulic radius, P bankfull wetted perimeter, θ_1 angle of left bank, θ_r angle of right bank, $d_{m\,a}$ maximum flow depth, R hydraulic radius of flow, P_a wetted perimeter of flow, f friction factor, a term related to cross-sectional flow geometry, R' effective hydraulic radius, D_b, D_r, D_1 median grain size bed, right and left bank sediment, σ_b, σ_r, σ_1, standard deviation of bed, right and left bank grain size frequency distributions).

channel adjusts its velocity, cross sectional, plan and longitudinal shape through erosion and deposition. For gravel bed rivers there are seven unknowns and it follows that there must be seven governing equations. These are given by the continuity, flow resistance, sediment transport, bank competence (2) and sinuosity (2) equations. Provided these physical processes can be specified mathematically then their simultaneous solution will uniquely define the bankfull dimensions of stable or unstable channels given the flow doing most transport (erosion/deposition), the input load associated with this flow, the bed and bank material and the valley slope (Fig. 6.4).

The operation of feedback mechanisms enables the channel to interact with neighbouring stretches of channel to adjust its input conditions. Research into the controls and rates of operation of these feedback mechanisms will eventually enable the development of a dynamic process—response model. Once this model is established computer simulations will enable the effect of any regulation strategy to be predicted both in time and space. With many schemes the degree of regulation will increase through time to match developing demands. Using this method both the immediate and long term effects can be investigated.

Given an accurate assessment of potential physical impacts their influence on other environmental systems can be appraised. In this case channel adjustment can have ramifications on fisheries, water quality, flood control, land drainage and amenity. Equally, it enables economic evaluation of channel improvement and maintenance schemes to be included in the project costs if it is predicted that regulation will cause instability. This exercise may in fact be more important in terms of modifying the original proposal than any sophisticated assessment of total environmental impact. Increased distribution costs may sufficiently raise the unit costs of water so that the scheme as originally outlined may not be a viable proposition.

Conclusions

Choice of method for the assessment of environmental impact should not only be influenced by the amount of available knowledge regarding environmental processes but also by the nature of requirements of the impact assessment. Sophisticated procedures may not always be appropriate in a preliminary survey. Equally, it could be argued that they are not justified when physical impacts are considered to be insignificant in comparison with biological and socio-economic impacts. Value judgements of this nature are dangerous, especially if they are made without any detailed insight of environmental processes. Certain minor changes in the physical environment may trigger important thresholds in linked environmental systems. This indicates the importance of establishing simulation models to explain environmental processes and responses and which, once computerised, can be used at any stage in the assessment programme. The ease with which models of this type can be applied would enable individual cases to be considered on merit and would avoid the controversial blanket application of controls based on the worst possible case.

Discussion

The question of short and long term effects of regulation on alluvial channels was raised by *Clayton* (East Anglia). He was particularly concerned with changes which may take place over 100 years or more and wondered how it was possible to assess these long term effects. *Hey* (East Anglia) responded by outlining some of the experimental work he had recently completed for the Severn—Trent Water Authority to assess whether the operation of the proposed Craig-Goch reservoir would affect the stability of the river Severn below the intake—outfall at Llanidloes. As theoretical considerations indicate [10] that the natural character of any river can be maintained provided abstractions and release take place at flows below the threshold of bed material transport, it was necessary to establish this threshold value. Experimental releases from Llyn Clywedog in June 1975 indicated that regulation based on projected demand in 1999 and average rainfall conditions would alter the frequency of flows above this critical threshold. Consequently, unnatural amounts of erosion and deposition would result over time. Initially, however, regulation would not be harmful to the channel because the projected release pattern did not immediately affect the frequency of flows above the bed material transport threshold. As demands increased through time, regulation would eventually affect the stability of the channel and, given the rate of increase in demand, it should be possible to assess when this would happen.

The question of public accountability was raised by *Woolf* (Lawyers Ecology Group) because he was interested to know in what form, if any, the results of this study were presented to the public before the decision was taken regarding dam constructions. *Hey* pointed out that the decision had yet to be made and changing circumstances had considerably altered the nature of the proposed scheme. In his report to the Severn–Trent Water Authority [11] he outlined the maximum safe abstraction and release pattern which would maintain the present channel characteristics. It has since transpired that revised population and demand figures indicate that demand will be much less than expected by the year 2000 and the scheme has been modified accordingly. It is now intended that regulation will take place at flows below bed material transported thresholds so the channel will be preserved in its natural state.

Notes

[1]   Water Resources Board, *Water Resources in England and Wales*, vol. 1 (Report), vol. 2 (Appendices), HMSO, London 1973.
[2]   R. D. Hey, 'Response of alluvial channels to river regulation', *Proceedings Second World Congress*, International Water Resources Association, New Delhi, vol. 5, December 1975, pp.183–8.
[3]   C. C. Inglis, 'Meanders and their bearing on river training', *Maritime and Waterways Paper No. 7*, Institution of Civil Engineers, 1947.
[4]   C. C. Inglis, 'The behaviour and control of rivers and canals', *Research publication No. 13*, Central Board of Irrigation, India, 1949.
[5]   M. Nixon, 'A study of the bankfull discharge of rivers in England and Wales', *Proceedings Institution of Civil Engineers*, vol. 12, 1959, pp.157–74.
[6]   P. Ackers and F. G. Charlton, 'Dimensional analysis of alluvial channels with special reference to meander length', *Journal of Hydraulic Research*, vol. 8, 1970, pp.287–315.
[7]   R. D. Hey, 'An analysis of some of the factors influencing the hydraulic geometry of river channels', unpublished PhD thesis, University of Cambridge, 1972.
[8]   M. G. Wolman and J. P. Miller, 'Magnitude and frequency of forces in geologic processes', *Journal of Geology*, vol. 68, 1960, pp.54–74.
[9]   R. D. Hey, 'Design discharge for natural channels', in R. D. Hey and T. D. Davies (eds) *Science, Technology and Environmental Management*, Saxon House, 1975, pp.73–88.
[10]   R. D. Hey, 'Response of alluvial channels to river regulation', op.cit.
[11]   R. D. Hey, 'Response of Upper Severn to river regulation', report to Severn–Trent Water Authority, August 1975, 47pp.

7 Ecological considerations in the preparation of environmental impact statements

B. MOSS

'Considerations' is a suitably flexible term to apply to the vague predictions and general statements which, by the nature of the subject, are as yet all that can be mustered for the ecological contents of impact statements. The final conclusion of a recent statement on the environmental impact of a new dam in Rhodesia was that '. . . the data required to write this statement is (sic) either not available or difficult to obtain.' [1]

Ecological predictions that have been made in all statements hitherto have been very general and in some cases obvious even to the layman. For example, the damming of a salt water estuary to form a freshwater lake inevitably will lead to replacement of salt marshes by open fresh water. And certainly, if the area be one frequented by migratory ducks and geese, this will reduce the available grazing by a known percentage. What it would be desirable to predict is whether the ecosystems of unchanged areas of grazing nearby will adjust in such a way as to accommodate more birds, or whether ecosystems not previously grazed will be then visited by ducks. In the latter case it would be desirable also to predict what secondary and greater order effects the ducks might cause. In general these things cannot be predicted.

It is an ecological consideration, in the sense of this chapter, to establish why predictions of any subtlety cannot be made. It is also germane to examine the philosophy behind the environmental concern underlying impact statements. Man is an animal competing for survival with other animals and has evolved survival mechanisms just as they have. The Alaska pipeline, insecticides and the M1 are to human populations what termitaria are to termites and territory establishment and defence are to red grouse and hippopotami. This topic is considered in the second part of this chapter.

The prediction of events in ecosystems

What are ecosystems?

Living organisms are not randomly distributed but occur in reasonably obvious arrays of particular species. These arrays are not fixed in time. They respond to climatic and other environmental changes by elimination of some members and adoption of others. Sometimes these come from elsewhere, sometimes from genetic change in existing members.

Nor are they fixed in space. Environmental changes may cause extension of the area covered by some arrays and retraction in others. Some 13,000 years ago most of Europe was covered in tundra, physiognomically similar to that of present day Alaska, Northern Canada, Northern Scandinavia and Northern Russia. This was because a sheet of ice previously covering the area was melting back, uncovering land but creating still very cold weather. Since then there has been a warming and replacement of the tundra by different sorts of forests, less well adapted to intense cold, but better adapted to milder climates. In recent centuries the forests have been replaced in many areas by grassland, the consequence of grazing by increasing flocks of domestic animals.

Arrays of co-occurring species and the physio-chemical environment in which they live are called *ecosystems*. They are very complex organisations with built in mechanisms to allow maintenance of this order while conditions remain steady. Also they have mechanisms which permit the organisation to change to meet changing environmental conditions.

Natural ecosystems, by the possession of these mechanisms, must represent the best adjusted living systems for each time and place – but best adjusted for what? The mechanistic explanation is one applicable to many levels of organisation even to the level of the evolution of chemical elements. Bronowski has pointed out that the tendency of subatomic particles at very high temperatures, such as those in the sun and other stars, is to aggregate into atoms of greater and greater stability. [2] A point is reached at which increasing size and complexity are not accompanied by increased stability, but by instability. A selective process, nuclear fission, then acts to eliminate the less stable individuals. There is thus a natural selection for maximum stability, or survival value. At the level where elements and their compounds aggregated into more complex units during the early evolution of life, some units must have been chemically less stable than others and would soon have disintegrated. The more stable persisted and passed on their stability to progeny as they grew and divided. There was a natural chemical selection for stability. [3]

At a more complex level, Darwin [4] and Wallace elaborated the mechanism by which maximum adaptation is attained in living organisms through increased reproduction of those individuals best fitted for their current environment. Stability and fitness at these higher levels means the ability to compensate for or to resist external disturbances tending to destroy the system. At the ecosystem level a similar selection operates and can be described as selection for maximum homeostasis. It seems inherent in all complex systems capable of changing or being changed, including different sorts of human systems, or societies.

Attainment of homeostasis depends on very great complexity at the appropriate level. Thus a typical ecosystem comprises many thousands of different species carrying out, within and between themselves and their environment, many hundreds of thousands of chemical interactions. Preservation of the complex structure which homeostasis demands requires energy, derived ultimately, on earth, from the sun. Most of the energy is channelled through relatively few of the species present.

Thus most of the energy input in a temperate forest is through ten or twenty species of trees. Many other species, however, are essential to the survival of these dominants, for instance in the dissemination of seeds by animals to ensure regeneration. Other less abundant species represent an 'information store' for the ecosystem. Holly is presently a minor species in British woodlands. However, if progressive climatic changes discriminate against regeneration of oak and other presently dominant trees, it may happen that holly or some other minority species will take over their dominant role, maintaining the energy flow and homeostasis of the forest system. In general it must be assumed that every species present has some significance in the functioning or resilience of the ecosystem, or else selection would have eliminated it. The problem is that in perhaps more than 99 per cent of species the detailed significance is completely unknown, simply because the system is too complex for our present abilities to investigate it. Hence our abilities to predict the future of current ecosystems are very limited.

What predictions can be made?

In its division of functions among species, an ecosystem is paralleled by division of labour among human societies. Effects of removal of an obvious and abundant component can easily be predicted in the short term, and perhaps long term. The effects of loss of a less numerous constituent may be completely unforeseen in the long term. We have enough experience to predict and plan for a short term strike of rubbish collectors, but are impotent when it comes to assessing the ultimate loss by emigration of leading cancer research specialists.

For ecosystems broad predictions can be made on the basis of past experience, if it exists. Were it now planned to build another large dam on a tropical African river, certain events would be expected. Flooding of bushland in the river valley would create nutrient rich conditions in the rising waters of the new lake as the old vegetation decomposed. Blooms of phytoplankton and perhaps of floating plants, if suitable candidates were present in the original river, would be expected. These would be accompanied by high fish production, and perhaps release of hydrogen sulphide from the deepest water.

Compared with the original case of Lake Kariba, [5] however, neither the pessimism concerned with the development of unnavigable floating weed mats, nor the optimism concerned with the high fish production, would be experienced. It could be predicted that on completion of decomposition of the bush and replacement of the initial nutrient rich water with less fertile incoming river water, the biological productivity of the lake would decline. It could also be predicted that the incidence of river blindness (onchocerciasis) close to the dam might increase. This would be because of the ideal conditions provided by the dam spillways for breeding of the biting fly larvae (*Simulium* species) which act as vectors for the nematode worms which cause the disease. Schistosomiasis (bilharzia) might also increase among human populations if the new lake provided an extended shoreline both attractive to human settlement and suitable for colonisation by snail vectors of the disease. The latter proviso might not be readily predictable however.

A large new lake would raise the water table for some miles distal to its shore. In areas with marked dry seasons, movements of large mammals seeking water and fresh foliage in the dry season might be foreseen.

To an environmental planner such predictions might be on exactly the scale he would wish, and even a professional ecologist might consider them a reasonable achievement. There is now considerable experience of the problems involved in the making of lakes by man. Many projects, however, are not repeatable often enough for general and predictable patterns to emerge. There are likely to be many fewer equivalents of the Alaskan oil pipeline and the Severn tidal barrage. Even in the cases of the more recent tropical man made lakes unexpected major ecological effects have occurred. Lake Nasser, on the River Nile, now collects much of the fine organic detritus and nutrients gathered from the huge catchment area of the river. Previously these nutrients had formed part of the food base of a sardine fishery in the eastern Mediterranean sea; this had not been suspected and a once flourishing fishery is now very much in decline. [6] Ecological predictions can only be made out of past experience and not *de novo*. Compared with the complexity of the continuum of ecosystems that covers the earth's surface, our experience is very small.

Even our past experience may have led to present misconceptions about the functioning of ecosystems. It has long been known that lakes come in a spectrum of fertilities, from the very infertile (or oligotrophic) to the very fertile (eutrophic). For fifty years [7] ecologists have believed that lakes became more fertile as they filled in progressively with sediment. This process of eutrophication was regarded as a natural consequence of lake development. Increase in fertility (eutrophication) of lakes by introduction of sewage effluent has been a common happening this century. It can be prevented by extra treatment or diversion of sewage, though this might be expensive. Those responsible for allocation of public funds have consequently found it quite reasonable to claim that the rather undesirable effects of extreme eutrophication are merely being accelerated but are inevitable anyway. In the last twenty years, evidence has been gleaned from studies on the chemistry and fossils in lake sediments that lakes do not inevitably become more fertile with time. Significantly, only in the past five years have such admissions been made in literature, [8],[9] in the face of conventional wisdom that matters were otherwise. Any environmental predictions made in an impact statement are thus subject to the proviso that they may be made on unsound premises, no matter how venerable.

Some ecological changes are theoretically impossible to predict. They concern the behaviour of individual species. Each species population in an ecosystem is subject to continuous selection for maintenance of fitness, i.e. ability to survive. The material on which selection acts is the range of slight genetic variants which comprise the individuals of the population. This genetic variability is produced by random mutation, which by definition is impossible to predict. A mutant may arise which is much better equipped to survive an environmental change than its close relatives, and it may multiply swiftly. Marked ecological changes can occur through the introduction of a particularly fit new genotype to an ecosystem. These are illustrated by the changes caused by introduction of a new species from one continent to another — the rabbit and prickly pear cactus in Australia are examples. That a particularly fit new mutant can arise from very small genetic changes in a species already present is illustrated by the rapid invasion of toxic metal spoil heaps by mutant genotypes of certain grasses. [10],[11]

In summary, the only predictions that can be made about ecosystems are broad ones based on previous experience. That which is not suspected cannot be predicted, and certain changes are unpredictable, for they are based on random events.

The significance of ecological changes caused by man

The ecosystems which have evolved for a particular place and time are those that have the maximum homeostasis for that place and time. It is meaningless therefore to talk about improving them. For instance, the intertidal organisms and ecosystems that occupy estuaries have become adapted, through natural selection, for existence there. Daily submergence at high tide and exposure at low tide are essential for their survival. Claims that removal of tidal fluctuation through the construction of a tidal barrage, for example, will benefit estuarine ecosystems [12] are wrong. Permanent submergence would lead to replacement of one ecosystem by another, but in no sense would 'improve' the original one.

Many ecosystems depend on periodic environmental fluctuations for their survival. The Florida Everglades is a wide freshwater marsh dominated by grass and sedge vegetation. A slow flow of water from Lake Okeechobee in the north through the marsh to the sea in the south-west maintains the marsh with its famous diversity of wildlife. [13],[14] The decaying remains of the marsh plants (peat) tend to build the bed up to above the water table. This permits pine forest to colonise just as it does on raised hummocks of limestone dotted around the marsh. However, the dry winter season, when water does not flow and the marsh dries out, is characterised by occasional light fires caused by lightning. These prevent deeper accumulations of peat forming without damaging the propagatory rhizomes of the main marsh plants, and also destroy any colonising pine seedlings. The marsh is thus prevented from succeeding to forest, and a diversity of habitat is maintained. There have been moves in Florida to regulate the amount of water reaching the Everglades in connection with the reduction of flooding risk in the developed lowlands near Lake Okeechobee in the wet season. The effects of these have been to prevent sufficient water reaching the marsh. Fires have been so severe that the marsh plant rhizomes have been damaged and the ecological future of the area is uncertain. Too much water, in the form of permanent flooding, would have an equally deleterious effect. The ecosystem has become adjusted through selection to the natural water balance and changes on either side will cause marked changes in the ecosystem.

Ecosystems react to environmental changes caused by man in the same way that they react to changes caused by any other agent — by adjustment or, in extreme cases, by extinction and replacement. Such reactions have been constant features of ecosystems since life began more than 3½ billion years ago. The differences between our present ecosystems and those dominated by dinosaurs, reconstructed from the Jurassic age, illustrate the pressures for change induced by progressive alterations in the physio-chemical environment. Arguably, the stresses induced by the progressive oxygenation of the atmosphere on ecosystems comprising solely anaerobic microorganisms in the early pre-Cambrian seas were much greater than the changes now being induced by man. The changes man makes represent, for human societies, the inevitable homeostatic trends common to all complex systems capable of change. In principle there is nothing unexpected about them. They became inevitable as soon as the ultimate adaptation for survival — the ability to manipulate the environment — had been evolved by man.

It may be that the changes man makes will be so far-reaching that his present abilities cease to be adaptive. The consequences must then be progressive genetic change — further evolution of man — or his extinction. A perspective view of ecosystem changes on a geological time scale encourages the view that the future of the world ecosystem, or biosphere, will be determined by subtler and more powerful forces than political lobbies. It is the alternation of day and night that induces the twittering of sparrows at dawn, not the reverse.

Discussion

Two speakers put forward a more optimistic view about the prediction of ecological impacts. *Goodier* (Nature Conservancy Council) felt that many of the ecological effects of dam construction in Africa could have been predicted, especially the incidence of bilharzia. In his opinion mistakes were made because of failure to make an adequate environmental impact assessment. *Moss* (East Anglia) accepted that many problems which by hindsight have been recognised, might have been predicted if an adequate assessment had been made. However he still felt that the magnitude of the problems could not be accurately predicted. Many jetties were built in Lake Kariba which are now either above or below the lake level. If the lake had been stabilised at some other level the weed bed area and the resultant bilharzia problems might have been reduced.

The distinction between the ideals of a complete understanding of the functioning of ecosystems and the requirements of an environmental impact assessment was raised by *George* (Nature Conservancy Council). In the UK there has been considerable research effort on the ecological impact of reservoir construction at coastal and inland sites. As a result of this research it has been possible to advise which proposed reservoir sites would be least or most damaging to wild life interests. Similarly, the Nature Conservancy Council have been able to make some predictions about what will happen to the reservoir, and what sort of bird life will colonise it when it is created.

For the purpose of environmental impact assessment, he believed that it is easy and possible to make ecological surveys which would enable predictions to be made. A more elaborate assessment based on a complete understanding of the functioning of ecosystems was not possible at the moment, but he felt that advice was required and had to be given in spite of limited understanding.

In reply, *Moss* admitted that he should have qualified the statement that it was impossible to make predictions, by adding the rider that it was impossible to guarantee correct predictions. It was all very well for Dr George to make predictions, but he did not know whether or not he was right.

Notes

[1] D. S. Mitchell, A. P. Bowmaker, P. L. Osborne, J. Ferreira and G. E. Gibbs Russell, *Environmental Impacts of the Darwendale Dam, Rhodesia*, Division of Biological Sciences, University of Rhodesia, Salisbury 1975.

[2] J. Bronowski, *The Ascent of Man*, BBC Publications, London 1973.

[3] S. W. Fox, *The Origins of Prebiological Systems*, Academic Press, New York 1965.

[4] C. Darwin, *The Origin of Species by means of Natural Selection*, John Murray, London 1859.

[5] A. J. McLachlan, 'Development of some lake ecosystems in tropical Africa, with special reference to the invertebrates', *Biological Reviews*, vol. 49. 1974, pp.365–97.

[6] See article entitled, 'Fisheries affected by Aswan Dam', *Commercial Fisheries Research*, vol. 32, 1970, p.64.

[7]   W. H. Pearsall, 'The development of vegetation in the English Lakes, considered in relation to the general evolution of glacial lakes and rock basins', *Proceedings of the Royal Society*, series B, vol. 92, 1921, pp.259—84.

[8]   B. Moss, 'Studies on Gull Lake, Michigan. Pt. II, Eutrophication — evidence and prognosis', *Freshwater Biology*, vol. 2, 1972, pp.309—20.

[9]   A. M. Beeton and W. T. Edmondson, 'The eutrophication problem', *Journal of the Fisheries Research Board of Canada*, vol. 29, 1972, pp.673—82.

[10]   A. D. Bradshaw, 'Populations of *Agrostis tenuis* resistant to lead and zinc poisoning', *Nature*, vol. 169, 1952, p.1098.

[11]   D. Jowett, 'Population studies on lead-tolerant *Agrostis tenuis*', *Evolution*, vol. 18, 1964, pp.70—81.

[12]   T. Shaw, 'Tidal power and the environment', *New Scientist*, vol. 68, 23 October 1975, pp.202—6.

[13]   M. S. Douglas, *The Everglades: River of Grass*, Ballantine Books, New York 1947.

[14]   P. Caulfield, *Everglades*, Ballantine Books, New York 1970.

8 Evaluating environmental impacts

B. CLARK

The Scottish Development Department and the Department of the Environment have sponsored a research project, the objective of which has been to develop methodologies for making a balanced appraisal of the potential impact of large scale industrial development on the physical environment, taking economic and social effects into account. The study has been concerned with proposed developments likely to be incompatible with existing land uses. Many of these large scale developments are likely to be either 'departures' from statutory development plans or fall under the 'call in' powers of the Secretaries of State for England and Wales and Scotland and as such tend to be in conflict with existing or proposed land uses.

The study has focused on the problems which planning departments must face when attempting to make a balanced assessment of the likely impacts of granting planning permission for industrial development. An attempt has been made to develop a methodology which encourages a systematic appraisal of impact under existing planning and related legislation. In developing the methodology emphasis has been placed on large scale industrial developments where it is necessary to consider environmental as well as economic and social effects. Techniques of appraisal, such as the work being undertaken in the United States as a result of NEPA, have been studied with a view to formulating techniques which are more appropriate to conditions in British planning authorities. An attempt has been made to present in summary form the various stages of the methodology of project appraisal which could be utilised as an aid to a structured evaluation of large scale industrial planning applications in Britain.

The proposed evaluation methodology

When considering a major development proposal a planning authority will

91

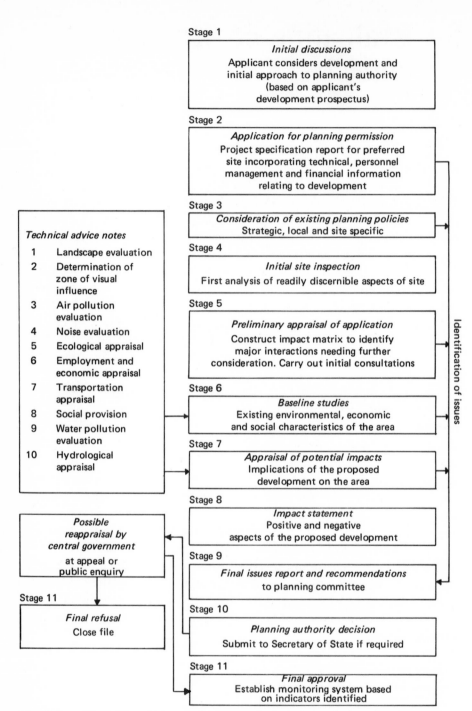

Fig. 8.1   An approach to project appraisal under existing development control procedures

92

wish to ensure that a thorough and systematic appraisal is made of the merits of the application and its likely impacts. The flow chart (Fig. 8.1) outlines the proposed evaluation methodology. It should not be thought however that the stages outlined will follow one another in strict sequence in all evaluation exercises. Indeed in many cases the stages will be concurrent.

Initial discussions with prospective applicants (stage 1)

In most instances a developer will wish to discuss the acceptability of a proposed project with the planning authority before submitting a formal application. At this stage the developer will normally disclose only preliminary details. Recognising that neither party will wish to commit themselves in these early discussions it is suggested that developers prepare a short prospectus about their project which would provide the planning authority with: (a) a list of alternative sites considered; (b) a list of the key siting criteria of the proposed development; and (c) brief details of the proposed development and the range of processes to be used when operational. The limited information available will restrict the scope of analysis at this stage but the planning authority should be able to make a preliminary assessment of the proposal in relation to existing planning policies.

Application for planning permission (stage 2)

Once a developer indicates his intention to apply for planning permission for a development considered to be of 'major significance' by the planning authority then the project appraisal mechanism would be implemented. The developer would be requested by the planning authority to submit a detailed project specification report with his application forms. All too often major development applications are subject to considerable delays in their processing. Delays tend to occur at various stages of evaluation if insufficient information is available to the authority. The project specification report would provide the planning authority with a wide range of information at the outset of the development control process and it would also facilitate the comprehensive appraisal of the environmental, economic and social consequences. The applicant should also benefit because submission of detailed information at an early stage could assist faster and more efficient decision making by the planning authority. A standard brief for the preparation of project specification reports will request that information should be submitted in the form of a technical report. Information will be requested on the following topics:

1   Details of the proposed plant and its processes.
2   Physical characteristics of application site:
(a)   land requirements;
(b)   site utilisation (and detailed plans at varying scales);
(c)   marine site characteristics (where appropriate).
3   Employment characteristics:
(a)   during construction phase;
(b)   when development is operational.
4   Financial data:
(a)   wage and salary levels;
(b)   expenditure on locally produced inputs.
5   Infrastructure requirements:
(a)   raw material demand;
(b)   transport requirements;
(c)   water demand;
(d)   electricity demand;
(e)   gas demand;
(f)   housing demand.
6   Environmental implications:
(a)   noise levels;
(b)   vibration levels;
(c)   gaseous emissions;
(d)   particulate emissions;
(e)   odours;
(f)   dust;
(g)   discharge of aqueous effluents;
(h)   solid wastes.
7   Emergency services:
(a)   fire and medical services;
(b)   hazard;
(c)   control of pollution at marine facilities.

It will be necessary for a planning authority to supplement the questions if other factors are considered appropriate. However, standardisation of areas where information would be required should be an invaluable aid to speeding decisions especially when the system starts to operate and prospective developers know what is required of them.

The major benefits to be gained from such an approach are that it would first aid the definition of initial issues, secondly aid the planning authority to decide upon the range of consultations that could usefully be undertaken, and thirdly provide the basis for deciding those aspects of the application which require detailed examination prior to any decision being taken.

Consideration of existing planning policies (stage 3)

It will be necessary for a planning authority in receipt of a major application to consider the range of planning policies and proposals that are likely to be affected and the extent to which they would have to be altered if development occurred. Close consideration should be given to: (a) strategic planning policies contained in the development plan; (b) local planning policies in the vicinity of the application site; (c) previous planning decisions in the vicinity of the application site and their implications; (d) current planning proposals in the vicinity of the application site; and (e) special development control factors which may act as a constraint on development in the vicinity of the application site — e.g. national park areas, areas of outstanding natural beauty, areas of great landscape value, sites of special scientific interest, ancient monuments, listed buildings, Ministry of Defence safety zones, aerodrome safeguarding zones, etc.

It may be useful to prepare overlays for each factor found to be relevant. Such a sieve assessment would help indicate the numbers, types and intensity of policy constraints acting upon the development proposal.

Initial site inspection (stage 4)

The site inspection is a fundamental part of any assessment work and there is no need to stress its importance for obtaining information about the proposed site and its surroundings, checking submitted plans and assessing if there are aspects of the application which require special consideration.

Preliminary appraisal of the planning application (stage 5)

Construction of an impact assessment matrix   The value of any assessment of impact will depend heavily on the thoroughness with which the appraisal work is carried out. Basically the method requires the investigation of the characteristics of: (a) the existing situation in the local area, and (b) the development proposal. The potential interactions between these two elements must be identified and analysed in detail.

On receipt of a project specification report, the planning authority should construct a matrix, which will provide a framework for identifying potential impacts. This matrix will act as a checklist to help the

Table 8.1

Example of an impact assessment matrix

Characteristics of the development

Characteristics of the existing situation	Construction																	Operation																			
	Land requirements	Site utilisation	Labour requirements	Company expenditure patterns	Raw material inputs	Transport of raw materials	Transport of employees	Water demand	Electricity demand	Gas demand	Population changes	Noise and vibration	Particulate emissions	Dust	Aqueous discharges	Solid waste disposal	Emergencies	Site utilisation	Permanent labour requirements	Company expenditure patterns	Raw material inputs	Transport of raw materials	Transport of employees	Transport of products	Water supply	Electricity supply	Gas supply	Population changes	Noise from plant	Vibrations from plant	Gaseous emissions	Particulate emissions	Odours from plant	Dust	Aqueous discharges	Solid wastes	Emergencies
Land																																					
Water																																					
Climate																																					
Land use																																					
Landscape quality																																					
Ecological characteristics																																					
Resident population																																					
Tourist population																																					
Employment structure																																					
Traffic movement patterns																																					
Electricity supply																																					
Gas supply																																					
Water supply																																					
Sewerage																																					
Solid waste disposal																																					
Transportation																																					
Finance																																					
Education																																					
Housing																																					
Health service facilities																																					
Emergency services																																					
Air pollution																																					
Water pollution																																					
Noise and vibration																																					

Instructions

1 Identify all actions that are part of the proposed development.

2 At every possible point of interaction between the proposed action and the present situation make a cross 'x' if an impact effect is possible.

3 Detailed appraisal work should be undertaken to assess each potential interaction.

4 The text which makes up the impact statement should be a discussion of the significant impacts within each box where interaction is indicated between the proposed development and the existing situation.

caseworker to obtain a comprehensive picture of the range of likely impacts, although it must be emphasised that such a matrix is not a substitute for analysis. An example of such a matrix is shown in Table 8.1. The characteristics of the development proposal are described on the horizontal axis, and the existing environmental, economic and social characteristics of the application site and its surroundings are shown on the vertical axis. Such a matrix should be drawn up on the basis of information known to the planning authority and obtained from the developer. When considering the various sections of the project specification report, the planning officer should place a cross in those boxes where he considers a possible action would cause a change in the existing situation. As it will be impracticable to produce an all embracing matrix which incorporates the characteristics of a wide range of development types and potential locations, the matrix will require modification by the planning officer depending on the proposed development, the application site, and its surroundings.

Consultations The matrix will play an important part in identifying the range of initial consultations which will be required. A copy of the matrix showing the range of interactions identified by the planning department together with the completed project specification report should be circulated to specialist groups for comment. In addition they will be asked to identify any interactions considered to be of significance. In this way the consultations should lead to the matrix being developed in greater detail as further potential interactions are identified.

Baseline studies of the existing situation (stage 6)

The objective of these studies is to establish the nature of the existing environmental, economic and social conditions in the local area likely to be affected if the development takes place. In practice much information will often be available if a detailed survey has been undertaken in the preparation of a plan which includes the development site. Depending on the nature of the site, the availability of recent data and other factors, it may prove necessary to undertake baseline studies to obtain a comprehensive picture of the site and surrounding area. The following is a summary of baseline study topics for which information will be required.

1 Physical characteristics of the site and its surroundings:
(a) land;
(b) water;
(c) climate;
(d) land use and landscape character.

2 Ecological characteristics of the site and its surroundings:
(a) habitats, communities and species.
3 Human activity patterns in the area:
(a) demographic aspects;
(b) employment structure;
(c) transport.
4 Infrastructure services:
(a) electricity;
(b) gas;
(c) water;
(d) sewerage;
(e) solid waste disposal;
(f) transportation;
(g) finance;
(h) education;
(i) housing;
(j) telecommunications.
5 Social and community services:
(a) health service facilities;
(b) emergency services – fire and ambulance.
6 Existing levels of environmental pollution:
(a) air pollution;
(b) water pollution;
(c) noise and vibration;
(d) radioactivity.

These baseline studies and updated local plan data will provide the planning officer with an understanding of the existing situation against which he will be able to assess the likely advantages and disadvantages of development proposals.

Appraisal of potential impacts (stage 7)

Whilst there is no method of systematically identifying and describing all likely impacts of a development proposal it is suggested that the following approach will go a considerable way towards providing a comprehensive approach of general applicability. To carry out an appraisal of potential impacts it will be necessary for the planning authority to draw together the detailed information contained in the project specification report and baseline studies. The matrix prepared by the planning authority should be referred to again at this stage of project appraisal.

In each instance where a likely impact was identified in the matrix during initial appraisal and consultations the planning authority should undertake analysis of the scale and acceptability of the changes involved. It will be important for the planning authority to establish not only the likely impacts of the development on the local environment and community, but also the extent to which these impose constraints during both construction and operation phases.

Appraisal should be carried out to establish the likely impacts identified in each box of the matrix. The construction and operational phases of the development should be dealt with separately. The planning authority should endeavour to identify whether the envisaged impacts are likely to be: (a) beneficial and/or adverse; (b) short term and/or long term; (c) reversible and/or irreversible; (d) direct and/or indirect; (e) local and/or strategic. At this stage of impact appraisal it is proposed that a set of questions should be considered by planning authorities. These questions will be related to the relevant sections of the project specification report and the baseline studies and their purpose is to assist the planning authority follow systematic lines of enquiry. It is envisaged that local authorities will supplement these by further project specific and site specific questions. A close consideration of these linked to the relevant sections of the project specification report and baseline studies should enable the planning authority to carry out an objective examination of the full range of implications of the development. If the planning authority does not have the necessary expertise it may be necessary in certain circumstances to employ consultants to consider these aspects.

Production of impact statement (stage 8)

The impact statement will draw together the conclusions reached on the potential impacts considered. Each potential impact investigated should be considered in turn and implications stated as succinctly as possible with discussion covering the following points:

(a)   a brief description of the proposed action;
(b)   likely impact of the proposed action;
(c)   any adverse effects likely as a result of the proposed action;
(d)   any beneficial effects likely as a result of the proposed action;
(e)   whether the impacts are likely to be short and/or long term;
(f)   whether the impacts are likely to be reversible or irreversible;
(g)   the range of direct and indirect impacts associated with the proposed action;
(h)   whether the impacts are likely to be of local and/or strategic significance.

The prospects for the area if the development does not take place should be discussed. This will enable decision makers to compare the potential effects of approving the application with the implications of the 'no change' alternative.

A summary sheet indicating the range of possible impacts can now be drawn up by the planning authority. A hypothetical example is shown in Table 8.2. No attempt has been made to use numerical weightings to differentiate the degree of importance or magnitude of impacts. Such weighting and ranking methods tend to provide a false sense of objectivity

Table 8.2

Project appraisal: impact assessment summary sheet

Potential impact effects of proposed development	Classification of impact effect	Descriptive evaluation of each potential impact effect
Loss of Zostera feeding areas for Brent geese	Insert where relevant: B $\quad$ = Beneficial A ✓ = Adverse St $\quad$ = Short term Lt ✓ = Long term R $\quad$ = Reversible I ✓ = Irreversible P ✓ = Primary S ✓ = Secondary T $\quad$ = Tertiary L $\quad$ = Local Sg ✓ = Strategic	The reclamation programme of 56 hectares associated with the development proposals would cause disruption of siltation patterns in the estuary. Inundation of Zostera beds in the north bay by water heavily laden with fine silts would lead to loss of approximately 60 per cent of this important habitat. It can be expected that there would be short term increases in the number of waders in this particular area; once the construction phase is complete and these silts are not replenished the number will return to its former level. The projected layer of anoxic mud (two to three inches deep) would probably not be reinvaded by Zostera, so that 60 per cent of this area would be permanently lost. The over-wintering Brent geese, which constitute 20 per cent of the world population, feed exclusively on Zostera and the reduced area of grazing would not support the present number of geese.

because they are themselves subjective judgements on the part of individual assessors. The core of any impact appraisal must lie in the detailed appraisal carried out wherever a potential interaction between the proposed development and the existing environment is indicated. The summary sheets are intended as a means of drawing together the technical information in these reports and presenting it in a descriptive manner which can be readily understood by all interested parties.

Final issues report and recommendations (stage 9)

This report will indicate the main issues that have become apparent and the extent to which they have been resolved. It should indicate the views of other local government departments, external organisations and individuals consulted during the appraisal and also representations received from members of the public. It should also contain a clear statement of points made by the applicant in discussions with the planning authority, particularly in relation to meetings held to resolve any problems raised in the impact analysis. This report along with the impact statement should be submitted to the planning committee and form the basis of the recommendation for approval or refusal of the planning application.

Planning authority decision (stage 10)

The planning authority will now be in a position to make its decision. It will have available: (a) a *project specification report* containing detailed information about the plant and its processes; (b) an *impact statement* containing detailed appraisals of each potentially important impact related to the study of the existing situation; (c) *summary sheets* describing impacts likely to result from the proposed development; (d) a *list of objectors* and those making representations with a summary of their views; (e) a *list of consultees* with summaries of their views; and (f) a *final issues report* indicating the planning officer's recommendation based on technical reports, consultations, and planning priorities in the area.

When refusing the application the planning authority must specify its grounds for the decision. If the developer appeals to the Secretary of State, a public local inquiry may be called to examine the case. Should an inquiry be called, the reports prepared during appraisal of the application should be forwarded by the authority for consideration by the Secretary of State. They would form the basic documentation in the event of a referral to a public inquiry and indicate those issues arising from the proposal on which differences of opinion between the various parties still existed. This should enable the inquiry to concentrate on the most relevant aspects of the development proposals and reduce the time taken to reach a decision.

When development applications are to be approved four factors relating to the future need to be considered. First, the possible dangers of giving permission for a major development with significant reserved matters. Secondly, the enforcement of conditions which may be attached to planning permission. Thirdly, schemes which should be established to consider specific aspects of development identified in the impact statement as requiring monitoring. Finally, the implications of the new development for future planning.

Conclusions

The various stages of project appraisal which have been outlined are an attempt to develop a methodology which is rigorous but which at the same time could operate under existing planning legislation. It is realised that in postulating a general methodology site specific and project specific considerations must be incorporated. In requesting more information than is customarily required from a developer when submitting his planning application, empirical evidence does suggest that many delays occur because of the need to obtain additional information during processing and evaluation of the application. It is also believed that if a developer was asked to produce his own project appraisal or 'impact statement' the local authority would still need to verify many of the statements. In suggesting the above methodology it is believed that whilst it might appear time consuming to a local planning officer it could facilitate a more structured approach to the appraisal of contentious planning applications. It would certainly only be utilised for a limited number of large scale industrial applications. It is precisely these types of development which usually require time, money and resources to process. It is hoped, therefore, that the proposals being suggested by the Aberdeen study team which will be published by the Department of Environment in a report titled 'Assessment of Major Industrial Applications − A Manual' will help to bring about an improvement in the evaluation of major developments.

Discussion

Clark's work is aimed primarily at providing a workable methodology for environmental impact assessment that could be applied to large scale development proposals within the existing statutory framework of development control in Britain. *Lyddon* (Scottish Development Department) agreed with Clark that there is a danger in trying to impress the American experience on British practice. He was concerned that the word 'impact' was too emotive, implying a hidden sharp shock, and preferred the phrase 'development impact analysis' to stress the emphasis on the consequences of change which was, after all, the essence of planning. [1] Given a well staffed planning authority and a developer with a social conscience, EIA was already possible since procedures for enacting this kind of review were in existence. For example, the Scottish Development Department has assisted local authorities to develop guidelines to review the effects of oil-related development in their areas, and although this is a non-statutory requirement it has proved effective.

Shaw (Norfolk County Council) agreed that EIA should not be mandatory and doubted that any new legislation was necessary for three reasons. First, it would delay development proposals still further, resulting in increased costs both of development and planning control at a time when all forms of unnecessary expenditure should be curtailed. This would only further reduce public confidence in planning. Second, the existing legislative basis for planning and development control is entirely adequate. The public enquiry should review all possible effects of a major development, while at an early stage of a proposal the Department of Environment can ask a developer to answer any specific questions it considers necessary to ask (a statement of issues). In really controversial cases the Environment Secretary can establish a planning enquiry commission with exhaustive and independent powers of investigation. This, however, has never been created because of the immense effort and time which would be expended on it. [2] Once a project is completed the local authorities responsible can monitor any environmental effects. If the planning authority does not like what is happening it can shut down a plant, for example, if it contravenes the conditions attached to the planning consent. *Biggs* (Confederation of British Industries) commented that such an extreme situation would be most unlikely since industry is at pains to consult with various local bodies and pollution control inspectorates before application for planning permission is made.

Thirdly, there is the matter of who provides the EIA. While there is a good case for this to be made by the developer, Shaw believed that only the planning authority can provide the proper balanced assessment. In any case the planning officer must give the final advice to the appropriate politicians. *Train* (Cremer and Warner) generally supported Shaw's arguments, but emphasised the critical importance of offering objective advice so that proper political decisions could be taken. Possibly the independent consultant, acting as a kind of honest broker, would be best here, he felt, since many local authorities take up adversary positions whenever amenities or hazards are involved, if only to counteract the self interested statements of the developer. In any case there are many very important but complicated technical issues associated with site selection and project design about which few planners are knowledgeable.

In reply to the criticism that his impact matrix was far too detailed and complicated, *Clark* (Aberdeen) emphasised the flexible nature of his matrix; only those issues regarded as important in the particular case need be studied and the matrix should help to pinpoint those. Obviously this will be of help to the developer, for he will then be more aware of the kind of factual specifications required by the local planning authority. As to the matter of advice and EIA preparation, the important point was not so much who did it as what questions were asked and how they were answered. All too frequently inadequate terms of reference led inevitably to improper assessment. *Train* observed that even at the site selection stage, political considerations might override technical matters, although the political issues could be adjusted when there were strong technical arguments for site selection. At stage 2 hardly any industry was in a position to give project specification. The criteria for judgement must be sufficiently broad banded to leave room for further detailed survey.

Notes

[1]   Train was not happy with this new wording. He felt that the proliferation of terms added to the confusion and encouraged imprecision. In any case, the phrase 'environmental impact assessment' was in line with EEC thinking.

[2]   The matter of the planning enquiry commission is developed further in Chapter 14.

9   Lessons to be learnt from case studies in London

M. W. A. CASSIDY

The increasing importance of environmental effects in planning has not been matched by the development of reliable and comprehensive methods for assessing their significance. Although work has been undertaken on parts of the problem only recently have attempts been made to bring together all the different factors in a way that will help planners, politicians and the public to make decisions.

Evaluation requires judgement: deciding which factors are the most important, weighing up the impacts that will fall upon different groups of people at different times, comparing environmental concerns with the social and economic. Such judgements are now made by planners, politicians and the public. Planners espouse the public interest as sanction for their judgement but often impose their own values. Politicians affect a concern for long term goals while behaving pragmatically. The public looks at local implications and may ignore the wider merits of proposals. At best, environmental evaluation may offer a common basis upon which some of these differences in attitude can be put to constructive use.

Local authorities are both poachers and game keepers in the environmental impact field. Many local authority policies and programmes as well as their physical development have considerable environmental impact and it is desirable for the same criteria to be applied to their own activities as to other people's proposals submitted to them for approval. It is significant that the goals adopted by the Greater London Council for its various programmes all make specific reference to environment.

The way in which environmental investment may be instrumental in achieving other goals and objectives has to be considered in project evaluation. Environmental factors are incorporated in projects to achieve goals like safety, health, efficiency and well-being. Most organisations adopt corporate goals and devise policies, with varying degrees of precision, to achieve them, but attempts to transform policies into effective criteria to evaluate performance − or to establish whether a project is consistent with objectives have usually failed. Yet the increasing adoption of environmental standards, at least as guidelines to action, offers considerable scope in the development of practical project evaluation techniques. Few authorities have begun to think seriously about the development of comprehensive environmental guidelines, or to evaluate the performance of their own programmes in environmental terms.

What form should this evaluation take? First, it should be comprehensive enough to be applied to various projects both nationally and locally. Second, it should be able to pinpoint undesirable effects (on the basis of irreversibility or equity or cost considerations), and third, it should enable comparisons to be made. Most importantly, it should afford decision making machinery including national, local, project and public interests a shared basis for debate, decision and review. A flexible framework that makes these contributions will need a different amount and quality of data at different stages and should not impose costs or constraints out of scale with the projects to which it is to be applied.

Given these many functions, and bearing in mind the many interests that will be exercised throughout the evaluation process, it is not surprising to find varying frameworks for environmental evaluation. Most importantly, there will be variations in the extent of aggregation attempted, in the relationship established between environmental and other considerations, and in efforts to translate all impact to some common unit like cost.

Traffic in London

The first case study covers the evaluation of traffic schemes in London. The story of London's roads is a familiar one. Neither the abandonment of the ambitious primary road proposals by the current majority party of the GLC nor the weighty ambiguities of the Environment Secretary's recent statement on the Greater London Development Plan have done anything to diminish the importance Londoners attach to reducing the environment impact of traffic.

Traffic management schemes, bus priority measures, pedestrianisation, lorry routes, all have environmental implications. As traffic is displaced from one street and reassigned to others, some people may be better off, others worse. A method was needed to evaluate the environmental effects of these proposals. Working in the local government context, close to decision makers and conscious of their exposure to the reactions of a well

106

informed public, it was clear that a purely scientific framework was unlikely to work. A balance had to be struck between scientific rigour and political relevance.

Transport proposals affect the environment in two ways. The direct environmental effects of road construction and improvement are largely confined to the immediate areas near new routes. These include the blight effect of uncertainty before construction; the disturbance due to property demolition and rehousing; the construction process itself; the physical impact of the road on the adjoining fabric in visual terms; the physical disruption necessary to readjust the local environment to accommodate the new route and the severance of existing communities and patterns of movement.

The indirect environmental effects of using roads, both existing and new, include noise from engines, transmission, gear boxes, tyres, horns and the slamming of doors; air pollution and smell; creating difficulties for pedestrians in terms of danger, delay and inconvenience; visual impact of vehicles both parked and moving; dust, dirt, traffic film and oil stains; and vibration.

Despite the considerable research that has been undertaken into the individual effect of traffic, there are major difficulties to be overcome if their aggregate effect is to be assessed. Some environmental effects resulting from the use of roads can be quantified, some predicted. Some are hazardous to safety and health, others just a nuisance. Some are perceived in their effects while others, possibly more damaging, go unnoticed. In these circumstances no assessment of impact is going to be complete. But progress may be made where measurements of the factors can be related to data on traffic flow, speed and composition and predictive equations derived. Preferably the areas for which such relationships are developed should be similar to the area being assessed. Where this is not the case, it may be necessary to undertake specific site measurements in order to adjust the predictive equations. It would be very convenient if all the environmental effects shared the same relationship with traffic flow, composition and speed. This would make it possible to use a single indicator for environmental effects, rather than having to deal with many. As it is, the relationship is different for each effect, as Fig. 9.1 shows.

It is important to recognise that different kinds of projects require different environmental evaluation. New road proposals need substantial analysis at every stage and their effects may be felt at great distances from the route. More modest traffic management schemes, however, are often implemented without much analysis.

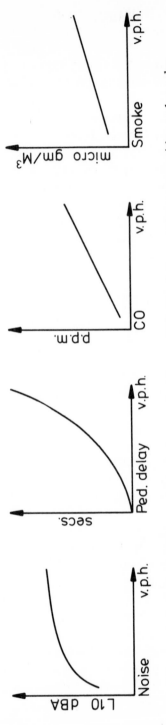

Fig. 9.1 Relationships between vehicle flow and noise, pedestrian delay, carbon monoxide, and smoke

There are four facets of evaluation that may be applied to the environmental effects of traffic:

1   Environmental standards may be used as a basis for determining the capacity of existing streets to accommodate traffic. Buchanan's *Traffic in Towns* studies [1] pioneered this approach with their proposals for hierarchies of streets, with primarily residential areas protected from through traffic. However, the logical application of standards to all people on all roads would produce very severe restraint, especially upon the main traffic carrying routes themselves. The costs of such universal application of standards as a basis for evaluating traffic proposals would clearly be of overriding importance. Another problem has been that somewhat arbitrary professional values have sometimes been added to the more acceptable health and safety standards. Questions of equity inevitably arise.

2   Comparison of the effects of alternative schemes may be a sufficient basis for evaluation. This enables more detailed studies to be focused upon feasible options and should eliminate wholly unacceptable solutions. It is usual to compare scheme effects with the existing situations but this assumes that the existing distribution of disamenities due to traffic is fair and reasonable. But the use to which roads are put is determined more by availability than suitability, so schemes which show a benefit for a majority may make things worse for people already badly affected. Lorry routeing, for example, often has this effect.

3   Having chosen a particular option on the basis of comparison, it may be necessary and desirable to predict more precisely the range of impacts. Legislation may require mitigating action to be taken, as under the Noise Insulation Regulations. Other ways may be found to mitigate the worst effects.

4   When a scheme is implemented there is going to be a discrepancy between predicted impact and observed impact. Schemes need to be monitored so that modifications can be made and so that predictive methods are constantly improved.

Capacity, comparison, prediction and monitoring will be needed in combination and at different stages of scheme development. The depth of analysis at each stage will depend upon the nature of the proposals.

Here are some examples of evaluation which consider particularly the way in which the results are presented to politicians and the public.

Table 9.1

Average environmental conditions during a.m. peak under three alternative traffic proposals

Street	From	To	Option A				Option B				Option C			
			L_{10}	PD	S	CO	L_{10}	PD	S	CO	L_{10}	PD	S	CO
Addison Gardens	Richmond Way	– Holland Road	69·5	1	46	3·0	69·5	1	46	3·0	69·5	1	46	3·0
Askew Road		all	79·5	50	87	8·5	79·0	35	80	8·0	78·5	32	78	7·5
Bagley's Lane		all	81·0	62	99	9·0	71·5	1	48	3·5	81·0	56	96	8·5
Beadon Road (i)	Glenthorne Road	– Hammersmith Grove	81·5	70	102	9·5	80·5	44	90	8·0	81·0	52	94	8·5
Beadon Road (ii)		rest	83·5	192	140	13·5	83·0	118	119	11·0	84·0	199	142	13·5
Bloemfontein Road	Uxbridge Road	– South Africa Road	79·0	21	75	6·5	79·0	23	77	6·5	79·0	18	73	6·0
Brook Green (i)	North side		70·5	1	47	3·0	70·5	1	47	3·0	70·5	1	47	3·0
Brook Green (ii)	South side		70·5	1	47	3·0	70·5	1	47	3·0	70·5	1	47	3·0
Brook Green (iii)	Eastern end		73·5	2	53	4·0	73·5	2	53	4·0	73·5	2	53	4·0
Butterwick		all	82·5	154	130	12·5	82·0	111	117	11·0	83·0	161	132	12·6
Conningham Road		all	76·0	8	63	5·0	74·5	4	57	4·5	75·0	4	57	4·5
Dalling Road	King Street	– Glenthorne Road	77·0	7	61	5·0	75·0	3	55	4·0	76·5	6	59	5·0
Dawes Road (i)	Munster Road	– Homestead Road	78·0	21	75	6·5	75·0	5	59	4·5	76·5	3	64	5·5
Dawes Road (ii)		rest	78·0	18	73	6·0	73·5	3	54	4·0	74·5	4	56	4·6

L_{10} – hourly L_{10} noise level in dB(A)

PD – pedestrian delay in seconds

S – concentration of smoke in microgm/m³

CO – concentration of carbon monoxide in ppm

Source: F. E. Joyce, H. E. Williams and D. M. Johnson, 'The environmental effects of urban road traffic, Part 2 – Evaluating alternative transport proposals, *Traffic Engineering and Control*, vol. 16, no.4, April 1975.

Table 9·2

Noise impact on dwellings under three options

18 hour L_{10} dBA	Number of dwellings affected					
	Option 1		Option 2		Option 3	
	1981 Prediction	Capacity	1981 Prediction	Capacity	1981 Prediction	Capacity
70 and above	280 (90)	480 (180)	80 (40)	200 (150)	50 (20)	100 (50)
72 and above	130 (40)	270 (100)	40 (20)	110 (80)	30 (0)	70 (30)
74 and above	20 (10)	120 (40)	10 (0)	50 (40)	10 (0)	30 (10)
76 and above	—	30 (10)	—	20 (10)	—	10 (0)

Note: Figures in brackets refer to the number of houses which would still be affected if noise screens are provided.

Source: 'Coventry transportation study: Report on phase one; The final analysis, Part 1: The results', City of Coventry, December 1972.

Table 9·3

Summary of person—time evaluation of a traffic management scheme

Group	Number of person-hours which:							
	Benefited		Had no change or mixed effects		Lost		Total person-hours	
	Daily	Weekly	Daily	Weekly	Daily	Weekly	Daily	Weekly
Residents	—	—	450	10,800	635	15,240	1,085	26,040
Workers	828	4,140	1,525	7,625	2,491	12,455	4,844	24,220
School users	—	—	428	2,142	2,909	14,547	3,337	16,689
Pedestrians	490	3,950	980	7,900	1,797	14,483	3,267	26,333
Vehicle occupants	1,017	10,644	48	507	836	8,753	1,901	19,904
Total	2,335	18,734	3,431	28,974	8,668	65,478	14,434	113,186

Source: K. Pearce and C. Stannard, 'Catford traffic management study', vol. 1, research report no.17, Department of Planning and Transportation, Greater London Council, July 1973.

1   Disaggregated prediction (Table 9.1) — Noise, pedestrian delay and air pollution are predicted for three options and the results

simply tabulated for comparison. Responsibility for evaluation is clearly with the decision maker alone.

2   Prediction of impact upon people (Tables 9.2 and 9.3) — This approach considers the numbers of people affected and the duration of effect. To facilitate comparison, thresholds can be chosen.

3   Dealing with non-quantifiable factors (Table 9.4) — Recognising that not all factors are as yet capable of prediction, it is possible to record all the impacts separating them out in some way.

4   Index of detriment (Table 9.5) — In this approach environmental detriment is assumed proportional to traffic flows. An environmental index is produced, based upon physical and functional characteristics that predispose a street to being vulnerable to traffic. This index is multiplied by weighted traffic flows and the resulting combinations of detriment index summed and compared for different networks.

Table 9.4

Sample of impact classifications: other classes are administrative, community, operational, activity distribution, and social

Monetary impacts

Agency costs	User costs	Neighbourhood costs	Community costs	Displaced costs
Right of way	Operating	Property values	Income	Replacement costs
Construction	Maintenance	Rents	Production value	Mortgage and
Auxiliary facilities	Parking	Assessments	Jobs	investments
Replacement housing	Insurance	Pollution	Assessment, taxes	Rents
Replacement of	Accident	Blight	Provision of	Title fees
facilities	Time	Accessibility	services	Moving expenses
Maintenance			Regional economy	Clientele loss
Revenue sources				
Relocation services				
Cost of capital				

Environmental impacts

Effects of traffic		Effects of roadway structure	
Air pollution	Noise	Water	Natural resources
Real estate values	Psychological effects	Drainage	Animal life
Material deterioration	Ability to concentrate	Diversion	Animal migratory paths
Power demands	Sleep	Erosion	Plant life
Mental depression	Nuisance	Access to light	Cultivated areas
Balance of nature			Uncultivated areas
Dust			Access to light
			Glare
			Soils
			Energy consumption

Table 9.4 (continued)

Aesthetic impacts		
View of the facility	View from the facility	Natural beauty
Lighting	Location:	Open spaces
dark scary areas	perception sequences	Greenery
cold light	Design:	Park system
monotony	rhythm	Boulevards or gardens
Location:	signing	Lakes
obstruction of sunlight		Wildlife habitats
change of air currents		
visual barrier		
Architectural quality:		
imageability		
dimensional balance		
beauty		
orientation		
psychological barrier		

Source: M. L. Manheim et al., 'Community and environmental values in transportation planning: Summary of findings and recommendations to the State of California', vol. 1, Cambridge, Massachusetts, June 1972.

Table 9.5

Index of detriment score for three traffic assignments

	Network		
Score	Fine	Medium	Coarse
Score or 'Index of detriment'	832,601	817,943	712,991
Total percentage of medium network score	102	100	87

Source: 'Traffic in Camden, study method and techniques,' London Borough of Camden, October 1971.

The assessment method developed in the GLC is intended to help make comparisons of alternative traffic management schemes. The bases of comparison are primarily the numbers of people affected and the significance and duration of the effect. In order to achieve comparability between environmental and other factors in any overall assessment, it was felt desirable to aggregate the environmental assessment, rather than offer the more traditional disaggregated statements of impact for many separate environmental effects. There is also a need to take into account particularly vulnerable or special streets or areas whose function or quality would be impaired by the effects of traffic, independently of the numbers of people involved. Local authorities in London differ, for example, in the importance they attach to conservation areas. Thus it must be possible for specific constraints to be imposed *a priori* on traffic assignments in pursuit of such policies.

The primary purpose of the method is comparison and so far traffic data alone has been considered in terms of flow, speed and composition. Environmental factors considered are noise, carbon monoxide, smoke and pedestrian delay. Predicting the emissions of environmental pollutants by reference to traffic flows is not sufficient on its own. Who will be affected, for how long and how significant will the effect be? While in the home, people are not exposed to danger from traffic accidents, except in the most unusual circumstances, but pedestrians generally will be. In other cases there is room for argument. The extent of vulnerability of people in vehicles certainly raises interesting questions. Are they vulnerable to vibration or not? If pedestrian delay is an environmental effect of traffic, is not passenger delay an environmental effect of pedestrians? Setting such conundrums aside for the moment, and considering the factors that can be predicted, all the activities vulnerable to noise and air pollution and pedestrian activities are in addition vulnerable to delay.

The way in which people use their time has recently received some attention but most analyses have traced people's behaviour on a personal diary basis rather than a locational one. Nevertheless it has been possible to develop a range of factors for different activities which can be multiplied by the number of people in each activity. For example, the average time spent at home in a twelve hour day from 7 a.m. to 7 p.m. is 5¾ hours, some 48 per cent of the period. Hence multiplying the residential population, derived from electoral rolls in the case study, by 0·48 a total 'exposure time' in person–days is estimated. In this way the pattern of exposure for a street is built up on the basis of the activities that front on to it.

Since some effects are perceived, others not, some affect health, others are a nuisance, it is clear that two quite distinct criteria of significance are available. First, what people themselves consider important, second, what public authorities consider appropriate taking into account both health standards and individual perceptions. Since no priority is accorded to non-perceived hazards, attitude surveys can only be regarded as offering partial guidance on the significance of impacts. In using priorities derived from attitude surveys there is also a risk that the people likely to be affected by a particular proposal may not be like the sample whose attitudes have been assessed and that, even if they were, they would have.

114

given different answers if they had been faced with the full implications of the proposal as it might affect them directly. Table 9.6 gives respondents' attitudes to traffic disturbance.

To overcome these difficulties the significance of impact has been based upon certain levels of impact already in use as reference levels in medical and environmental analysis. These are public authority criteria. At this stage private perceptions of hazard have not influenced the weighting of factors but it is possible and appropriate that, as more is known of people's priorities among the factors, these can be taken into account. The weighting of health compared with amenity effects will remain largely a matter of judgement.

In Table 9.7 four different levels of significance of impact have been

Table 9.6

Respondents' attitudes to traffic disturbance

	Percentage of respondents	
	Bothered at all	Seriously bothered
Overall traffic	64	21
Individual disturbances:		
i Pedestrian danger	69	27
ii Noise at home	49	9
iii Noise out	54	16
iv Fumes at home	7	3
v Fumes out	47	23
vi Dust and dirt	36	15
vii Vibration	27	8
viii Parking	21	12
Any of these eight disturbances	88	
Any disturbance when outside the home (i, iii, v above)	82	–
Any disturbance when in the home (ii, iv, vi, vii, viii above)	66	–
Any noise or fumes (ii–v above)	73	33

Source: F. D. Sands and Miss V. Batty, 'Road traffic and environment', in *Social Trends,* no. 5, HMSO, 1974.

Table 9.7

Significance of impact table for four environmental factors, with brief explanation of assumption

Environmental impacts	Noticeable 1	Undesirable 2	Highly undesirable 3	Severe 4	Assumptions
Noise (in L_{10} dBA) Arithmetic average of 8 hour L_{10} levels*	55	70	76	84	1 55 L_{10} dBA, which is roughly comparable to the noise of rustling leaves, is assumed as 'noticeable'. 2 70 L_{10} dBA, as an average of 8 hour L_{10} levels, is approximately equivalent to 68 L_{10} dBA as an average of 18 hour L_{10} levels. The latter represents a specified level above which, in certain circumstances, compensation may be allowed under the Land Compensation Act. We have suggested, therefore, that this should represent an 'undesirable' level. 3 76 L_{10} dBA, as an average of 8 hour L_{10} levels, represents about twice the loudness of a maximum desirable 8 hour L_{10} level of 65 dBA. The 76 L_{10} dBA is also reported to be a noise level at which people seriously complain, hence, assumed as 'highly undesirable'. 4 84 L_{10} dBA, as an average of 8 hour L_{10} levels, represents about 4 times the loudness of the maximum desirable level of 65 dBA. Also, as it is similar to the noise from a busy motorway with 2,000 vph, this level could not possibly be tolerated in an urban situation, therefore it is defined as 'severe'.
Pedestrian delay (mean) (in seconds)	7.5	15	30	120	1 7.5 seconds' delay is assumed 'noticeable' drawing on our own experience. 2 15 seconds' delay is assumed to be sufficient to tempt people to take risks in crossing the road randomly. Therefore it is detmined as 'undesirable'. 3 30 seconds (twice the above) can be seen logically to increase substantially the risk taken by pedestrians and is therefore defined as 'highly undesirable'. 4 120 seconds' delay (= 2 min.) represents a situation where crossing at random points is almost impossible. Thence the great potential danger to pedestrians, and the grounds on which this level was determined as 'severe'.

Carbon monoxide (in ppm)	7	8	15	30
8-hour average*				

1 7 ppm (= 8 microgr/m³) represents a level of 2 ppm below the 'limiting level' (recommended by WHO); therefore this is assumed 'noticeable'.

2 8 ppm (= 10 microgr/m³) is recommended by the WHO Experts Committee as a 'limiting level' (i.e. not to be exceeded). It therefore seems consistent with our condition of 'undesirable'.

3 15 ppm (= 17 microgr/m³) is 1·7 times the above 'limiting level', therefore established as a level at which the effects could be considered to be 'highly undesirable'.

4 30 ppm (= 35 microgr/m³) is reported by the WHO Experts Committee to be the level required to reach 4 per cent carboxyhaemoglobin concentration – a situation against which it is generally agreed that individuals should be protected. Therefore determined as 'severe'.

Smoke (in microgr/m³)	80	120	200	300
8-hour average*				

1 80 microgr/m³ of smoke in conjunction with the same concentration of SO_2 are reported by WHO Experts Committee to lead to reductions of visibility and to general annoyance, therefore determined as 'noticeable'.

2 Over 100 microgr/m³ of smoke in conjunction with the same concentration of SO_2 are assumed to cause respiratory difficulties to children (WHO Experts Committee), therefore 120 microgr/m³ have been determined as an 'undesirable level' in terms of the public at large.

3 250 microgr/m³ of smoke in conjunction with the same concentration of SO_2 are assumed to worsen the conditions of patients with pulmonary disease (WHO Experts Committee); to keep a safety margin 200 microgr/m³ have been determined as a 'highly undesirable' level.

4 500 microgr/m³ of smoke in conjunction with the same concentration of SO_2 are assumed to lead to excess mortality and hospital admission (WHO Experts Committee); to prevent this situation occurring we have assumed 300 microgr/m³ as a 'severe' level.

* The 8-hour average represents an hourly average for the impact over the active part of the day.

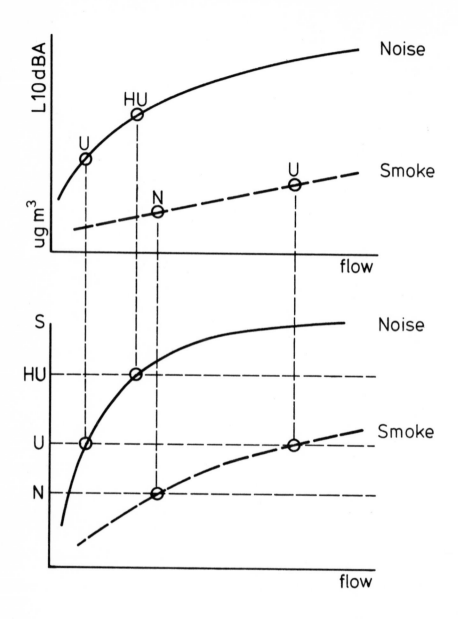

Fig. 9.2 Converting environmental factors to a common scale (S = severe, HU = highly undesirable, U = undesirable, N = noticeable)

identified on each impact scale. 'Noticeable' impact suggests a level at which the impact is apparent but acceptable. 'Undesirable' suggests the point at which levels become unacceptable. 'Highly undesirable' refers to the point upon the impact scale where seriously adverse effects may occur. 'Severe' suggests levels of impact that ought to be avoided.

Assuming that the factors are considered equally important, from the comparable points on the different scales it is possible to derive a common scale upon which the degree of annoyance arising to an individual from each separate impact can be expressed as a single index (Fig. 9.2). Hence an aggregate annoyance index can be produced by summing the relevant annoyance indices. For outdoor situations, where four factors are considered, the aggregate index may range from 0 to 6, and for indoors, from 0 to 4·3, according to traffic composition, flow and speed. Table 9.8 illustrates the range of aggregated annoyance indices for a 31 kph speed for indoor conditions. Although the use of an abstract number to indicate the combined impact may be difficult to interpret at first, it is easy to relate each point on the scale to decibels, parts per millions, etc. For example, the disaggregate impacts for 95 per cent PCUs, 5 per cent HGVs, at 31 kph, equivalent to the top line of Table 9.8, are given in Table 9.9.

Taking into account the person–days affected by the proposals and the significance of the effect street by street it is possible to derive an index of the change due to the proposal. This is simply the product of person–days affected and the aggregated annoyance index.

This approach has been applied to proposals for a 'speedbus' route in London, from Parliament Hill Fields to Peckham Rye. The concept of 'speedbus' put forward by London Transport is to afford such priority to buses on a particular route that the savings in resources on existing services in terms of vehicles and staff are sufficient to run an additional, frequent, limited stop service over the whole route. Two levels of bus priority were considered, the first incorporating the maximum possible extent of measures to assist buses, while the second proposes more measures than are usually considered reasonable, and modifies the more extensive elements of the first. It was possible to set out for existing conditions and each option the annoyance indices and the number of person–days in each street and hence calculate the change in impact. Table 9.10 gives these figures for a section of the speedbus route itself. In a similar way, the individual streets affected off the route can be assessed and total amounts of change recorded. For the off route streets the totals are given in Table 9.11.

While presentation of annoyance indices tends to underestimate the real impact of change, reliance upon people affected tends to overestimate.

Table 9.8

Range of aggregated annoyance indices for indoor conditions,
speed 31 kph

Composition (percentage)	250 vph	1,000 vph	2,000 vph	3,000 vph	4,000 vph
95 PCU, 5 HGV	0·91	1·90	2·55	3·06	3·33
50 PCU, 50 HGV	1·51	2·54	3·29	3·98	4·28

Table 9.9

Example of disaggregated impacts, noise, smoke, carbon monoxide,
related to different flows comprising 95 per cent private car units and
5 per cent heavy goods vehicles at 31 kph

250 vph			1,000 vph			2,000 vph			3,000 vph			4,000 vph		
dB(A)	ppm	mgm³	dB(A)	ppm	mgm³	dB(A)	ppm	mgm³	dB(A)	ppm	mgm³	dB(A)	ppm	mgm³
70·0	7	60	76·5	9	69	79·5	12	81	81·5	14·5	93	82·0	17	105

Table 9.10

'Speedbus': comparative impact of speedbus options on the route

	Existing		Option 1		Option 2	
	Peak	Off-peak	Peak	Off-peak	Peak	Off-peak
Annoyance index	2·41	2·03	1·87	1·49	2·07	2·03
Person–days affected	552	883	517	868	523	872
AI × person–days	1,330	1,792	967	1,293	1,083	1,770

However, this problem is overcome by giving the product of annoyance
indices and people affected. The results are given in Table 9.12. This
offers the clearest expression of comparative impact. In absolute terms of
person–days affected and level of annoyance the effects on and off the
route come close to balancing one another, while the percentage figures
show by how much the average improvement on the route is greater than
the average deterioration off the route. However, while this presents the
general balance sheet for an area, it will often be necessary to take into
account the effect on individual streets so that the spread of impacts can

Table 9.11

'Speedbus': comparative impact of speedbus options off the route

	Existing		Option 1		Option 2	
	Peak	Off-peak	Peak	Off-peak	Peak	Off-peak
Annoyance index (weighted average of 19 streets)	2·22	1·84	2·39	1·89	2·29	1·87
Person–days affected	3,683	3,894	3,710	3,846	3,685	3,836
AI × person–days	8,189	7,151	8,867	7,276	8,449	7,161

Table 9.12

'Speedbus': comparative overall impact expressed in annoyance indices times person–days with percentage change (+ benefit, − disbenefit) shown in brackets

	On route	Off route
Option 1	+862 (+28)	−803 (−5·2)
Option 2	+265 (+12)	−270 (−1·8)

be considered. This can be most easily achieved by classifying the streets subject to changes from the existing conditions into groups related to increments in the annoyance index.

Power stations in London

In 1973 the CEGB applied to the Department of Trade and Industry for consent to construct three new power stations in the Greater London area. The larger two stations proposed, at Barking and Brunswick Wharf, were very large and very visible. Together with other stations proposed for the 1990s they would emit into the atmosphere every year some 300,000 tons of oxides of nitrogen, 20,000 tons of particulate and some trace metals, and a million tons of sulphur dioxide. Other environmental factors demanded attention. The urban design implications of buildings of the scale and bulk proposed needed consideration as did the transport effects.

How was the Greater London Council, as local planning authority for power stations in London, to respond? The members took the view that the whole question of power generation in and for London should be reconsidered. The approach recommended by the author and accepted by the council was that, before agreeing to the new plant, the council would need to be assured that (a) the new plant was necessary to meet realistic estimates of demand; (b) if so, it would make the best use of fuel; and (c) if so, it would not have any adverse effects upon the health of Londoners, upon the conditions of London's fabric or upon local amenity.

In short, the council considered its response in terms of a hierarchy of questions. If need could not be demonstrated it really was not worth putting a lot of effort into evaluating the hypothetical effects of plant that might never materialise. On the basis of the estimates of demand prepared, using up to date forecasts of population, employment, floor space, etc. (which had been offered to the CEGB) there was no urgent need for new plant in London. Figure 9.3 shows these various forecasts. The government's energy conservation policies, the increase in price of Middle East oil, the downturn in prospects for economic growth and the economic pricing of electricity all tended to confirm the Greater London Council's forecast of demand.

The CEGB undertook new demand forecasts earlier this year and these turned out very close to the council's. The way was then clear for joint discussions between the CEGB and the GLC, there being time to consider together the range of questions that the council had raised. These discussions are now under way. Forecasting methodology, district heating potential in London, air pollution implications, are all being considered. It remains to be seen whether agreement on all these points can be reached, but it is clear that the approach adopted is likely to produce a more appropriate solution for London's electricity needs than could have been anticipated from an environmental evaluation alone.

To achieve cost effectiveness in evaluation it is thus essential that the right questions are asked at the right time. Although most projects have multiple impacts many have a primary purpose. Statutory undertakers, such as water authorities and regional electricity boards, have duties to provide a service at minimum cost. A hierarchical approach which takes into account economic and social as well as environmental factors is often therefore appropriate. Clearly the questions raised about London's power stations may interrelate, but until agreement is reached on need the detailed examination of the others is likely to prove unnecessary. Conversely, if full evaluation is postponed until the end, it may be shown that a project dismissed earlier on grounds of cost or location offered the flexibility to contain the constraints at least overall cost.

122

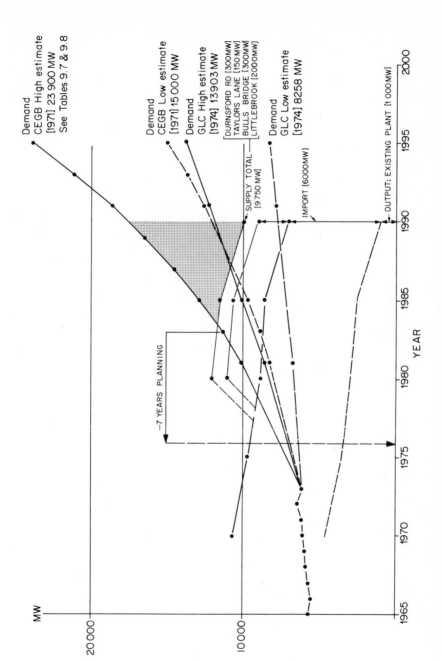

MW

Demand
CEGB High estimate
[1971] 23 900 MW
See Tables 9.7 & 9.8

Demand
CEGB Low estimate
[1971] 15 000 MW

Demand
GLC High estimate
[1974] 13903 MW

DURNSFORD RD [300MW]
TAYLORS LANE [150 MW]
BULLS BRIDGE [300MW]
LITTLEBROOK [2000MW]

Demand
GLC Low estimate
[1974] 8258 MW

SUPPLY TOTAL
[9 750 MW]

IMPORT [6000MW]

OUTPUT: EXISTING PLANT [1 000MW]

20 000

10 000

—7 YEARS PLANNING

YEAR

1965   1970   1975   1980   1985   1990   1995   2000

Fig. 9.3   Relationship between forecasts of electricity demand and the need to build power stations

123

Conclusion

Costs of project evaluation appear to be rising dramatically. Public consultation has contributed to this as decisions are deferred pending the availability of more information. Projects may be implemented in some cases experimentally and effects monitored as a basis for eventual decisions, but such monitoring may cost more than the project. For example, a recent traffic management scheme in south London cost some £4,000 to implement and nearly £6,000 to prepare before and after evaluation studies. Purely predictive exercises cost much less, of course. The environmental part of the speedbus exercise cost only £2,000 in staff time compared with possible implementation costs of more than £1·5 million. There may be some merit in developing guidelines for the cost of decision making, but there is as yet no agreed basis. Possible considerations include: (a) proportion of scheme costs; (b) degree to which project is unique and whose evaluation cannot be based upon experience elsewhere; (c) seriousness of anticipated effects and the risk in making a wrong decision; (d) extent to which projects and their effects can be modified; (e) reliability of predictions of effects and the robustness of project to accommodate to future change; and (f) technical complexity.

The seriousness of project impact, the perception of impact by public bodies and private individuals and the interdependent effect of environmental impact in different combinations need further study. It is not a matter of proliferating the lists of environmental factors as they become quantified, but rather of examining classes of impact and the way each impact has its effect. Projects often have different effects during construction from those in use and the time horizon for impact studies must allow for this. Different groups of people, too, will be affected, and methods of reconciling public responsibilities for non-perceived hazards and private perceptions of nuisance will be needed.

There is little systematically maintained information on existing environmental conditions. This leads inevitably to *ad hoc* data collection for project evaluation and to difficulty in establishing the effectiveness of national or local policies. A limited range of indicators of environmental quality is needed, based upon health criteria for non-perceived hazards and upon attitude studies for aspects experienced and perceived directly. There would thus be a common and objective basis with which the seriousness of impact anticipated from a particular project could be compared when taken with guidelines, levels of impact implicit in the scale of the project and the resources involved.

124

Discussion

This chapter outlines some methods which are used by professional advisers to help local authority politicians decide on the environmental feasibility of various proposals. The difficulty with this approach, noted *Searle* (Earth Resources Research), was that one could not equate the various criteria. The trouble was that the public respond to perceived annoyance such as noise and delay, while ignoring potentially serious hazards like toxic fumes. *Lord Zuckerman* concurred, arguing that the methodology might help political judgement, but it certainly was not based on scientific assessment. *Clayton* (East Anglia) pointed out that the same individual could easily suffer two or more effects at different times of the day; indeed, they could well be beneficiaries of traffic schemes during the workday and sufferers at night and on weekends. Thus even this procedure could not weigh up the final political response.

Cassidy (York Rosenberg Mardell) replied that the techniques described were still experimental procedures subject to continual refinement. They were primarily aimed at helping local politicians to make better decisions on the basis of comparative impact. He conceded that they were only the 'environmental' part of a more comprehensive assessment which looked at the wider social and economic gains and losses. The advantage of these techniques was to determine preliminary feasibility, using experimental test cases if necessary, before expensive and inevitable commitments were made. Nevertheless the wider social and political ramifications were still not covered. These form the subject matter of chapters 10, 11 and 12.

Note

[1]   See C. Buchanan, *Traffic in Towns*, Penguin Books, London 1963.

10 Some social and economic implications of environmental impact assessment

D. E. C. EVERSLEY

Looking at the spectrum of literature concerning environmental impact assessment (EIA), one is immediately struck by the fact that it ranges from 'pure science' (i.e. exercises which in themselves contain no judgements, only conclusions provable by the orthodox canons of physical or biological sciences) to 'political science' which in this context means the superimposition of value judgements of a policy making kind on the findings of the pure scientist.

In pure science, as opposed to applied science, it is possible to conduct an investigation into the consequences of a project [1] in terms of environmental change, expressed entirely in quantitative terms. The adjective 'quantitative' does not necessarily mean absolute precision; impacts may be measured in terms of ranges of probabilities which may be assigned quite wide limits, and time scales may be elastic. Nor does 'quantitative' change exclude some assessment of quality, and therefore possess some undertones of subjective judgement; but in the 'pure' case such qualitative assessment is always subordinate to the measurable characteristic. Thus if we say the air is 'pure' this may refer to the absence of pollutants, but if we say it is 'good' we may also mean that it feels fresh, rich in what is mistakenly called ozone, or smelling of pine needles, or stirred by a gentle breeze as opposed to being still and dead, or stormy and moisture laden. The good scientist will always try to avoid any judgement which he cannot prove from first principles. Recently some attempts have been made to evaluate the 'quality of landscape' in some areas of Britain, [2] and although precise scales were claimed for this exercise there was clearly a subjective element in it because this is the nature of experiencing landscape.

Nevertheless, the common characteristics of most of these scientific attempts to evaluate the impact of projects is that they are essentially related only to changes within the natural environment, though to be sure such assessments are also man related. That is to say, even the 'purest' scientist will concede that the conservation of species in its former habitat must be related to man's ability to observe it. However, such a concession may be of the most grudging kind: for instance, tracts of primeval woodlands are preserved only for those with passes from the Nature Conservancy, and the habitat of rare species of orchid are known only to a few initiates, as are the eyries of the reestablished eagles of the Lakelands. To many scientists the presence or absence of a number of kinds of fish in a tract of water is a *Ding an sich* unrelated to the question of whether anyone other than the specialists has ever seen or counted the species, let alone as to whether recreational fishing is possible or desirable.

Traversing the spectrum further, we find that many examples of EIA are positively man related; that is to say they conceive the objective of the exercise from the start to be the maximum retention (or even extension) of man serving facilities. Thus purity of water is related to the quality of drinking water; the use of insecticides to the effect on human diet; the construction of power plants is related to the assumption that power, in one form or another, will be needed. The search for an optimal road alignment is conceived in terms of accepting the need for traffic flows; and the siting of a water reservoir is seen as a necessity created by the organisation of a man orientated society.

At the other end of the range we find the scientist who is essentially part of the scheme of societal governance. He accepts that the decision to undertake a project as a matter of policy is immutable, and that his place in the management team is to work out the method of implementing this project in such a way as to satisfy a number of criteria already socially and politically acceptable. These include delivery at least cost, minimum intrusion into historic townscapes or protected landscapes, maximum conservation of resources for future use, and so on. It will be seen that such an orientation involves the acceptance (not necessarily unquestion-ingly) of the ideal of a social good which can be attained in an optimal manner. Here EIA becomes the scientific equivalent of cost—benefit analysis in economic science. Some economists might claim that they, too, have some absolute values, but on closer inspection these will turn out to refer either to sections of their calculations which relate to the impossibility of putting money values on unique objects (e.g. an historical monument *in situ*), or societally imposed limitations on financially compensating some people for their losses as the result of a piece of project implementation because of the intangible 'community' values which may be involved.

EIA in historical perspective

The idea that resources are finite is of relatively recent origin. For most of its existence mankind has been concerned with the discovery, conquest and subsequent exploitation of empty spaces (or those inhabited by inferior species who were considered to be of no account). Throughout its history capitalism has seen relatively short bursts of shortage of investible resources alternating with a glut of capital waiting to be invested, and for 200 years in the Western world, and still today in developing countries, the idea of a shortage of labour was confined to momentary periods of expanding activity.

Nor do we find, in the past, any feeling of great reverence for what exists. The prevailing attitude until this century was that what was old was useless, probably unhygienic, and unquestionably ripe for removal if it stood in the way of progress. Only where superstition (or faith) stood in the way, temples, holy groves or churches might remain unscathed, though the scientific and rational mind made short shrift of consecrated ground or buildings, statues, paintings or candlesticks. The idea of a 'museum' is a very recent one, and official protection for historic buildings, monuments, let alone townscapes or landscapes, belongs to the last few minutes of the recorded history of 'civilised' society. [3]

It is perhaps as well that this should be so. Had our forebears known or cared about pollution, visual intrusion, an admiration for the ancient as such, we should certainly not have created the Victorian world which we now so profess to admire, let alone the modern, contemporary, industrial state, which we profess to despise but which, especially for our scientist, is his *raison d'être* as well as livelihood. We should certainly never have had any railways or trams, nor would we have had electricity outside Faraday's laboratories; we should be growing crops in the manner of aboriginals, and our lives would most certainly be nasty, painful and short. We should not have been allowed to manufacture chemicals, let alone petrochemicals, or experiment with drugs. X-rays would have stayed in Wilhelm Roentgen's laboratory and radium in the Curies'. We should not have been allowed to keep horses in city streets – which were noisy on the cobblestones, dangerous to health, accident prone, and traffic congesting, as well as perpetuating inequality.

Thus it is only the attempt to spread the benefits once reserved to the very few — comfort, convenience, mobility, cleanliness — to larger numbers of people that has produced the anxiety about the environment (coupled, of course, with population growth and the 'discovery' that resources were not going to last indefinitely, or at any rate not be available at low cost). This discovery has been sudden, and like many such explosions of knowledge or self knowledge assumed the dimensions of a cult. In other words, something which began as a scientific exercise has, in the course of a decade, become an irrational prejudice, largely sustained by laymen and pseudo-scientists, and assumed all the characteristics of the pre-scientific world of superstition from which the positivists tried to liberate us a hundred years ago. [4]

It is one of the characteristics of such messianic movements that the false messiahs make the largest impact (and profits). Thus the typical manifestation of our day is not the sober kind of evaluation which dominates the activities, let us say, of the NERC, but the doom prophecies of doctors, biologists, model builders of all persuasions, and downright amateurs. Instead of warning us against the effects of eating certain kinds of fungi, we are now told that the ingestion of sugar, alcohol, fruit juices, frozen cod, animal protein, soya beans, white bread, eggs, potatoes, chocolate, tea, coffee or butter will do lasting damage to our bodies if not our souls. We are told that bonfires, supersonic planes, aerosols, fruit sprays and waste heat from power stations will poison the atmosphere, biosphere and ionosphere, and will make us all die from cold, heat or too much or too little oxygen, nitrogen, hydrogen or helium. There is danger in fluoride, food preservatives, tranquillisers, stimulants, antidepressants and aspirins. It appears that to go hungry, thirsty, and live out our lives in pain, surrounded by parched, stunted and blighted crops is better than to live longer, reduce infant mortality, and eradicate malaria and smallpox. The fact that in this country we do live longer, choose not to work some days rather than be forced to absenteeism through tuberculosis, have reduced deaths from violence and accidents, counts apparently for nothing. It is not a sign of progress, but of our acceptance of false values, materialism, neglect of spiritual advantages, and in any case only a mirage since it is based on borrowed time; it has all been achieved at the expense of future generations and the premature exhaustion of finite resources. Since technology must now stand still, further substitutes cannot be found, nor resources augmented: to exploit North Sea oil now rather than leave it to be discovered by our great-grandchildren is typical of the earth piracy which thoughtless economists and politicians have forced upon us.

Now this type of argument has been dismissed by Lord Ashby (p.5), amongst others, as being the work of 'individual zealots'. Unfortunately it is this sort of idea which receives widespread coverage through the more irresponsible media and therefore it affects policies. So the fact that these prophecies can actually swing the balance in favour of inaction, or at least indefinite delay, makes these travesties of genuine EIA a necessary extension of the subject under review.

The social nature of EIA

The stress on the need to pause before committing oneself to projects, and to abandon them at the slightest hint that they are in some way environmentally detrimental, has important social and political consequences. However well intentioned the original exercises, in practice the approach can be shown to work inequitably, in favour of some minority sections of the population, special interest groups, and not for the 'public good'. It is now clear that 'public good' is in itself incapable of being defined and it has rightly been lampooned by liberal economists. Nevertheless, all our political thinking is still basically utilitarian, and whilst the tag about the 'greatest good of the greatest number' leads immediately to the same absurdity which we encounter when we take 'the public good' as an idea in itself (i.e. pseudo-quantification) it does enable us to make the transition to modern cost—benefit analysis. It will be remembered that one of the principal objections to the calculations made for the Roskill Commission on the third London airport was that it 'overvalued' the time of travelling businessmen. In other words, instead of treating everyone's time as being equally valuable, it presumed to say that the time of a minority who both earned more and travelled more was worthy of more consideration than the time of other people who earned less and travelled less. [5] Yet there is some logic in this, and not necessarily a value-laden logic, for it uses the market value of a man's time as an indicator of comparison. Translated into terms of the 'public good' in relation to a project, however, can we allow the same to be true of the comparison, let us say, of the interests of a specialist investigator of certain rare species of algae, and those of the population of a valley city which is short of drinking and washing water? Is it true that we apply neutral market evaluations if we say that the interests advanced by rock climbers are in every case to be considered more important than those of motorised but idle folk who wish to visit the foothills without having the skill or inclination to climb the heights?

This turns out to be the cardinal question. All EIA is basically defensive: it is about preserves, about territorialism, about exclusion, non-access, non-use of resources. Its yardsticks are invariably those internal to the situation itself. That is, the integrity of a territory is not to be violated if, as a result, something happens within that territory which alters the status quo, reduces the enjoyment of those who happen to be the previous or present users of that territory, or even, if there are several such groups of users to choose from, selects that group as deserving prior consideration whose use of the area is least likely to disturb the status quo. There is nothing wrong with this logic – except the pretence that it is value-neutral. It is not. It is essentially élitist in the sense that it places those who by reason of their education, their physical fitness, their social background or their common interest in a 'higher' pursuit, not quantitatively, but qualitatively above those whom our system has failed to educate, whose childhood environment has not taught them to appreciate what is good and what is not; those who by reason of age or infirmity or just ignorance cannot use facilities in a certain way, and who shall be excluded either from access or from the benefits conferred by what we have called a project, on no other grounds than that they are inferior.

Naturally, it would be added, it is hoped to educate their children in future, in mind and body, to attain the same standards as are now enjoyed by a minority. But this is a fallacy if it is adduced in the course of an EIA exercise, because if greater masses are educated, paternalistically, to share certain current middle class values, the need to reduce access (i.e. to ration it, preferably by price) becomes even more urgent. In other words, those who do not have it now cannot win in the future. Those who are in possession now, must, if this logic is followed, remain privileged. [6]

The social alibi

Much of this window dressing of EIA lies in the pretence that it is a way of preserving values (or resources) for the masses and for posterity, and that the urban poor, for instance, would be the greatest sufferers in the long run if we now allowed remote valleys to be flooded, oil wells to be drilled, or roads to be constructed. The logic of this argument seems to be that it is better for the have nots to be excluded from present enjoyments, so as to preserve an amenity and resource which in theory they could then enjoy in the future, but there is a fundamental fallacy in this logic. If the amenity (resource) is truly to be preserved, future access (exploitation) can always be prevented by reference to a yet more remote future. It is a

131

different matter if something can be achieved by a slower rather than a more rapid exploitation of an area or resource, but this is seldom the argument, though it is often advanced for slower regeneration of outworn old cities. It is inherent in the 'small but beautiful' philosophy, with its emphasis on slower speed and smaller scale, and there may well be a point of substance here. However, even this line of argument fails to measure the losses caused by present sufferings (i.e. benefits not received) against the problematical future gains, perhaps of a different set of people. Above all, this kind of reasoning always presupposes that those on whose behalf these decisions are made are consenting parties, and will do willingly without their present enjoyments for the sake of future benefits to be enjoyed by others (and, naturally, already available in abundance to the decision makers themselves). But this is not a question which can be put to those affected.

One of the fundamental reasons for this situation is that the methodology of cost—benefit analysis, in so far as it deals with the future, is incapable of including most of the unknowns in this equation of present benefits forgone in favour of future ones. In other words, neither scientific methodology nor a concept of fairness or natural justice can be used to adjudicate between the claims of present and future generations, especially since those who are alive now are mostly not conscious of what they may be missing, or see their deprivation in only very partial terms; and the generations for whom we are supposed to be protecting the natural or built environment are not yet born, and we cannot foretell their numbers, needs or tastes. Therefore a great deal of this discussion must inevitably come back to the value judgements of individuals who are the decision makers (or protectors) now, and who, as their only legitimate standpoint, need to defend their personal interests. All appeals to other interests must be problematic if not metaphysical.

We must not underrate, for all its lack of scientific pretensions, the force of the appeal of these value judgements, masquerading under the guise of the public interest. Thus, whilst official policies have gradually sapped the inner cities socially and economically, appeals for their physical conservation have intensified in strength. The well-to-do have acquired the improved houses formerly occupied by the working classes and are thus the chief beneficiaries of the prohibition of change. However, these benefits are not, as usual, costless — the price we pay is the absence of opportunities either for new dwellings for low income inner city workers or, more seriously, job opportunities for the semi-skilled and unskilled.

Whose city, whose countryside?

Choosing as a subtitle for these paragraphs the combined titles of two recent books [7] draws attention to the much less problematical conflicts of interest which have been evident in this country in recent years. In examples from this book which illustrate past battles for the environment, some 'won', some 'lost' (from the ecologists' standpoint only) there is rarely any realisation of who bears the cost of protecting the existing landscape. Thus there have been many demands for the existing super-grid to be put underground, because of the environmental intrusion of the pylons and cables. Yet the truly astronomical costs of putting 400 kv cables underground (or even 100 kv, as under the Malvern Hills) now reckoned in several million pounds per mile, whatever method is used, means an additional charge on the consumer — or else a larger deficit for the CEGB, and hence extra charges on the taxpayer, and large debts. In the past rural dwellers and poor townsfolk have begun to enjoy a reasonable price for electricity as a consequence of a national system of production, distribution and charging of electricity supplies. [8] That people have chosen then also to use electric power for heating, cooking, washing their clothes, ironing and other purposes, has, according to one school of thought, increased their leisure, lightened their burdens of heavy physical work, freed their homes internally from the pollution of open coal fires and paraffin stoves; and generally increased their choices. According to the other school, cheap electricity has been bought at the cost of ruining the landscape, polluting the atmosphere and earth with fly ash, and reduced our fossil fuel reserves.

Who is to arbitrate between these claims? A sensible compromise is sometimes reached. In Sussex the Dungeness to Fratton line of the 400 kv grid crosses over 120 miles of mostly very beautiful countryside. It does so in a 'dog leg' fashion, more expensive than a straight line, but much cheaper than underground, with each pylon expertly situated by one of the country's leading landscape architects, so that it avoids all concentrations of habitations, and most of the areas of outstanding natural beauty. The 'victims' in this case were some owners of splendid but isolated country mansions, whose view of the Downs from their terraces was admittedly spoilt by the pylons and cables; but at that time such minority interests, however loud their voices in the establishment, could be overruled in favour of a greater majority of people whose daily enjoyment of their less splendid micro-environment is not so much affected by this alignment.

Such examples are rare. Mostly such lines are routed in deference to the vociferous demands of minorities. We see only too clearly how the supposedly scientific environmental impact assessment has no room for the evaluation of those innumerable intangibles affecting people's life styles which are profoundly affected by the apparently praiseworthy, or at least innocent, preference for 'saving the countryside'.

Take the example of the high rise building policy advocated largely on the grounds of 'making Britain more self sufficient' and 'preserving our rural way of life'. It has been calculated that each acre saved cost the nation about £220,000. [9] This did not include the social costs of forcing families into high rise dwellings, nor the negative environmental impact of the buildings themselves. Such abstractions as 'making ourselves self sufficient in food', or 'saving our rural heritage', are purely subjective value laden assertions or, in the case of the desire to save imports, non-economic judgements based on very special calculations about the value of our trade with countries which have vast exportable food and raw material surpluses. Here scientist and economist might collaborate fruitfully, but with rare exceptions [10] this has not happened, and 'saving the countryside' has become an end in itself, so that the practitioners of EIA can without difficulty pronounce the scheme 'better' if it consumes less land, without reference to other policy consequences which might follow.

One also notices, as an outside observer, that the practices to which EIA are applied very often concern the forwarding of projects which have significance for large numbers of people, especially disadvantaged urban minorities. Projects which benefit the advantaged minorities are less controversial. Thus it does not seem to be questioned that large acreages of land and many miles of shoreline are ruined, probably for generations to come, for 'defence' purposes: denied for recreation and agriculture, and detrimental to natural life. Nobody minds the intrusions of Shoeburyness, but there was wide objection to Maplin. Apparently neither land nor resources are considered scarce when it comes to the building of very large houses for very wealthy people, or the erection of luxurious and, to some minds, highly intrusive office blocks. Some observers find it ominous that a great deal of ecological research work in recent years has been sponsored by the great petro-chemical combines, themselves no mean despoilers of coastal and some inland areas.

The redistributive effects

With the exception of a relatively small band of British and American economists [11] who have made the effort to link EIA and cost–benefit procedures into a coherent whole, and whose impact on policy decisions so far appears to be negligible, we are then faced with scientific practices which leave the redistributive effect out of account. So long as all land, buildings, and human activities are treated as if they were tradable commodities [12] there is always a presupposition in favour of the market, which is not renowned for its ability to redistribute. [13] Yet redistribution lies at the heart of the social and economic policy of government and increasingly, in times of economic stagnation, falling real incomes, and high unemployment, should take priority over market considerations, let alone the 'pure' scientific approach described earlier. As the general situation worsens, so people's anxieties about their future deepen, and bitterness and divisiveness in society increases. [14]

Why then have governments of all persuasions allowed so many concessions to the environmental pressure groups, many of whom shelter behind the supposedly value free EIA techniques? The answer probably lies in the 'popular' pressures of the media which, though they speak only for themselves, have the capacity for making life unpleasant for governments. Recently, too, there has been increasing anxiety on the part of economists (especially in the Treasury) that further large scale development, however desirable for the individual beneficiary, is undesirable because of the overall negative effect on inflation, the balance of payments, and therefore the long term prospects of the economy as a whole. This is a very weighty argument, so it is pertinent to ask whether this is a passing phenomenon or not. Certainly the abandonment of large intrusive projects is not an unmitigated blessing, as their opponents claim. In other words, if for other social and economic reasons it should prove desirable to have more fast and safe roads, another large airport, or a Channel Tunnel, then EIA procedures are perfectly acceptable as a way of minimising environmental disturbance without raising costs to prohibitive levels. 'Prohibitive' means a state of affairs where the project is so expensive as to preclude its use, or usefulness, to the least well off sections of the population, i.e. where it becomes a regressive form of investment, leading to redistribution from the poor to the rich.

Basically there are only three ways out of the conflict of interests which is involved: either one allows market mechanisms to determine whether or not a project is executed, or one relies on the democracy of noise and pressure, or one finds a rational way of making decisions. Looking at the history of the last few years, it would appear that the first option has been almost universally rejected, and while the last was allegedly tried, the difficulties of arriving at such a rational process and the fact that no options were in the end value free, reduced governments, time and again, to an acceptance of the anarchy of planning by decibels.

So we are left with the rule of the squeaky wheel, which is thoroughly undemocratic. It is also potentially dangerous, and more so as resources dwindle. In the United States some of the more blatant attempts by the environmental lobbies to stop river pollution by bankrupting industrial concerns into closure and thus aggravating unemployment have somewhat reduced the effectiveness of this sort of pressure group. In Britain the closure of plants has recently been more usually due to their inability to sell their products, thus creating a climate in which environmental considerations have not been in the forefront.

The obligation to provide alternatives

One's faith in the rationality of environmental impact assessment would be much greater if every report, however technical, instead of stopping short of pointing out the adverse consequences of doing this or that accepted automatically that there are also adverse consequences to total inactivity, and went on to provide an alternative solution. Otherwise the whole exercise simply becomes a delaying device which of course may well be the objective of some of the groups now in business.

However, this is not politically acceptable. A typical case concerns the London urban motorways. First conceived as an essential part of the Abercrombie strategy for Greater London at the end of the war, they were politically acceptable and economically possible as late as the middle sixties. Opposition then arose and they were finally abandoned by the London administration which took office in 1973. The panel of enquiry into the Greater London Development Plan had suggested modifications; the Secretary of State, after endless delays, produced a minuscule adjudication [15] which failed to make clear whether new roads were to be built or not. Meanwhile the financial resources to undertake the work disappeared. The GLC thereupon decided on its alternative of 'lorry routes' [16] which would make heavy transport run through selected roads, except if they had to pick or drop loads elsewhere. Not surprisingly, those through whose roads the already heavy traffic would have been increased by this measure strongly objected, and the whole scheme was quietly dropped. By now we are back at the situation Abercrombie said he wished to avoid at all costs -- that heavy traffic concentrations should build up in residential streets. Added to this, the GLC is now producing schemes of bus lanes and closing roads to all traffic

136

except buses and taxis, thereby greatly increasing private car traffic in formerly relatively quiet streets. As might have been foreseen, the effect of relatively cheap 'management' schemes of this sort is just to increase the ingenuity of drivers in finding quiet backwaters through which they can drive at high speeds. In such a situation the bankruptcy of EIA or CBA in the face of political inaction may be evident — but this in itself does not prove that a costless, and at the same time socially just solution, *could* have been found. The scientist will claim it is not his task to say whether a particular policy is, in the widest sense, feasible or infeasible; his job is merely to say whether it is technically possible and, if so, what would be the price of environmental deterioration that some section of the community would have to pay.

To be fair, social scientists behave in exactly the same manner. If there were anything so pseudo-scientific as social impact analysis, no doubt this would invariably condemn in advance any plan to change the status quo as being detrimental to some section of the community, present or future. Since urban sociologists, deeply divided as they are amongst themselves, are at least unanimous in equally damning every form of urban renewal which has so far been tried, one would also be inclined to ask them what alternative they have to offer other than inaction. But then we immediately have the same problem: like scientists they claim it is not their task to provide alternative solutions, merely to criticise, in advance or later on, anything that has been planned or even executed.

Norms and expectations

Taking the social history of the last hundred years as a whole, nobody now disagrees with the proposition that the physical standard of life of the vast mass of the people of this country has changed enormously — and most people would say, for the better. All but a relatively small minority of households now dispose of their own dwelling, are not overcrowded, have a fixed bath and indoor toilet, running hot water, and adequate heating. [17] The great majority of households either own their houses or have the security of tenure from a local authority. Most households have cars and the vast majority have television sets and refrigerators. Almost everyone takes holidays with pay, at least three working weeks in the year, and practically nobody works on Saturdays unless they do it for overtime pay. Because this change of experience has happened, change has become the norm and expectations have been raised. This is a fundamental process and probably an irreversible one. The urge to better oneself and one's children is probably universal to the human condition. So the attempt to stop the process at any one point of time would be disastrous and a nonsense. Yet this is the implication of much that follows from the negative attitude associated with so much EIA work. The only alternative if we really do think that our landscape and townscape is in some way irrevocably destroyed if we alter any more of it, would be a more even distribution of what there is so that everyone is given an equal chance. Scientists cannot work out what this would involve in the way of more punitive taxation or severe rationing, by price or quantity, of the goods and services which are the subject of these rising expectations. They would say that this was a matter for the much despised politicians.

If indeed it is true that we are threatened by an environmental catastrophe, then the political preparation of measures to avoid this moment of doom requires more determination than one expects from politicians. The difficulty is that one cannot really, as an outsider, place any credence in the prognostications of the scientists, and is therefore disinclined to adopt the stance of 'enough is now'. A few years ago we were solemnly told by the FAO and their propagandist pupils that by 1975 the majority of the world's population would be nearing death from starvation. People do die from starvation, or rather they die from diseases which they cannot resist because they are undernourished, but this seems to happen in countries where there is civil war, or mass expropriation of the native peasantry, or where aid grains do not reach them. It is precisely the apparent inability of scientists to understand what are truly biological phenomena, and what events are the result of political or administrative malevolence or incompetence, that inures the public against too ready acceptance of their statements.

Thus the responsibility lies with the scientists themselves to make themselves credible in the eyes of those who are concerned with economic and social conditions. This requires a much wider education for the providers of EIAs than, apparently, they at present possess. Amongst other things they seem to lack historical perspective. It is not, after all, those populations which have kept to the economy of the jungle and the steppe which have survived. Instead, our generation enjoys the fruits of the labours of those who initiated the industrial revolution, introduced science into everyday life, and, after initially vitiating the air and water with waste and by-products, were gradually brought under control by legislation. This process has been going on for 115 years, at least in this country, and each year the safety precautions become more stringent, despite the allegations of inefficiency and bribery which are rife. [18] There is always more room for more effort. The basic feature of this type

138

of social organisation has always been a widespread (though by no means universal) consensus about the necessity for change, adaptation and the concomitant constraints, by legislation and voluntary action. Whilst it is true that there are now louder voices against more change, and whilst these voices make use of scientific methods to prove their point, it is also true that the cessation of growth must be accompanied by the petrification of current inequalities, if not a worsening of the situation, and the result must be increased social bitterness.

Political realities and scientific expertise

The observer coming from a social science background is bound to be increasingly suspicious of a whole complex of tendencies of which the growth of environmental impact assessment is only one. In practice it cannot be separated from a very one-sided sort of conservationism, nor can we ignore its political lack of responsibility. As indicated there seems to be no good logical, let alone theoretical basis for leaving things as they are for the sake of a future generation, if this is done at the expense of those who go without at present. Moreover, whilst it is always easy to say 'no' to any project, it is an act requiring considerable courage to say: yes, there will be some damage, but on balance the social and economic advantages would benefit more people than would be hurt by this damage. It would require a definite political judgement as well as courage to say that because those whose interests might be adversely affected by the project are on the whole very much better off than those who could benefit from it, our democratic head counting alone becomes even less relevant when we introduce the value judgement implied in desiring fairer systems of distribution.

The work presented in this book has been thorough, but any admiration for the ingenuity of the *homo mensor*, in this case, is much reduced when one realises the policy vacuum in which the work is done. To claim that this is the *only* atmosphere (or lack of it) in which good scientific work is done is to condemn the outcome to sterility. If the social consequences of *not* proceeding with projects, and proceeding with some reasonable speed, are not taken into account, then the exercise is invalidated. That this applied also to the economists' CBA is no excuse for the biologist or geophysicist. The economist usually errs in his judgement by wrongly weighting costs and benefits, or by omitting sections of the population more indirectly affected by the project, or its absence. The scientist errs when he simply disregards the place of the project within human society, never mind weighting it wrongly. However, to run away from the problem by pretending that the final decision must lie with those who wield political power is not merely a form of cowardice but it robs the scientific practitioner of credibility.

It is more than likely that we have passed the zenith of the most virulent conservationist movement which did so much to promote this form of scientific study. Preoccupation with the starker realities of economic decline will probably accelerate the demise of this particular fashion. Yet it would be a pity if it were all buried. No doubt in the past we have been careless, spendthrift, and often too prone to wreck good landscapes or buildings, whether in the pursuit of individual gain, or in the name of the social good. But relative to the real problems of our time — the wanton killing of human beings by deliberate acts of war, civil war, and terrorism; the persistence of inequality between nations, and within countries between different groups — the kind of problems of pollution, erosion, intrusion, or resource exhaustion which are the subject matter of EIA seem rather to pale into insignificance. One says 'seem' because it is a matter of opinion, in other words a personal value judgement. There are people who think that rare orchids matter more than human lives, or that the preservation of a Victorian building is worth a few traffic accidents. We are all entitled to these judgements. The mistake lies in pretending that they are anything other than value judgements, and giving them the sanctity or at least respectability of unassailable scientific fact.

Notes

[1]   The term 'project' is used to describe any act which in some way has a bearing upon the physical environment. It can be a piece of construction, alterations to existing buildings, changes in a water course or such minor changes as regulations regarding the use, access to, or rate of depletion of an existing resource.

[2]   See for example, K. D. Fines, 'Landscape evaluation: a research project in East Sussex', *Regional Studies*, vol. 2, 1967, pp.41–5; and 'Landscape evaluation and planning policy: a comparative survey of the Wye Valley area of outstanding natural beauty', *Regional Studies*, vol. 7, 1973, pp.153–60.

[3]   For a discussion of the origins of the building preservation movement see W. Ashworth, *The Genesis of Modern British Town Planning*, Routledge, London 1954; and for various commentaries on more recent development, see *Built Environment,* vol. 3, January 1974,

pp.13–30.

[4]   The classical positivist statements is in W. W. Reade, *The Martyrdom of Man*, 1872.

[5]   See J. G. V. Adams, 'Westminster: the fourth London airport?', *Area*, vol. 2, no. 1, January 1970, pp.1–9.

[6]   For a modern statement of the thesis that landscapes should be protected for the educated minority, see J. Parsons, 'Population and liberty', *Population and the Quality of Life in Britain*, Royal Society of Arts, London 1975.

[7]   R. Pahl, *Whose City?* London, London 1970, and G. Haines, *Whose Countryside?* Dent, London 1973.

[8]   The cost of electricity to these people is possibly less than one third of what it was thirty years ago.

[9]   See P. A. Stone, *The Structure Size and Costs of Urban Settlements*, Cambridge University Press, Cambridge 1973.

[10]   The one exception is the work done by G. P. Wibberley and R. H. Best at Wye College, Kent.

[11]   See D. W. Pearce, Chapter 11.

[12]   R. Barras and T. A. Broadbent, 'An activity–commodity formalism for socio–economic systems', Centre for Environmental Studies research paper no. 18, London 1975.

[13]   K. Boulding, *Redistribution to the Rich and to the Poor*, Wadsworth, Los Angeles 1972.

[14]   Lord Ashby disagrees; he feels anxieties are in the process of being lessened.

[15]   See the statement by Rt Hon. Anthony Crosland MP on the Greater London development plan, HMSO, London, October 1975.

[16]   See its discussion paper entitled 'Lorry routes', Greater London Council, 1975.

[17]   This statement is not meant to sound complacent; the plight of the remaining minority must not be underestimated.

[18]   See Counter Information Services, 'Courtaulds inside out', anti report no. 10, London, November 1974; and J. Bugler, *Polluting Britain: A Report*, Penguin Books, London 1972, especially pp.3–31.

11 Measuring the economic impact of environmental change

D. W. PEARCE

Within the framework of conventional economic theory, the 'environment' is as much a commodity as are the normal goods and services we find incorporated in our national economic accounts. The rationale for seeing the environment as a commodity is a powerful one, although not unchallengeable. This rationale can be briefly assessed by considering the three main functions of natural environments.

First, the environment supplies natural resources. The economic argument tells us that a resource preserved in the environment must obey the same rules that we would apply to capital investment. Essentially, a resource in the ground has an increasing value over time as the demands for its use grow. Hence, from the purely private standpoint of the resources owner, a resource should be exploited only if its current value (the price that can be secured on the market, less costs) exceeds the discounted value of the expected future price. Otherwise it should be left in its natural state. In this way 'conservation' becomes, to the economist, equivalent to capital investment, for investment means forgoing consumption now in order to reap greater expected gains in the future. In the same way, leaving a resource in the natural environment rather than exploiting it is tantamount to forgoing the use of that resource now (consuming it) because we expect its future value, viewed from the current standpoint, to be greater. If we extend the argument to a social standpoint and away from the narrow grounds of private profitability, the same logic holds. What we now require is that we exploit resources – i.e. consume them – only if the current social value exceeds the discounted magnitude of expected future values. We may note in passing that this provides the rationale for the so-called 'optimal rate of depletion' of natural resources, a rate that, as long as we accept the use of discounting, is unlikely to be zero. [1]

Second, the environment acts as a receiver of waste products. The first law of thermodynamics tells us that whatever is extracted by way of natural resources from the environment must (eventually) be returned to it, albeit in a transformed state. Roughly, then, the amount of waste entering the natural environment at any one time is equal to the amount extracted in that time, allowing for the embodiment of resources in the capital stock of the economy. The environment has, for most wastes, a counterpart to degrader capacity — an 'assimilative capacity'. As long as the flow of wastes is less than this capacity the environment degrades the waste and restores itself to its initial state. This is a grossly simplified statement, but it serves our purposes for the moment. Given that the environment has this capability, the economic argument is that it is irrational not to use this capacity as long as it is cheaper than the alternatives. Thus, if waste is not disposed of to the environment it must be treated or recycled. Both these activities utilise resources. They cost money. From the private standpoint, then, it is illogical to use these alternatives if the straightforward dumping of waste is cheaper. At the social level, the same relationship holds except that we must now ensure that all the social costs of disposal, recycling and treatment are included in our analysis.

Third, the environment supplies amenity in the form of natural habitats for leisure activities and pure appreciation. Again, the preservation of such amenity is, on the standard economic argument, justified only if the values placed on that amenity exceed the value of the environment in some alternative use, e.g. as a source of mineable natural resource.

These three arguments demonstrate that there is a kind of internal logic to the economist's approach to environmental problems. Whether that logic holds in practice is something we shall try to evaluate in this chapter. The common link in the economic approach to the three aspects of environment is the weighing up of costs and benefits. Quite simply, the way in which the environment is used should be determined by the maximum difference between benefits and costs, allowing for all the alternatives. To abate pollution due to waste disposal is a resource using activity. Hence, we have to consider *abatement costs.* The benefits of abatement accrue in the form of the values placed by people on reduced pollution. Hence, we are also interested in the savings in *damage costs.* The nature of the meaning of 'cost' is important here. Economists are criticised for their use of money values more than anything else, yet these criticisms invariably rest on a basic misunderstanding of the role of money values in economic analysis. Essentially what the economist tries to do is to record people's preferences for or against environmental change. Since we cannot have repeated political referenda on each and every issue, the economist looks to the behaviour of individuals to see if this reveals their preferences. Since individuals choose between alternatives every day of their lives, the potential for studying preferences is enormous. While choice in the market place is the most obvious and lucrative source of information, individuals also make choices about non-marketed goods such as environmental amenity, clean air, quieter habitats, and so on. Accordingly the principle involved is no different whether there is a market or not. What the absence of markets does is to make the *practical* task immensely more difficult, as we shall shortly illustrate.

Finally, the continuous preference monitoring system that is provided by markets and by behaviour in non-market contexts permits some measure of the *intensity* of preference. Thus, a political voting system operating on the basis of 'one man, one vote' would socially sanction a policy if 51 per cent of voters just prefer it while 49 per cent are deeply opposed to it. Economic votes, on the other hand, permit some measure of intensity of feeling. This is because a vote *for* something is measured in terms of individuals' willingness to pay for it, while a vote *against* it is measured, in cost—benefit analysis anyway, by a requirement for compensation. This provides us with the cost—benefit rule: benefits are measured by willingness to pay and costs by the requirement for compensation. Costs are also further linked to the willingness to pay concept since the requirement for compensation should bear some relationship to a benefit forgone. Thus, the capital cost of a project measures approximately the benefit that would have been obtained had the money been spent on something else. This is the economist's concept of opportunity cost. The entire system of concepts can then be formalised by saying that if, for any environmental change, the aggregate of all individuals' willingness to pay for the change exceeds the aggregate of all individuals' requirement for compensation because they do not like the change, then that change is socially worthwhile. The rationale here is that, if benefits exceed costs, the beneficiaries *could* pay the losers the compensation they require and still have something left over. This means that the beneficiaries would still be in a state of preferring the change while the losers would not be indifferent to the change since they will have been compensated for any loss suffered. [2]

Having set the scene for the cost—benefit appraisal of environmental change, we can now consider two limitations: (a) theoretical, and (b) practical. These will be considered in the context of pollution problems only, but there are direct parallels in the field of natural resource economics. [3]

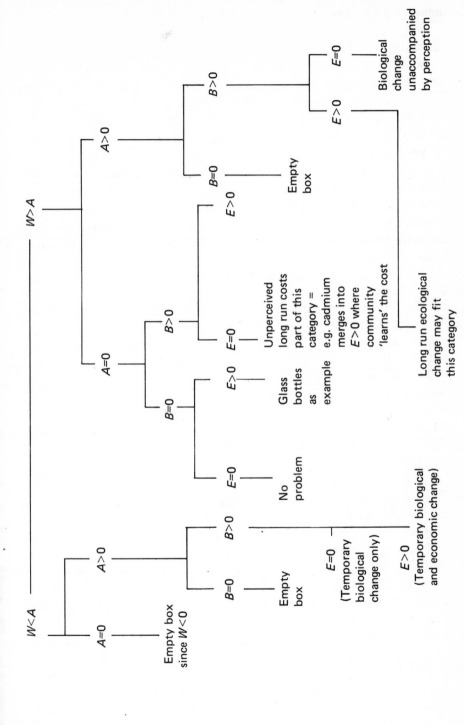

Fig. 11.1   A classification of pollutants

The theoretical limits of cost–benefit analysis

Probably the chief limitation of the conceptual framework of cost–benefit analysis in the context of pollution is the presumption that pollutants are homogeneous. In fact they have different dimensions which demand that they be treated differently. Some attempt has been made elsewhere to classify the nature of pollutants in an economic context. [4] It cannot be claimed that the classification developed is a very tight one, but it is sufficiently useful to illustrate the problems.

Figure 11.1 suggests a classificatory framework according to various parameters. First we define two contexts, one in which waste emitted to the environment is less than the environment's assimilative capacity, and one in which it is greater. We then suppress the first case, not because it is unimportant, but because it is not germane to the purpose in hand. In the second context we consider whether the pollutant in question has a biological dimension — defined as a situation in which some biological change occurs of whatever kind — and whether it has an economic dimension. From the opening remarks in this chapter it should now be clear what 'economic dimension' means — it exists if any one (or more than one) individual expresses a preference for or against a pollutant. If we omit the unlikely case in which people prefer pollution for its own sake (and not because of the associated benefits the pollution creating process generates), we are dealing only with costs. The costs imposed by pollution are known in economics as instances of *external effects* — costs imposed by one party on another in such a way that the polluter is not motivated to account for them in his own behaviour. This gives us the complete taxonomy shown in Fig. 11.1.

From the figure we may select three contexts. The first is where assimilative capacity A is zero — i.e. there exists no counterpart degrader capacity in the environment — and where externality E exists, but where no biological effects B are discernible. The obvious case is that of glass bottles. Here the problem is one of litter nuisance and the cost–benefit calculus has a direct application in that we shall require to weigh up the costs of abating the nuisance (e.g. the cost of a clean-up campaign) against the benefits. For this category of pollution economic analysis has direct relevance.

The second context is where A is zero, B is positive — i.e. biological changes do occur — but where E is apparently zero because the costs are unperceived by the sufferers. We may recall that unless a preference against pollution is recorded economic analysis dictates that no action be taken. However, economics acknowledges the existence of 'merit wants' —

commodities which are provided not so much in response to consumer demand but because some super individual body, the state perhaps, deems that they should be provided. Free primary education is an example. If the provision of primary education was determined by the desires of children of primary education age one imagines that very little of it would be provided! In the environment context we need to consider whether the same argument applies. The suggestion here is that it does apply to this second category. We may take the example of cadmium. The ingestion and inhalation of cadmium is painless and unperceived. Moreover it is not, except for the more dramatic cases, specifically related to proximity to the sources of cadmium emission, i.e. apparently 'safe' populations can have positive rates of intake. [5] Additionally, while there is a natural process of losing cadmium from the body the exit rate is less than the intake rate. There being no natural decay process, cadmium therefore accumulates in the body. To date it has been implicated fairly positively with renal disorder and speculatively with hypertension, cardiovascular disease, and even cancer. Accordingly we have a situation in which consumers exist in a state of ignorance which is associated with some probability of disease later in life. Since exposure is not correlated generally to location, there is little opportunity to relocate in order to avoid cadmium, even if consumers are aware of the problem. To make matters worse, since cadmium has no counterpart degrader population in the environment, it accumulates as a stock in the environment. The damage it does is then related not just to the flow of new emissions but to the total existing stock. As such, the cost of abating the problem has to be calculated in terms of cadmium emissions now *and* the cost of reducing the past stock. It would appear that it is technically impossible to reduce the stock by significant amounts, giving us an effective abatement cost of infinity. If we now try to apply our cost—benefit framework to cadmium we quickly see that it is applicable only in the loosest sense. If costs are infinite and if damage is finite (assuming a finite value to human suffering and life) cost—benefit dictates that we do nothing about the situation. Of course we can argue that if it is technically impossible to do anything about the stock we should concentrate on the flow of new emissions. The cost of controlling these will be finite and the damage will also be finite. Accordingly, we would expect cost—benefit to dictate some 'optimal' rate of emission which will be positive (unless we value suffering at infinite sums). Yet this leaves us with a so-called optimal rate of flow which is inevitably an addition to the stock and hence to perpetual future damage. What cost—benefit dictates is a shifting of a perpetual burden of cost onto future generations, and it is fairly clear how this arises. Quite simply, the

147

practice of using positive discount rates is entirely consistent with securing short term gains for current generations at the cost of infinite losses to future generations. The magnitude of this problem is perhaps not widely appreciated. Nash has given the example of a project yielding net benefits over a 50-year period of £85,000 in present value terms, using a 10 per cent discount rate, but which generates annual costs of £1 million for year 51 onwards to infinity. The standard cost—benefit approach would sanction that project simply because the discount factor reduces the future costs to insignificant amounts. [6]

The argument is that this example is not a fanciful one, for what is true of cadmium is true of mercury, and may be true of some nuclear wastes and countless new chemicals. One can therefore sympathise with those who say that what is required is a cost—benefit calculus that calls for outright prohibition of emissions of such pollutants. On the other hand, we can also see that the social disruption that such requirements would cause would be immense and no one can assert that the damage done is more than probabilistic. Perhaps the safest and mildest conclusion is that the physical monitoring of such pollutants should occur on a far greater scale than is currently the case, and that such monitoring should be heavily weighted towards *anticipating* damage. Finally, we need to know far more about the physical relationships between pollutants and health hazards. One thing is clear, however, and that is that individuals are no longer in a position to assimilate the kind of information they would need in order to take avertive action against all the probabilistic hazards of modern technology's pollutants. In the framing of environmental legislation we need to bear this point strongly in mind.

The third category of pollutant selected from Fig. 11.1 is the category where A exceeds zero, where biological effects are present and where externality exists. For many of these pollutants cost—benefit analysis is no doubt directly applicable. For some, however, we may note an impact which economists have generally ignored but to which some earlier papers have drawn attention. [7] Figure 11.2 shows the analysis in simplistic form. In the upper half of the diagram waste emissions W are shown as a function of the output of the commodity responsible for the pollution, *and assimilative capacity A* as some fixed quantity. The lower half of the diagram shows a curve of marginal net private benefits *MNPB*. This curve is the difference between private benefits and private costs, but in terms of first differences. Perhaps the easiest way to think of it is in terms of a firm's marginal profit curve — the extra profit earned from producing one extra unit of output. To simplify matters we further assume that if $W <$ A, there is virtually instantaneous degradation of the waste so that no

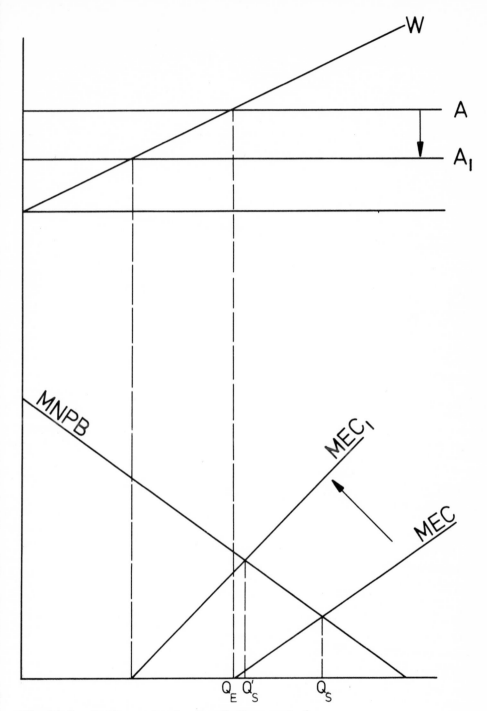

Fig. 11.2   Optimum levels of pollution control

149

externality occurs. This is an obvious simplification but it has been shown elsewhere that it makes no difference to the final analysis when the assumption is relaxed. [8] Accordingly, the marginal external cost curve, the extra cost to third parties brought about by an extra unit of output; begins at the point where $W = A$. More strictly, this is the earliest point at which it can begin because it will be recalled if individuals exhibit no 'dispreference' for the pollution there is no economic cost. [9] If we apply cost—benefit analysis to the problem we get the result that we should operate at the point Q_S where marginal external cost equals marginal net private benefit. This is the condition for maximising the difference between benefits and costs.

What is missing in this analysis is some consideration of what happens to assimilative capacity if waste exceeds that capacity. The essential point is that the capacity will itself be a function of the excess of waste over assimilative capacity. To put it another way, pollution reduces the capacity of the environment to receive further waste. This effect would appear to be fairly well documented. [10] In terms of our diagram it means that if we operate at any point to the right of $W = A$ we shall generate a shift downwards in the assimilative capacity line in a later period. The output Q_S meets this condition even though it appears 'optimal' from the application to cost—benefit analysis. The shift is shown in Fig. 11.2 as the movement from A_0 to A_1. If this shift occurs the impact of waste on the reduced assimilative capacity is all the greater. If individuals are highly sensitive they will react by showing a greater intensity of preference against pollution. The marginal external cost curve will shift to the left as shown and will be steeper in slope (since the ratio of W to A has increased). There will be a new apparent social optimum dictated by cost—benefit and this will be at Q_S. However, this new optimum is just as unstable as the first one and hence the process begins again. There appears to be one final solution, namely that the socially optimal output will eventually be zero — the economic counterpart of the 'doomsday conclusion'.

Has cost—benefit failed to identify the true optimum? In one sense it has. Inspection of the diagram, however, suggests that provided a long term view is taken we could operate at point Q_E from the start and thus avoid the dynamic instability involved in the repeated adjustment of output levels to apparent social optima. Further, there appears *prima facie* evidence that Q_E is consistent with the maximisation of long run net benefits. Whether this is correct remains slightly uncertain, not least because of the impact that the introduction of a discount rate has on the analysis. [11] It seems to point to the need to integrate ecological analysis with cost—benefit analysis or, at least, for economists to take a 'longer view' than they normally might.

The implications of the limits for measurement

The taxonomy of pollution has been considered at some length because it has clear implications for the measurement of the economic impact of environmental change. It should be clear by now that, to the economist, measuring 'economic impact' means measuring preferences for or against that change. The suggestion is that if we confine ourselves to situations in which we have a 'nuisance' such as litter and where biological change, if it exists, is perceived and understood, we face no *conceptual* problems in applying cost—benefit approaches. Where the impact goes unperceived, and particularly where there are no processes to reduce pollutants, cost—benefit seems to have a limited role *unless* we accept that current generations have the moral right to shift on to future generations burdens that *could* be of immense magnitude. This is a weighty moral problem but one can do no more than suggest that it is perhaps *the* greatest moral problem faced by current generations. Finally, we suggested that there may be some dynamic external effects which will go unacknowledged by orthodox cost—benefit analysis. If, as hinted, there is some 'ecological optimum' (Q_E in Fig. 11.2) which can be defined as the output level giving the maximum economic benefits compatible with the avoidance of ecological instability, then it may be that sophisticated cost—benefit analysis will identify that optimum. It may also be the case that cost—benefit becomes redundant in this situation (a) because of the impossibility of predicting and measuring the relevant shifts in the parameters involved, and (b) because a purely physical analysis might identify a long run optimum, for example by identifying the equivalent of the $W = A$ point in Fig. 11.2.

What is being suggested, in contrast to the normally accepted viewpoint in cost—benefit analysis, is that there is still a long way to go in dealing with the *conceptual* problems of applying cost—benefit analysis to environmental problems. It is not just a matter of perfecting the 'state of the art' in measuring damage costs. It is a matter of ensuring that, before we hasten to measure what we can, however we can, we investigate in far more detail the fundamental problem of applying cost—benefit. It may well be that at the end of the day cost—benefit is vindicated. My argument is that we still need to have this demonstrated.

The practical limitations of cost—benefit analysis

The previous sections have concentrated on the theoretical difficulties faced in measuring the damage done by pollution. While these difficulties are important, they still leave considerable room for the application of cost—benefit techniques and, as many commentators have remarked, cost—benefit is perhaps the best technique we have for ordering our thoughts on the gains and losses associated with environmental change. However, when we turn to situations in which there appears to be a conceptual case for measuring damage we face other difficulties. That there should be problems will come as no surprise to anyone who has ever tried to engage in any social measurement exercise, and simply because there are problems does not mean that we should abandon the idea of measurement.

To give some idea of the 'state of the art' in practical measurement we can take the example of noise. This is particularly relevant because (a) it has been selected as perhaps the most important pollutant in modern society by the Royal Commission on Pollution (an arguable judgement, but certainly plausible in terms of the numbers of people affected), (b) it is readily perceived and hence seems to fit our category where cost—benefit can be applied, and (c) it has attracted perhaps the greatest amount of attention from economists who have sought to measure the damage from pollution. In short, if we find ourselves forced to the conclusion that we have failed *in practice* to measure the damage from noise, we shall have to conclude *either* that we stand no chance of ever measuring the damage from other more complex pollutants, *or* that the state of the art is currently primitive. The latter conclusion is, in a sense, an inevitable one but totally unfalsifiable: no one can say if we shall ever satisfactorily measure the damage from pollution. The suggestion here is that, given forseeable technique and knowledge, if we have failed to measure noise nuisance damage, we have failed in general to measure the damage from pollution.

The case of noise nuisance

The following is a brief survey of the state of the art of measuring noise nuisance damage. The main approach is the property price approach since this has been the subject of most research.

Property price approaches

General theory The essence of the property price approach to noise

152

nuisance evaluation is that individuals can 'buy' peace and quiet by choosing to locate their homes in peaceful areas and by opting to work only for employers who locate their activities in such areas. Accordingly observation of the behaviour of people who vary in their sensitivity to noise should enable us to estimate their implicit (positive) valuations of quiet and hence their implicit (negative) valuations of noise. If, to take an extreme example, a consumer is able to choose between two houses identical in every respect except that house A has a peaceful location and house B a noisy location, then the existence of noise sensitive people should mean that the price of A (P_A) exceeds the price of B (P_B). The differential $P_A - P_B$ would provide a *prima facie* measure of the extra value of peace and quiet attached to house A. This generalised approach requires us to accept that:

(a) individuals *are* free to choose in the manner supposed;
(b) noise is *not* a ubiquitous 'public bad' but a localised one;
(c) noise, or 'quiet', can be measured quantitatively in a fashion similar to that for amounts of other commodities;
(d) the effects of noise on house prices can be disentangled from the many other effects on house prices.

As far as assumption (a) is concerned, it is evident that many people will not be able to move house with the comparative ease required by property price models. We need therefore to investigate the effects of limited mobility in this approach and this is the subject of some later sections. Assumption (b) is necessary because property price models would not reveal significant or meaningful house price differentials if individuals who are averse to noise are unable to find quiet areas. Walters [12] asserts, however, that 'aircraft noise is a local and not a ubiquitous phenomenon', but this author has pointed out [13] that the localised nature of aircraft noise is not sufficient to warrant application of partial equilibrium techniques if noise in general, from whatever source, is widespread. The United Kingdom Royal Commission on Pollution has estimated that some ten million people in the UK are exposed to 'unacceptable' noise and that this figure could rise to thirty million in 1980. If this is true the housing market would have to be in a remarkable state of flux to accommodate the avertive behaviour of so many rational people.

Assumption (c) is an important one. For an individual without monopsony power the price of any commodity is the same however many he buys. If apples in the market are priced at x pence each, the amount spent is a simple multiple of quantity bought and the constant unit price paid. But, given the way noise measures are constructed, one would expect units of noise to differ according to how many of them one already has, i.e. the (negative) price of 1 unit of *NNI* added to an existing 50 units should be higher than the (negative) price attached to an additional unit on top of 40 *NNI*. In this respect we would expect the price—*NNI* relationship to be non-linear. Walters argues that the evidence from the information collected in the investigation of London's third airport supports the assumption of linearity, i.e. a constant price per unit of noise measure. Since the information on which this argument is based is itself questionable, and since no other investigation appears to support the linearity hypothesis (though they do not really refute it either), Walters' argument is, as he readily admits, open to doubt.

As far as assumption (d) is concerned, it is clearly *technically* feasible to separate the effects of noise on house prices from other prices determining factors. Whether the actual efforts made so far have been successful in this respect is questionable. One adjustment mechanism open to the consumer is to move house to avoid or diminish noise nuisance. The most sophisticated house price differential (*HPD*) models have in fact incorporated the relocation decision into the property price analysis. Although there are numerous modifications to the basic *HPD*/relocation models, we concentrate on the two closely related but most sophisticated models, those of the Roskill Commission team [14] and Walters. [12]

The 'Roskill' model We may first categorise the types of persons affected. These are:

1 People who are 'natural movers' — i.e. who will be moving anyway for reasons unconnected with noise. If noise increases as these people sell their houses, we can expect house prices to fall and they will bear this loss. For these people, consumers' surplus, S, the excess of subjective valuation of house price over actual price, is zero.

2 People who move *because* of noise. For many people the value they place on their home exceeds the market valuation by the amount S. Hence they lose both the depreciation on the market price of their house (D) and S by moving. In addition they will incur removal costs, R. For these people it must be the case that the cost of noise, N, if they remained, exceeds $S+D+R$. Consequently, $S+D+R$ is a minimum estimate of the costs to this category of sufferer.

3 Those who *stay* and tolerate noise. They suffer a cost, N, which is their subjective valuation of the noise. Technically, $N < S+D+R$ for

these people and, of course, N could be zero.

4   Those who move in to the noisy area to replace natural movers and those who have moved because of noise. If these people are fully aware of the new circumstances, it would be reasonable to assume that they are at least compensated by D, the depreciation on property that they now buy. In fact D could exceed their requirement for compensation, in which case there would be *benefits* for this category. The general assumption, however, has been to set costs equal to zero for this category.

The estimate of D was obtained by the CTLA Research Team from Gatwick estate agents (Gatwick was thought to be similar to the four sites chosen for short listed consideration). D was thus a direct estimate of how estate agents thought noise *alone* would affect house prices. The estimates of D vary according to house price category. Three categories were chosen − high, medium and low − with absolute price levels being estimated from rateable values. Estimates of D varied for each house price category and for each noise zone. The estimates of D were validated, *ex post*, by reference in Inland Revenue data.

The estimate of R was obtained independently from professional removers and was taken to include the 'disruption' costs of moving. The actual figure used was 16 per cent where $R = 0{\cdot}16P$.

The estimate of S was obtained from a survey of householders. S was assessed as a sum of money required by householders to induce them to move, not as the sum householders might pay to retain their peace and quiet. Actual estimates of S were obtained by a questionnaire approach to people living in areas considered to have close resemblance to the actual sites under consideration. People were asked to give an estimate of the market value of their property and then to say how much they would require to induce them to move. The difference between the latter and the former gave the *householder's surplus*, as it was called. The final average surplus was 52 per cent of property price, i.e. $S = 0{\cdot}52P$.

Finally, an estimate of N was required. N is that 'sum of money which would just compensate . . . [the house owner] . . . for the nuisance suffered and make him as well off as he was before'. [14] The actual estimation of N was quite complex. In particular, we need to know N because it determines the proportions of residents who move *because* of noise (i.e. they move if $N > S+R+D$, but stay if $N < S+R+D$). In terms of the *movement rule*, S will be the measure of how much the consumer is *willing to pay* to buy back quiet and stay where he is. The procedure for estimating N was as follows: the distribution of annoyance scores over the population in each *NNI* was taken from the Wilson Report. [15] For each distribution the median is associated with the value *D* such that *D* is assumed to measure noise disbenefit.

This procedure is repeated for other *NNI*, enabling Table 11.1 to be derived.

Table 11.1

Noise nuisance and property value depreciation

Annoyance score	*NNI* for which the score is median	Corresponding percentage depreciation		
		Low	Medium	High
1	32	2	4	6
2	40	4	9	15
3	49	10	15	26
4	55	13	20	35
5	60	15	22	38

These disbenefit measures can now be fed back to the distributions within each *NNI*, with the percentage depreciation being expressed in absolute terms in each case. There are the absolute values of *N*, and they will now appear as a distribution for each *NNI* category. To obtain estimates of those who move ($N > S+R+D$) we look at the distribution of householders' surplus. For example, $S = 0$ for 11 per cent of people in medium priced houses (S is invariant with respect to *NNI*). $D = 9.4$ per cent for the average priced house of £6,000 and $R = 16$ per cent of property price. Hence, $S = 0$; $D = £564$, and $R = £960$. Hence $S+R+D = £1,524$. Now $N > £2,000$ for 21 per cent of people in the 40–45 *NNI* medium house price category, so that some 21 per cent of people have $N > S+R+D$, and these people are predicted to move.

Accordingly, by securing independent values of S, R, and D, and by deriving N from D, the model is able to predict the *sizes* of the relevant categories noted above.

It was accepted that the *relative* valuation of 'peace and quiet' would rise over time, because of a presumption that the income elasticity of demand for quiet exceeds unity. Thus if real incomes can be assumed to rise at x per cent per annum, the real value of quiet can be assumed to rise at some rate nx per cent per annum, where n is the income elasticity of demand for quiet. In fact, the house depreciation data themselves suggest a relationship whereby noise costs vary (approximately) as the square of income, making $n = 2$ in the above formulation. In the CTLA study, a value of n of about $1 \cdot 7$ was used.

Criticisms of the 'Roskill' model

The role of expectations   The validity of the 'Roskill' model depends critically upon the 'rational' behaviour of householders and on a perfectly functioning housing market. Rationality is fundamental to all economic analysis, but it is always pertinent to ask if sources of irrationality exist and, if so, how they affect the validity of the model. Sources of imperfection are even more important. It will be seen that many of the methodological criticisms of property price models centre on the imperfections of housing markets.

One such problem is the expectations of the inmovers. As we saw, these people have zero losses or may experience a gain due to the fact that their subjective valuations lie above the depreciated property price. But the validity of this point depends on the expectations of the inmover, with respect to noise, being fulfilled. Since, virtually by definition, inmovers do not experience their new surroundings for any significant period of time there is no reason to suppose that they predict correctly the net advantage of the environment. As Paul [16] points out, planning authorities frequently restrict residential building around airports; there would be little point in this if the authorities did not expect inmovers to make precisely the kind of mistake noted above.

Noise pervasiveness   If noise nuisance occurs in such a way as to affect *all* areas, or all areas to which noise sensitive residents can move, then the change of residents predicted by the 'Roskill' model will not occur. That is, if noise behaves like a global, or near global, public bad, property price differentials will not emerge even though noise sensitive residents are clearly worse off.

How far noise pervasiveness of this kind prevents the previously described model from operating as it is supposed to depends entirely on evidence about which residents move and which do not even though they would like to. As yet such evidence is limited in amount, but there is some evidence to suggest that noise sensitive residents do not move as expected. [17]

The use of D to estimate N   There is no *particular* reason to suppose that the median of the noise annoyance distribution is associated with the measure *D*. That this assumption was never substantiated was accepted in the final report of the CTLA. The earlier argument used by the CTLA

157

research team was that there would be an equal number of buyers and sellers of houses, the residents of which thought N exceeded D. Consequently, if we plotted a distribution of such people, 50 per cent would think $N > D$, and 50 per cent would think $N < D$. Hence the median of such a distribution should coincide with D. As Paul points out, however, this is not the relevant distribution; what matters are all those residents in noise affected houses, not just those in houses bought and sold after the noise has occurred. [16] Those who stay and suffer the noise also lose part of their surplus.

The relevance of NNI   The way in which noise annoyance is measured is not part of this report, but it is important to observe that if the measures of noise in common use are, for one reason or another, unsatisfactory, the economic models based upon them will also be open to error. One recent attack on the use of such measures as *NNI* requires comment. This criticism has been advanced by Hart, [18] and directly contradicts the assumption that *NNI* (and hence other noise measures, since such measures tend to be transformations of each other, albeit complex ones) is a cardinally indexed entity. [19]

The *NNI* index is expressed as:

$$NNI = \frac{}{PNdB} + 15 \log N - 80$$

$$\text{and } \frac{}{PNdB} = 10 \log \left(\frac{1}{N}\right) \sum_i 10^{\frac{L_i}{80}}$$

where L_i = peak noise level in perceived noise decibels (*PNdB*) for the ith aircraft;

$\dfrac{}{PNdB}$ = logarithmic average of noise loudness;

N = number of aircraft heard on an average summer day;

80 = a constant corresponding to zero annoyance.

Hart begins by doubting whether the implications of such an equation can be correct. It implies, for example, that annoyance doubles if N quadruples from 1 to 4; but also only doubles if N rises from 20 to 80, or from 80 to 320. This is clearly an absurdity. Hart then shows that, using the original data from the Wilson report, only 20 per cent of the variation in noise annoyance between people was ever explained by noise loudness and numbers of aircraft. Hart traces this unsatisfactory explanatory power to the method of assessing annoyance scores themselves. He argues that the questionnaire technique actually used could never have elicited correct answers, particularly because they were asked in such a way as to preclude the *number* of aircraft from affecting annoyance in a sensible fashion. Hart also points out that annoyance ratings are *ordinal*, but *NNI* is a *cardinal* index. However, ordinal measures are determinate only up to monotonic transformations, while cardinal scales are determinate up to linear transformations. Basing a cardinal measure on an ordinal scale is illicit. Finally Hart observes that 80 *dB* can no longer be regarded as corresponding to zero annoyance. Hart suggests that deviations from 70 to 75 *dB* would be more suitable (and even this seems high), which means that current *NNI* measures will *understate* noise nuisance.

Although Hart's critique was not aimed at the cost—benefit work based on measures such as *NNI* (it was concerned with the so called 'minimum noise routes'), its importance is that it may suggest that *NNI* is a quite unreliable statistic upon which to base any economic model. If this is true, it brings completely into question the 'Roskill' noise—cost model as it was *actually* estimated.

Movement rates   All property price models depend on the assumption that noise sensitive householders will move out of a noisy area, to be replaced by 'imperturbables'. If the number of annoyed persons wishing to move out is very much smaller than the number of imperturbables wishing to move in, the price of noisy property will not change, or at least will change only marginally. This is because the price differential is determined by the turnover of those properties put up for sale and *not* by the total stock. We need to know how many movers there are in any one area and whether the number varies according to the noise level. Using data from the second survey of aircraft noise carried out at Heathrow Airport in 1967, Starkie and Johnson [20] argue that mobility is not significantly different between noise bands. If they are correct, a basic assumption of the *HPD* model is shown to be false.

The Walters model

The most sophisticated development of the property price approach is to be found in Walters. [12] The outcome of Walters' approach is an actual valuation of noise which, it is argued, can be applied to most noise generating or noise abatement programmes. The significant feature is a valuation *per unit of noise* which is held to apply regardless of where on the noise scale the increase or reduction in noise occurs. Clearly if such a unit value of noise could be derived it would simplify immensely the problem of integrating noise nuisance valuation into standard cost—

benefit approaches.

First, a utility maximising model is developed in which 'quiet' appears as one of the commodities the consumer can choose. Essentially a constant–returns Cobb-Douglas utility function is assumed, giving rise to a unitary elastic demand curve for quiet. In this way quiet (and hence noise) is not seen as an attribute of housing as in other property price models, but as a continuum such that the consumer can choose the *amounts* of noise he wishes to experience given his preferences for other commodities. This is important because in other models, dubbed 'attribute' models by Walters, the consumer is judged to be choosing between noise and quiet which in turn are seen as polar extremes of each other.

Walters aims to find a demand function for 'quiet'; this he does by deriving such a function from the utility maximising model. If this demand function can be estimated, we have a direct means of valuing noise. Strictly we secure only a minimum estimate since what is paid for quiet reflects the consumer's willingness to pay for the marginal unit of quiet only. We require, of course, an additional estimate of the consumer's surplus on intra-marginal units of quiet if there are significant changes in the amount of noise.

Where P is the price of quiet, Q is the amount of quiet, and y is income, the consumer spends a proportion of his income, $P.Q/y$ on quiet. From the utility maximising model we can show that this proportion is equal to b, the 'taste' for quiet. *Hence,* b, *a direct measure of the value of quiet at the margin, can be obtained by looking at the proportion of income a consumer (household) spends on quiet.* If the amount of quiet experienced by a consumer changes, that consumer will adjust his behaviour in such a way as to maintain the *amount he spends* on quiet constant; this result is a direct outcome of the unitary elasticity of the demand curve for quiet and, in turn, this unitary elasticity results from the specific form of utility function assumed. In this way, the distribution of b across individuals is invariant with respect to the price of quiet and the relative supply of quiet.

For small changes in the amount of noise, or for changes which affect only a small proportion of housholds, the price of quiet, P, can be assumed to stay constant since it is the overall market demand and supply of quiet that determines the price of quiet. This amounts to assuming that noise pervasiveness is not significant or, to put it another way, that noise is a localised and not a global public bad.

Accordingly, we require a direct measure of $P.Q/y$, and this will be the 'value' of the marginal unit of quiet. Since income measures are not usually available as an independent piece of data in property price studies, Walters proposes the use of house prices themselves as a measure of 'permanent income' This is justified by the fact that the elasticity of demand for housing itself tends to be minus unity such that the amount people spend on housing tends to be a constant proportion of their total income. In this way we can alter the problem to one of looking at the expenditure on quiet as a proportion of house prices. If the price of quiet can be thought of as being a constant, the effect of a change in the *supply* of quiet (through noise generating or noise abatement investments) will be such that the depreciation in the market price of property will measure the change in expenditure on quiet. In short, for a *given* income level and *given* noise level D, the house price depreciation, will measure b, the value of quiet. In practice Walters accepts that the imperfections in housing markets, wrong expectations etc. will mean that the value of b would not be the same for each income category in each noise group. There will in fact be a distribution of b within each income group and noise level. Walters' procedure is to take $P.Q/y$ (the observed expenditure, which in turn equals D) to be the mean or median of this distribution of b. This was in fact the assumption of the 'Roskill' research team.

In Walters' approach D becomes the critical variable that requires measurement. After surveying the available literature on the effects of noise on property values, Walters concludes that noise has a definite effect on house prices and that, expressed in a particular way, these depreciation values are similar for each of the studies carried out and can be considered reliable. He expresses the information on depreciation in the formula:

$$NDSI = \frac{\text{Difference in percentage depreciation}}{\text{Difference in } NNI}$$

where $NDSI$ is termed the 'Noise Depreciation Sensitivity Index'. To see how this is calculated, consider the example of a 10 point change from 40 to 50 NNI in the Gatwick area on high priced houses (the figures are taken from CTLA, 1970). We find that such a change alters depreciation from 3·3 per cent of the price of the high priced house, to 13·3 per cent. Hence the $NDSI$ for this house price (income) category is:

$$NDSI = \frac{13·3 - 3·3}{50 - 40} = 1$$

To see how the $NDSI$ is modified and then used, we proceed as follows. First, NNI (and hence other noise measures which are transformations of NNI) can be taken to be a direct measure of Q, the amount of quiet. Walters establishes the cardinality of NNI so that the $NDSI$ is not affected by the level at which the level of quiet (noise) changes. Second, we interpret the *NDSI* as the percentage of income (house price) the consumer will pay for a unit (one *NNI*) increase in the amount of quiet. If we write P_h for house price, and recall that *NNI* measures Q, the *NDSI* formula becomes:

$$NDSI = \frac{100\,D_2/P_h - 100\,D_1/P_h}{Q_2 - Q_1}$$

But we have already established (from the utility maximising model) that $P.Q = D$, with P constant. Hence *NDSI* can be rewritten as:

$$NDSI = \frac{100(P.Q_2 - P.Q_1)P_h}{Q_2 - Q_1} = \frac{100.P}{P_h}$$

If we then look at the empirical studies on house prices (Walters looks at five studies for the USA, and the 'Roskill' study for the UK) we can correct the *NDSI* for differences in P_h in the studies to see how closely *NDSI*s correspond. Recall that what we are doing is seeing what the percentage of income is that a consumer will spend to buy an extra unit of quiet. Walters argues that the resulting *NDSI*s do show similarity — with value of between 0·4 and 0·7 for the USA, and value of 1·0–1·3 for the UK, all based on a standardised $25,000 house.

Finally, we need to see how *NDSI* can be used. Borrowing Walters' example, if we have 20,000 houses affected by noise such that *NNI* increases from 30 to 45 and the average price of a house is £8,000, we obtain, assuming an *NDSI* of 1, the compensation required as:

$$C = NNI.\ NDSI.\ P_H.\ H.\ 1/100$$

where H is the stock of houses affected. i.e.:

$$C = 15.1.£8,000.20,000.1/100 = £24 \text{ million}$$

The attraction of Walters' model is that it provides a theoretical rationale for adopting house price depreciation as a measure of the value of (the marginal unit of) quiet. Simply observing that house prices may be different in noisy areas compared to quiet areas cannot justify the use of those differentials unless it can be shown that they relate to the necessary measure of compensating variation. In addition, Walters' model argues that there is a fairly systematic and comparable effect of noise on house prices regardless of where the noise occurs and where on the noise scale the change in noise takes place.

The problems with the model are numerous and Walters acknowledges throughout that these are only rudimentary beginnings in what he hopes will be a sustained research programme. The salient problems are (a) that the utility function used implies an income elasticity of demand for quiet of unity whereas the evidence, if it can be believed, suggests an elasticity of from 1·7 to 2·0; (b) that the information used to establish some general values of the *NDSI* is itself weak, so that it might be better to attempt a recalculation of *NDSI* for each study — i.e. essentially to estimate D for each specific case; (c) that the observed value of b for any homogeneous income group is taken to be the mean of the b_i distribution and information is lacking by which to substantiate this assumption (although Walters suggests it is consistent with some of the socio-psychological data); (d) that it presupposes a particular equilibrating mechanism in the housing market which seems unlikely to occur in practice given the immense constraints on movement and adjustment. It is not clear that the b_i distribution captures all these constraints; (e) that it presumes noise to be a localised public bad whereas the true situation is perhaps closer to one of being a global or near global public bad; and (f) that it justifies the cardinality of *NNI* on the basis of very few observations (see below in the section on empirical applications).

The state of the art in estimating pollution damage

While the previous section has only briefly surveyed one of the approaches to estimating noise damage in monetary terms, [21] it suggests that the degree of confidence to be placed in the estimates so far obtained cannot be great. If we extend the investigation to the valuation of noise from traffic as opposed to aircraft the results are even less impressive. Indeed they seem to suggest virtually no progress at all in that context. What is true of noise is also true of air pollution where house price approaches have also been used. Admittedly figures of monetary value *are* obtained, but the real difficulty is to know just how much faith to place in these values since there is no real validation procedure, no way of really testing whether these are the 'right' values because of the multiplicity of problems that continue to exist with the methodologies adopted and the information. Further, with other 'perceived' pollutants such as the more obvious forms of air pollution there are associated health hazards and these are extremely difficult to value in monetary terms. While research into the valuation of pollution damage must clearly continue, it seems impossible to avoid the conclusion that to date the monetary measures obtained cannot be used for practical policy purposes.

Is there an alternative? One possibility is that we need not require estimates of monetary damage at all. This argument suggests that it is more important to know the costs of abatement. If the decision maker can be presented with a range of costs with the associated impact on pollution levels, plus some further indication of what the changes in pollution levels mean (for example in terms of health, or fish stocks, or visual amenity), he can decide the appropriate 'optimum' level of pollution. Such an approach is very far from the ideal that cost–benefit analysts would like, not least because they see it as one more mechanism for divorcing actual decision making from the revealed preferences of the individuals whose lives are affected by those decisions. The dilemma is a real one – either we opt for suspect monetary valuations which have little scientific claim to validity, or we abdicate responsibility to the civil servant and the politician. Ultimately, of course, theirs is the responsibility; no cost–benefit analyst would suggest otherwise. It is perhaps slightly sad that we cannot present more detailed estimates of damage so as to ensure that decisions are executed on the basis of information on what individuals want. There is no escape from this dilemma at the current time. At the very least it is imperative that we considerably expand our research into the costs of abating pollution – research which, sadly, is minimal in the United Kingdom.

Notes

[1]   For various views on the optimal rate of depletion, see the essays by J. Kay and J. Mirrlees, G. Heal, and I. Pearce, in D. W. Pearce (ed.), *The Economics of Natural Resource Depletion,* Macmillan, Basingstoke 1975.

[2]   This constitutes a so-called 'potential Pareto improvement' and is formally equivalent to the Kaldor–Hicks compensation test. This brief outline glosses over numerous problems, not least that the test does not require compensation *actually* to be paid so that the losers really are worse off. However, there are signs that legislation is moving towards the idea of securing actual compensation transfers between gainers and losers – see, for example, the Land Compensation Act 1973. The various problems with the cost–benefit rule described above are discussed in C. A. Nash, D. W. Pearce and J. Stanley, 'The evaluation of cost–benefit analysis criteria', *Scottish Journal of Political Economy*, vol. 22, no. 2, June 1975, pp.121–34.

[3]   For an excellent critique of the standard welfare maximising approach to natural resource depletion, see T. Page, *The Economics of a Throwaway Society*, Resources for the Future, Johns Hopkins Press,

Baltimore 1975.

[4]   See D. W. Pearce, 'The limitations of cost—benefit analysis as a guide to environmental policy', *Kyklos*, vol. 29, 1976, pp.97—112. See also D. W. Pearce, S. Ghatak and A. Ghatak, 'A synthesis of cost—benefit analysis and ecological decision criteria for solving environmental problems', paper presented to International Institute of Applied Systems Analysis, workshop on decision making with multiple conflicting objectives, Vienna, 20—24 October 1975.

[5]   For more detail, see C. A. Nobbs and D. W. Pearce, 'The economics of stock pollutants: the case for cadmium', *International Journal of Environment and Planning*, vol. 5, no. 5, 1975, pp.611—8.

[6]   C. A. Nash, 'Future generations and the social rate of discount', *Environmental and Planning*, vol. 5, no. 5, 1975, pp.611—8.

[7]   The papers involved are best seen as a continuum developing the theme — later papers develop and sometimes correct and modify earlier ones. They are: D. W. Pearce, 'An incompatibility in planning for a steady state and planning for maximum economic welfare', *Environment and Planning*, vol. 6, 1973, pp.267—71; 'Economic and ecological approaches to the optimal level of pollution', *Social Economics*, vol. 1, 1974, pp.146—59; 'Economics and ecology', *Surrey Papers in Economics*, vol. 10, July 1974; 'The limitations of cost—benefit analysis as a guide to environmental policy' and 'A synthesis of cost—benefit analysis and ecological decision criteria for solving environmental problems', op.cit.

[8]   See D. W. Pearce, *Kyklos*, op.cit.

[9]   Readers may care to repeat the analysis with the marginal external cost curve beginning to the right of the $W = A$ point; it merely strengthens the conclusions.

[10]   G. M. Woodwell, 'The effect of pollution on the structure and physiology of ecosystems', *Science*, 24 April 1970.

[11]   For one approach which does incorporate a discount rate see the paper by Pearce, Ghatak and Ghatak, op.cit., note [4]. The analysis becomes highly complex. Note also that assimilative capacity can be increased by suitable investment of funds in some cases — e.g. augmenting streamflow. Models allowing for this are being developed at Leicester University.

[12]   A. Walters, *Noise and Prices*, Oxford University Press, London 1975.

[13]   D. W. Pearce, 'The price of peace and quiet', *Times Literary Supplement*, 23 May 1975.

[14]   Commission on the Third London Airport (CTLA), *Papers and Proceedings*, vol. 7, HMSO, London 1970.

[15]   Committee on the Problem of Noise, *Noise — Final Report*, HMSO, London 1963.

[16]   M. E. Paul, 'Can aircraft noise nuisance be measured in money?', *Oxford Economic Papers*, November 1971.

[17]   I. D. Griffiths and F. J. Langdon, 'Subjective response to road traffic noise', *Journal of Sound and Vibration*, vol. 8, 1968.

[18]   P. E. Hart, 'Population densities and optimal aircraft flight paths', *Regional Studies,* vol. 7, no. 2, 1973, pp.137—51.

[19]   Walters presents the case for cardinality in *NNI*, but accepts that *NNI* itself is biased against the influence of *numbers* of aircraft annoyance. See Walters, op.cit., note [12].

[20]   D. M. Starkie and D. M. Johnson, *The Economic Value of Peace and Quiet*, D. C. Heath, Farnborough 1975.

[21]   For a detailed survey, see D. W. Pearce, *Social Cost of Noise*, OECD, Paris 1975.

12 On putting the environment in its place: a critique of EIA

E. BROOKS

This chapter is concerned primarily with the relevance to the political decision maker of 'the idea of comprehensive assessments of the wider (and less easily measured) environmental impacts of proposed general policies and particular projects.' [1] In particular it seeks to assess the practicability and value of building environmental assessment into 'a proper cost—benefit account which includes *all* the relevant components of project evaluation, including economic, political and sociological aspects', [1] and of using such a very broad and (it is hoped) balanced framework for policy implementation.

It has been suggested that two distinct forms of environmental deterioration occur. First there is pollution whereby the residuals of economic and social activity have a damaging impact upon the human habitat. Secondly there are the misallocative effects of land and water planning whereby certain populations suffer adverse consequences within their specific environments. [2]

In practice however these two forms of degradation frequently combine or overlap, as when an urban motorway emitting noise and fumes into the environment is so located that it concentrates its environmental pollution upon a limited population. More generally we can identify a spectrum of environmental impacts from the global at one extreme to the individual at the other. The effect upon global gases of the destruction of the Amazon rain forest would fall into the former category, while the person whose window is obscured by new high rise flats next door would fall into the latter.

The degree to which an impact is area specific, and on what scale of intensity, might well be critical in determining its sensitivity and bearing upon the political process. We must immediately qualify this assumption by recalling that individuals and regions are far from equal in their ability to protest and to take remedial political action. Moreover, if somewhat paradoxically, a protest might be easier to articulate and focus where the scale of engagement is more parochial and manageable. How does the world citizen protest about the destruction of the Amazon rain forest, and to whom? By comparison, the Westway agitation stemmed from a small local community where protest could swiftly be mobilised against a perceived local enemy.

In one sense this is saying no more than that an environmental impact assessment would need to be appropriate to the scale of the project and its areal propensity to pollute. But if the object of the exercise is, among other things, to arouse public awareness of the potential for damage before it is too late, we immediately face the difficulty that different publics exist and might well perceive their interests in mutually contradictory ways. An environmental impact assessment of Concorde, say, which was confined to Great Britain (e.g. the noise pollution at Heathrow), would be able to ignore the sonic boom problem by making the assumption that Mach 1 would not be exceeded until the plane had left British air space. Thus the British public's concern would be muted and less likely thereby to resist the pro-Concorde lobbies based upon employment prospects or technological ambitions. The public which stood to suffer from sonic bangs — the nomads of the Arabian desert perhaps — would probably lack the foreknowledge to express their opposition in good time. Even if they (or more likely some desert oil employees) managed to find out in advance that a London–Bahrein route was being promoted, their lack of a constituency voice in the country generating the pollution would weaken the effectiveness of their influence over events. A somewhat similar position applies in the case of plutonium manufacture and disposal, where the ultimate environmental effects may well be global and of exceptional hazard; yet the institutional machinery for assessing the wider environmental impact of national economic and technological policies hardly begins to exist. Moreover, individual countries have strong security as well as economic incentives to resist intervention by any global constituency claiming to speak on behalf of the planet.

More fundamentally, is it even theoretically possible to invoke a planetary optimising policy towards the global environment? Quite apart from the daunting number of variables involved, and the clairvoyant abilities required of those seeking to measure any long term impact upon the earth's environment, we meet the same problem which at the micro-scale was illustrated in the Roskill Commission's cost effectiveness appraisal of the third London airport. [3] In that case each project involved a spatial income redistributive effect; or, to put it crudely, one man's peace had to be traded for another man's tumult. There were of course many variables in addition to noise, such as the structural damage to ancient churches, but in each case some more or less arbitrary weighting was applied to generate allegedly meaningful costs (or more strictly opportunity costs and shadow prices) which could then be grossed and used to justify policy decisions.

It has frequently been pointed out, and justifiably, that the weightings were prone to favour the rich, whose time is manifestly more 'valuable' than the poor, yet those who argue for egalitarian principles are being no less arbitrary than the realists who do at least measure an existing rather than a hypothetical world. What we have to recognise is that there are no right rules of the planetary game, at least in terms of weighting the various contenders via specific handicaps, yet the weights we actually give them (e.g. all men are equal, or one white Rhodesian is worth twenty blacks) can profoundly affect the way in which environmental impact is measured. In the case of Westway and similar urban motorway schemes there has long been an implicit weighting which penalises the local downtown residents. Similarly the postwar schemes of urban clearance which have left large areas of our inner cities looking like bomb sites for decades are in effect an expression of the political worth and power of those whose local environment is so degraded. Or, to put it yet another way, a truly comprehensive cost—benefit evaluation of a project is inherently a political testament and should not be confused with an objective or neutral piece of disinterested advice.

Those who have followed the argument so far might here protest that even an avowedly partisan advocacy can have scientific value if the assumptions made can be identified and used to correct the polemic. In other words, an environmental appraisal of Concorde which restricted its assessment of sonic boom to the impact over Great Britain alone would stand revealed as a partial and to that extent misleading document. Or an analysis of a suitable location for London's next airport which, like Roskill, was based on assumptions that logically supported a site by the Thames at Westminster,. [4] might lead one to scrutinise the formula for weighting ancient churches (such as Westminster Abbey) with healthy scepticism.

It would be churlish to deny that the Roskill Commission was of considerable scientific value in this negative sense. As the greatest and easily the most expensive cost—benefit assessment ever conducted in Britain, it was instrumental in revealing the immense complexity of the variables involved in both time and space. In retrospect it can be seen to have been a clairvoyant charlatan; it failed to foresee the energy crisis which dominates the mid-seventies, and its assessment of Britain's investment potential was, like the Channel Tunnel project, based upon a fanciful optimism. The consolation that the economic climate deteriorated so swiftly that big and carefully costed projects like the Chunnel were virtually stillborn misses the real point: had the Yom Kippur war broken out two or three years later, Britain might have had to practise a much more expensive infanticide instead of abortion upon such projects.

Returning to the claim that any cost–benefit analysis is better than none as long as the assumptions are made clear, we may doubt whether they invariably are made clear, or can be so readily extricated from the *mélange* of facts and suppositions which underpin the recommendations. We have already commented upon the vastly diverse publics whose environments risk change and possible deterioration. Many of these publics and their political spokesmen are unlikely to have access to the detailed information and calculations used and, as the belated exposure of Concorde's noise levels at take-off shows, [5] those who stand to benefit from a specific project may prove reticent in coming clean with the full evidence. In short, our political publics can readily be misled by interest groups, and elaborate and complex costing exercises which wrap up the tendentious reasoning in spurious and pseudo-mathematical formulae can be positively dangerous when handled by an innumerate politician.

Much of the foregoing has been critical, at least by implication, of any attempt to widen still further the formal statutory requirements for environmental appraisal within a cost–benefit analysis. The scepticism is partly academic and partly political. On the former count it stems from the essentially *unpredictable* as well as complex world of man/land interaction. Multivariate futurology is, to put it no higher, an inexact science. On the political count disquiet arises simply because of the difficulty of measuring environmental impact by any single and objective yardstick. Politics is to do with the articulation and reconciliation of human conflict, and the environment is one of the goods whose allocation is disputed in a world of marked inequalities. Each human group has its own environments perceived as acceptable, unacceptable or optimal, and the search for a single national (or global) optimal is likely to be as taxing as that for the Holy Grail.

Against this general background of scepticism or at best caution towards the alleged benefits of comprehensive environmental impact assessment, it is fair to point out that British economic and physical planning since the end of World War II has fairly happily accommodated an awareness of place when decisions were being made. Planning controls after 1947 were by international standards fierce to those who sought to despoil the British landscape, and the packs of private watch-dogs (Green Belt societies, the Council for the Protection of Rural England, the Conservation Society etc.) were quick to buttress and encourage the statutory constraints operated by local government, water undertakings, the Factory Inspectorate, and similar state bodies charged with environmental responsibilities. Most recently of all there has been public discussion of structure plans drawn up by local authorities under the 1968 Town and Country Planning Act, in which environmental issues are specifically introduced as a backcloth for assessing recreational and other policies. [6]

It would be wrong to conclude that the British mixture of statute and case law, common law, custom and convention is beyond criticism, but it has proved reasonably accommodating to the articulate pressure groups which still flourish in our democratic arena. However it must be said that British institutions are more skilled in conducting post-mortems upon completed projects than in reviewing and monitoring schemes during their conception and labour pains. The Public Accounts Committee is a good example of such formal check upon the mistakes of earlier years, and although it can be criticised for its posthumous role, there is the merit that such enquiry – if known to be searching and effective – can be a deterrent against the careless or the criminal anxious to avoid exposure subsequent to the offence.

Here the question arises of what actually constitutes an offence. Infringement of environmental standards can only occur if standards are laid down, just as the criminal is defined as someone who commits a crime by offending against some recognised law. A water authority could prosecute someone who discharged effluent into a stream only if there were already in existence explicit laws which defined the maximum permissible pollution. This may seem a fairly obvious truism, but one could proceed to argue that the ultimate defence of environmental standards must essentially be sought in clarifying, extending and making more feared (by appropriate punishment) the general body of environmental law. The firm or nationalised industry which broke that law could immediately be prosecuted – and not necessarily at the completion of the offending project, but perhaps at an early stage in its gestation. The onus of proof would admittedly be upon the prosecution, but if the law is reasonably unambiguous and penal it is unlikely to be flouted frequently or wilfully.

This 'constraining' approach to safeguarding environmental standards is not of course incompatible with the American attempt via EISs to smoke out the environmental implications of federal policies. The law may indeed by a form of countervailing power at the service of those at risk from juggernaut state institutions, but it would be perverse to deny that popular countervailing power depends critically upon the knowledge possessed of leviathan's plans. It would be no less perverse however, to believe that an agency wishing to promote a particular scheme would take undue pains to reveal its environmental warts. Far more likely would be a tendentious piece of advocacy which, as already suggested, could be so cunningly quantified (i.e. mystified) that its potential opponents might be lulled into complacency.

Two conclusions seem to follow from this summary reasoning. First, the production of an environmental impact assessment by the protagonist or sponsoring agency must be seen as an inherently propagandist document, a piece of special pleading which needs to be submitted to the arena of adversary confrontation (the law itself, perhaps, or such quasi-legal arenas as public enquiries or the House of Commons). Without an antagonist, the protagonist not only wins but does so in a blaze of selfrighteousness. The second conclusion follows on immediately from this gladiatorial model: the contenders must be evenly matched. The strength of the Public Accounts Committee for example lies in the ability of lay Members of Parliament to draw upon the expert advice of the Comptroller and Auditor General's Department. The politician's interrogation of the mandarins from each great spending department would be hopelessly emasculated were this armoury of criticism not to hand.

The analogy may not be altogether precise, but it helps focus attention upon the need to see any comprehensive (and almost certainly very complex) environmental assessment by an initiating body as the political football rather than the final goal of the planning process. Expert advocacy demands expert scrutiny and possibly rebuttal, and the more complex the project and its environmental assessment the more necessary it becomes to ensure a critical appraisal. As this author has argued elsewhere, it is advisable to set an expert to catch an expert, [7] and the development of the Central Policy Review Staff in recent years may be seen as one such attempt to bring countervailing prime ministerial power to bear against the expert but partisan advocacy of major Departments of State.

Such observations do not invalidate the case for a wider and formal deployment of environmental issues during the initiation of a departmental project, but the politician must − as the representative of the cynics as well as the innocent among his constituents − query the image of a Whitehall dedicated to the pursuit of truth.

Let us assume, finally, that the appropriate political machinery has been devised for scrutinising the EIA, and that the whole futorological exercise has been completed. What then follows will depend presumably upon the findings of the assessment as modified during scrutiny. If the project is seen to risk human survival, it is hoped it will be rejected, while if it promises a land flowing with milk and honey it will be acclaimed, albeit with suspicion and amazement. Most projects however will fall in the middle band of the desirability spectrum, and the politician's task will be that of balancing the environmental risk, say, against the economic or maybe military gain. It is hard to disagree with the superficial proposition that the more he knows the better his decision is likely to be, but this implies that some objective way of comparing chalk and cheese is lurking in the cost—benefit formulae, and that he can strike a manifestly 'better' or for that matter 'worse' balance. To know everything may be to forgive everything, but it can also confuse everything unless there is some common yardstick for evaluating a host of multifarious data.

To take the point a stage further, should the politician necessarily block a proposal because it is seen to have serious and damaging environmental effects? He might argue that overriding considerations of national security are involved — the defoliation of much of Vietnam presumably fell into this category — or that economic considerations outweigh ecological anxieties. The current Brazilian assault upon the Amazon rain forest is the macro-version of the reservoir built at Cow Green to 'save jobs'. [8] In such cases it is doubtful whether sophisticated exercises in weighting Cow Green's alpine flora, or Vietnam's indigenous population, would have made much difference to the outcome. Ultimately the politician, or more precisely the political decision maker, has to take the plunge into a pretty murky sea of troubles, and once immersed has frequently to swim for dear life.

One danger of adding yet further cross currents and whirlpools in the shape of ill charted environmental hazards is that of procrastination without any commensurate benefits. Another may be to give 'the environment' a negative or restrictive role *vis-à-vis* economic growth — instead of seeing environmental degradation as a challenge to be overcome by technological innovation. One advantage of the traditional method of learning the hard way, by experience of mistakes, is that one does at least learn. Had early man carried out an EIA on a project to rub two pieces of wood together, he might well have desisted on the grounds that forest fires were threatened. More seriously it can be argued that the essential justification for trying to see environment as an economic commodity, by such devices as fines or charges for the deposition of illegal residuals, is that such pricing policies encourage market forces to operate, not least in the field of technological innovation.

This does not pretend to have exhausted the political case for and against EIA as an integral part of comprehensive cost–benefit project evaluation. A sceptical approach to the value of such a proposition has been adopted, although much of the critique is rooted in a disenchantment with cost–benefit analyses generally rather than with the proposition that environment needs to be injected into the cost–benefit calculation. Without wishing to deny the self evident proposition that major projects can have important environmental implications, the author remains unconvinced that these implications can be perceived other than dimly in advance. Instead of putting the emphasis on complex preliminary calculations by the initiating agency, it is concluded that the major safeguards need to be sought in the political and legal monitoring processes of democracy itself. In particular we must review the institutional checks and balances upon spending departments, and the penal constraints of statute law.

Discussion

The polemical nature of Eversley's assertions in Chapter 10 about the social irresponsibility of scientists caused *Lord Zuckerman* to remark that the number of scientists who practised the art of pseudo science was relatively small and, in his view, largely concentrated in such groups as the British Society for Social Responsibility in Science. However, he agreed that many environmental quality standards were determined by another scientific minority, who were in many ways equally as ignorant of the facts and were not always respected by their peers. Nevertheless, remarked *Eversley* (Centre for Environmental Studies), both minorities captured public attention and certainly influenced policy; the vast majority of moderately opinioned scientists appear either to have no views at all or never to express them. His call for greater involvement by this group from all branches of science was echoed by *Train* (Cremer and Warner) who felt that the very subjective nature of amenity valuation required the tempering hand of both political and scientific moderation so that extremism could be brought under control.

Brooks (Liverpool) and *Pearce* (Leicester) did not agree over the proper role of politics in environmental impact assessment. As a former politician, Brooks could not accept that political judgements could be made simply or even primarily on the basis of quantifiable information. He believed that the great political arguments were about values, not facts, and involved all kinds of consequences that could not possibly be quantified. Politicians assess alternatives in terms of good and bad; they delight in the controversy of value judgements and conflicting ideologies. True, the outcome of political decisions often favours the articulate over the inarticulate, but that is largely due to the pattern of political forces which have resulted in many people becoming politically disenfranchised. Politicians act in response to vision and outrage as well as reason; they do not look over their shoulders all the time to make sure there is an army of experts at hand telling them the best way forward.

Pearce, however, argued that cost–benefit analysis can be of use to the politician who can adjust the weights attached to various outcomes. The proper role of the expert is to provide the politician with a decision framework flexible enough to indicate various possible circumstances. He agreed that there were certain things which were not quantifiable with the present state of the art – amenity and recreational benefits, for example – but this did not mean that the quantifiable framework should be entirely abandoned.

The case analysis of people's reaction to noise (see Chapter 11) caused *Kinchin* (Atomic Energy Authority) to ask whether the unexpected degree of immobility was due to the dislike of social disruption caused by moving. *Pearce* replied that even when these factors were built into the model, there still remained an inexplicable unwillingness to move. In fact the evidence he had was that people, far from being indifferent to noise, actually increase their distaste for noise the longer they stay in the affected area. These findings, he believed, implied not so much that people are not disturbed by noise; more likely they are unable to articulate their discomfort and do not know how to react in a bewildering political system.

Eversley's point that had EIA been in force in the Stone Age human society would never have progressed at all, prompted the correction from *Hammer* (Commission of the European Communities) and *Woolf* (Lawyers Ecology Group) that EIA is and never will be intended as the sole arbiter for decision making. Its primary purpose is to identify where and when certain unpleasant consequences could occur and thus alert the policy makers to possible corrective courses of action. EIA need not stop economic growth and human progress, but it should help to make them more pleasant and fair. Thus, they argued, to try to include pseudo scientific inexactitude into such a procedure would defeat its objective. Value judgements can only enter the process once this assessment is made. *Lord Zuckerman* entirely agreed. Where the scientist enters, he noted, is in the area of predicting specific consequences that are measurable from specific points of view such as health, crop productivity or landscape erosion. Outside this area the scientist must recognise that he is articulating values.

The common view of both *Pearce* and *Brooks* — that people are voiceless partly because of the nature of political decision making — was shared by *Eversley* who argued that the people who suffer because a project is stopped are those who remain silent and hence those whose values and preferences cannot be contained either in the economic or political calculus. When the costs of, say, a power or water project are raised in order to reduce the environmental effects, the brunt of the repercussion is borne by the marginal consumer, the person who is just coming within reach of electricity or water at a price he can afford. The rest do not actually suffer, but only slightly rearrange their expenditures. If these marginal consumers remain silent and unidentifiable, how possibly can their losses be calculated? *Pearce* believed that conceptually and technically, this was not a difficult problem; if properly reformed so as to weigh the incidence of gains and losses on various groups, the method of cost—benefit analysis could incorporate such effects quite adequately.

Brooks strongly demurred. The domain of politics is not a matter of sophisticated accountancy, but of creative moral evaluation and leadership, a pursuit of goals that are ultimately not mathematically measurable. The politician should be a person of imagination and conscience whose vision should not be blurred by mathematical mumbo-jumbo masquerading as political justification. Vision, he added, may be an attribute that is difficult to quantify, but without it the people perish and that would be the ultimate disbenefit. The kind of social costs to which Eversley was referring are simply *bad* and politicians should denounce them as such and endeavour to change the system.

Notes

[1]   See the preface to this volume.
[2]   See J. S. Bain, *Environmental Decay: Economic Causes and Remedies*, Little, Brown, Boston 1973, pp.178—229.
[3]   Royal Commission on the Third London Airport, *Final Report*, HMSO, London 1971.
[4]   See J. Adams, 'Westminster: the fourth London airport?', *Area*, vol. 2, January 1970, pp.1—9.
[5]   See, for example, the report in the *Sunday Times*, 19 October 1975.
[6]   See, for example, the 'Ecological appraisal of Cheshire', published

by the Cheshire County Council in 1974.

[7]   See E. Brooks, 'Lies, damned lies and statistics', in J. T. Coppock and C. B. Wilson (eds) *Environmental Quality*, Scottish Academic Press, Edinburgh 1974, pp.196–207.

[8]   For a study of the Cow Green case, see R. Gregory, 'The price of amenity', in P. J. Smith (ed.) *The Politics of Physical Resources*, Penguin Books, London 1974, pp.144–201.

PART V

Implications

13 Education requirements for impact reviews

C. WARD

It seems that for people who hope that we shall evolve a more participatory kind of society, and even for some who do not, there is a great and abiding principle which applies in every sphere of life: the principle of *transparency of operation.* This was the principle of the Model T Ford. Henry Ford may not have been a believer in a participatory democracy, but he wanted to make a car so simple that, as he put it, 'any hick up a dirt road could mend it with a spanner.' Government has never paid much attention to this principle, any more than the modern motor industry does. Government provides social benefits for those in need, but makes it so difficult for them to apply that vast numbers of people do not receive the assistance they require, nor are they allowed to know the basis for allowing or disallowing their application. Opacity of operation is a long established governmental principle, which is taken to an extreme in the case, relevant for us, of environmental pollution.

Several years ago Jon Tinker remarked that 'If a factory owner should choose to pour a thousand gallons of cyanide into a river, the maximum fine the courts can impose is £100. But if a river inspector analyses a sample of this effluent, and mentions the results to a member of the public, he can be sent to prison for three months. Far too often the Prevention of Pollution Acts function as Acts for the Protection of Polluters.' [1] Soon after he wrote that the penalty for the first of these offences was considerably increased, thanks to various scandals about cyanide dumping. The second remains, and as Mr Tinker says, 'this mania for preserving industrial secrecy at the expense of public participation and at the risk of public safety runs right through British pollution law and procedure.' [2]

In the field of planning of course the participation of the public is now written into the legislation. If you were asked to name the founding fathers of the town planning movement in this country, you would undoubtedly say Ebenezer Howard and Patrick Geddes, and it is noteworthy that neither of these men, the first a professional shorthand writer and the second a biologist, would have qualified for membership of the Royal Town Planning Institute. Most ordinary people would imagine that environmental impact assessment was being done for us already by the members of the planning profession, on account of all the wisdom it has accumulated since it grew out of its amateur childhood. After all, there are a lot of planners. Professor J. R. James, formerly chief planner in the Ministry of Housing and Local Government, remarked last year that since the reorganisation of local government there had been a 70 per cent increase in planning staff (even though many jobs were still unfilled) at a cost, in his view, 'which cannot and should not be borne by the taxpayer and ratepayer.' He thought that if the general public knew this, and knew the salaries paid, it would be more angry, confused and resentful than ever. On 31 March this year 19,502 full time and 485 part time staff were employed in local authority planning departments in England and Wales.

With all these planners it is not surprising that they have developed techniques for doing what ordinary people would regard, assuming that they understood the words, as environmental impact assessment. There was cost—benefit analysis for instance. Talking about its use by the Roskill Commission, Peter Self concluded that it strengthened 'the existing tendency to convert genuine political and social issues into bogus technical ones'. [3] And David Eversley warns us against the misuse of pseudo scientific management tools in planning, and the dangers of objectifying value judgements (see Chapter 10).

Is environmental impact assessment just such another smokescreen as far as the public is concerned? Is it just the latest way of offending against the principle of transparency of operation? Already there are firms of professional consultants 'doing' assessments, and what are the views of the public concerned worth, against their professional expertise? One of the things people found unacceptable about cost—benefit analysis was the way it had to attribute cash values to everything. In the Roskill Commission there was the equation of a Norman church with its fire insurance value, while the DoE 'has recommended to local authorities that the cost of deaths in road accidents varies from £20,000 to £24,000 to enable them to discover whether a road safety investment is justifiable.' Reporting the recent DoE symposium on environmental evaluation at the University of Kent, *The Surveyor* remarked:

If one derives indices (ordinals) for noise, view, pollution etc., can one add them together as if they were cardinal numbers? Should one perhaps multiply them? It is enough to say for the moment that, however little some people trust them, numbers are going to be the basis of environmental evaluation. But they will, as critics of the Staffordshire structure plans brought home, have to be numbers which the majority of us who are innumerate can understand.

The DoE study team has concluded that EIA should be an early part of the planning process for major projects, that it should be an objective statement rather than a decision document, that the planning authority should bear responsibility for it but should work together with the developer and that there should be every opportunity for public participation. It is the participatory aspect that is important, not the education of the professionals. A few years ago Cynthia Cockburn of the Centre for Environmental Studies prepared a report summarising the literature on the education of the planning profession, called 'Opinion and planning education'. After this we had a report from a panel of distinguished professionals and academics with the title 'Education for planning: the development of knowledge and capacity for urban governance', and soon after that a paper from the RTPI called 'Implications of changes in education and membership policy'. What impression would be gained from this endless flow of reports on the education of planners by an ordinary member of the public, particularly someone who had listened to the debate over the last five or six years on public participation in planning? He would be puzzled, since many of the words now used do not mean what his past experience has led him to believe they meant. For example, the unfamiliar word 'governance' is not for the authors synonymous with 'government'. It is a word they have found it necessary to use in order to acknowledge the role of the community as a whole in decision making. 'Planner' does not mean what our reader thought it meant: it means *any* (my emphasis) person contributing to urban governance through the planning process; while 'planning', authors explain, has been altogether divorced 'from its common physical and spatial policy context.'

The ordinary reader might be forgiven for assuming that the text based on these definitions was to be about everybody's education in decision making on resource allocation, and would be disappointed as he read on to find that the report turns out to be yet another manual on the education of a technocratic élite. The signatories of the 'Education for planning' report were the top practitioners and academics of the planning profession, and if their definition of the word is altogether divorced 'from its common physical and spatial policy context' one might very well wonder why it is necessary for us to consider the educational requirements for impact assessments, unless we are envisaging some entirely new profession of impact assessor, like fire assessing or quantity surveying.

If such a new professional specialisation were invented, the likelihood is that, having set up a professional institute, a journal, categories of membership and an examination structure, it too would fall victim to what the Americans so rightly call 'role inflation', a fate which has already befallen the planning industry.

One would have to be quite unbelievably complacent or thickskinned to ignore the low esteem that the ordinary public has for what it regards as 'the planners', or to ignore the literary barrage in the last few years which has demolished many of the inflated pretensions of the planning profession. However, the reaction of the profession is to imagine that some improvement in its own education, a broader base, a higher standard of entry, a longer period of training, more research, more science, more knowledge, more planners, a higher rank in the pecking order in County Hall, is somehow going to put everything right.

The subject which is coming more and more under fire, and which is going to be attacked even more in the future when we get round to 'objective' environmental impact reviews, is the very nature of professionalism in these matters, precisely because the greater the claims for expertise and the allegedly scientific judgements of the experts, the less opportunity there is for the ordinary citizen to influence decisions. Ivan Illich, the most damaging of the new critics of the professionalisation of knowledge, remarks that:

> It makes people dependent on having their knowledge produced for them. It leads to a paralysis of the moral and political imagination. This cognitive disorder rests on the illusion that the knowledge of the individual citizen is of less value than the 'knowledge' of science. The former is the opinion of individuals. It is merely subjective and is excluded from policies. The latter is 'objective' — defined by science and promulgated by expert spokesmen. This objective knowledge is viewed as a commodity which can be refined, constantly improved, accumulated and fed into a process, now called 'decision-making'. This new mythology of governance by the manipulation of knowledge-stock inevitably erodes reliance on government by people . . .
>
> Over-confidence in 'better knowledge' becomes a self-fulfilling prophecy. People first cease to trust their own judgement and then want to be told the truth about what they know. Over-confidence in

184

'better decision-making' first hampers people's ability to decide for themselves and then undermines their belief that they can decide. [5]

The author agrees with his observations. Consider, for example, an instance which is often cited in the discussion of environmental impact assessment. Professor Lee and his colleagues at the University of Surrey were commissioned by the Department of the Environment to study the effect of motorway building on the surrounding community: a study of severance. They found that the 'centre of gravity' of communities and their shopping patterns adapted to the new situation much more rapidly than had been supposed; that the environmental impact was less severe than was hitherto thought. Professor Lee described his findings to his professional peers at the Architectural Psychology Conference at the University of Sheffield in October 1975. He was subjected to quite a barrage of hostile questioning, querying his methodology and the validity of the results, and raising the issue that there was a danger that his findings would be used out of context by the public authorities and 'stretched' beyond their scientific validity, just as for example IQ tests have had claims made for them in the educational or job selection worlds which would never have been made by their originators. If he had found that the impact of urban motorways on the surrounding communities was absolutely disastrous, no one there would have queried his methodology. As to the relevance of his findings, if his fellow environmental psychologists, who were unlikely to be directly affected by any particular road building decision, were highly critical of the whole exercise, would it carry any weight at all with the Deadsville Motorway Action Group? Contrary to what Illich says, wouldn't they describe the whole exercise as a whitewash job for the authority, and wouldn't they find some other expert in survey techniques to declare that the findings were invalid because of some methodological flaw?

There is not the slightest reason to question Professor Lee's professional integrity nor to query the way in which the exercise was carried out, but it is seen as yet another example of Peter Self's remark about the 'tendency to convert genuine political and social issues into bogus technical ones.' We know that in the last fifteen years virtually every city in Britian has carved itself up to provide an inner ring road, since the city engineers have regarded it as their first duty to keep the traffic flowing at all costs. In London an incalculable amount of expensive staff time and positive forests of paper were expended on the ringway motorway proposals. Politically it was a bipartisan matter, but vast numbers of citizens acting on unscientific self regarding criteria decided that they didn't want it. They made their own environmental impact assessment and concluded that they didn't want, after the experience of Westway, any more inner urban motorways. It became a political issue, possibly to the surprise of the politicians. One party, then the ruling party in London, made noises suggesting that the ringway would be kept out of certain areas – those which voted their way. The leader of the other party, at that time in opposition, announced that if his party were returned the proposals would be abandoned. It was of course a nicely judged stroke of electoral genius. Here were the two parties coming before the voters to win their support on the issue of how much of *their* road plans they would let *us* off if we voted for them. And the party that promised the mostest won the votes.

Anyone can think of large scale proposals with an environmental impact, where decisions are arrived at after employing every kind of specialist wisdom, and which have been overturned as a result of the opposition of groups of outraged citizens. In the metropolitan area alone, quite apart from the London motorway proposals, there have been the siting of the third London airport, the redevelopment of Covent Garden, of Piccadilly Circus and Trafalgar Square.

What price expertise? What price environmental impact assessments? The lesson is that the awareness and environmental sophistication of the ordinary citizen is much more important than the educational experience of the professionals, including their education in any specific techniques we may evolve for impact reviews. The CES report on planning education mentioned above starts with the assumption that a planner is *any* person contributing to urban governance, and immediately ignores the implications of this and goes on to confine itself to discussing the education of a professional élite.

We are *not* concerned with the education of the professional elite. That would be far more difficult than the daunting task of educating the public, precisely because the professionals have so strong a vested interest (in terms of status, income and promotion) in their own professional wisdom. Professor Derrick Sewell [6] remarks that 'One consequence of the increasing reliance of society upon professionals has been the alienation of the public in the policy making process. This has led to adverse reaction in several parts of North America, in part because the public feels it has a *right* to be consulted, and in part because the professionals have often seriously misjudged what the public wants or how it would react to what is provided.'

As a result of his statistical survey, Sewell feels able to generalise about

186

the characteristic attitudes of engineers *vis-à-vis* those of public health officials. He even relates his findings to the number of years a professional has spent in the job: 'Modifications of policies or expansion of responsibilities would obviously further complicate his task, a task which he believes is complicated enough already!'

Ideally the right people to conduct environmental impact reviews should be 'the public' *itself*, and an assessment produced by the planning officer with the collaboration of the developer – who in the British situation is likely to be, in any case, central government – the same local government, or a publicly owned corporation, should not be regarded as an impartial, 'scientific' evaluation by the people whose interests are affected. In the case of a development with an apparently adverse effect on the local population, the very fact that the assessment has been prepared by the local planning officer will effectively destroy *his* credibility, and this will be regretted by some.

There is an alternative, which is that the local community, in the form of the multiplicity of interest groups, pressure groups, all those self appointed and unrepresentative spokesmen of local feeling, should be the formulators of an environmental impact assessment. In 1972 a conference was held in Newcastle by an organisation called Tyneside Environmental Concern on the theme of planning for people. Robert Allen expressed the view that people and organisations in the region should draw up their own plan for the region which, apart from anything else, would be the yardstick against which they measured and evaluated the proposals that emerged from private capital or public enterprise. His view of 'NE 2073 – A future for the North-East' was that:

> Farmers, housewives, industrialists, trades unionists, planners, lawyers, scientists, miners, factory-workers – anybody and every body, professionally or privately – in Northumberland, Durham and the North Riding of Yorkshire, are invited to form committees to develop a 'Blueprint for the North-East'. They will be invited to imagine that the North-East is a semi-independent region, with sufficient self-government to formulate its own agricultural, educational, development, employment, housing, transport and urban renewal policies – in other words free to do what it likes in all those areas that would not have direct effect on other regions. The committees will discuss how the region could meet basic demands – for food, shelter, health, etc. and how to stabilise and contain 'surplus' demands – more and bigger roads, reservoirs and so on. They will try to decide the optimum population for the North-East,

how satisfying employment can be given to its citizens without causing ugliness and ill-health, and what social reforms are necessary – what is the best social structure for the North-East.

The assembled citizens of the North-East failed to take up his message. Nevertheless, the notion that the best people to undertake an environmental impact assessment are the people who live there is an obvious and sensible principle, so why doesn't it work out that way? The answer is that some people know far better than others how to manipulate the machinery in their interests. Reyner Banham remarks that 'when the Workers Education Association was young, one of its main functions was to help the workers to survive and prosper through exploiting the machinery of a bourgeois democracy. It was the never-acknowledged aim of the WEA to equip its members with bourgeois know-how.' He goes on to describe the WEA syndrome at work in efforts to involve the public in planning decisions in Los Angeles. The planners, he says:

> . . . were going into the streets, into the ghettoes, into the suburbs and on to the beaches to get the word from the consumers of planning themselves. The people were delighted, and they came up with a long list of complaints and things which they thought needed to be done. 'How can I find a parking space downtown?' 'How can I get the Mexicans out of my neighbourhood?' All kinds of live issues like that, which for good liberal professional reasons, don't appear in the planner's vocabulary at all . . . Then, of course, the planners saw that the thing to do was to explain to the people what planning was really about, and out came those handy little booklets explaining high and low density, high rise and low rise, cluster and distributed. But the people just walked away. The book just didn't tell you how to get the Mex out of your neighbourhood, or how to find a parking lot outside a shop downtown. Once the rules of the game were known to both sides it was seen to be no game. Like, bad thinking stopped play.

There are a number of morals to be drawn from Professor Banham's cautionary tale, but the most important one is the one he misses out: the object of education for participation *is* to equip everyone with that lovely bourgeois know-how, so that, in his example, the Mexicans can fight for their place in the sun, and the downtown dwellers can resist the parking demands of the out of town commuters. 'Education' in this context means effective community self organisation, and we haven't yet discovered the best recipe for that; maybe there is none.

Last year, at the seventy-fifth anniversary conference of the Town and Country Planning Association, a chief planning officer remarked, 'We tried an exercise in participation, and it was just a colossal waste of time, and of money.' He was talking as though both planners and public could adopt entirely new roles overnight, and it was pointed out that it may take another quarter of a century to evolve a genuinely participatory system of planning. In many ways the kind of procedures that seem to be envisaged militate against participation because they involve yet another barrage of expertise. In the context of a no growth economy they almost look like a new way of providing an income for the expensive consultancy firms. The fact that assessments are to be drawn up by the planning authority *with* the developer, or, more likely, with his consultants, may make the planner even more suspect in the eyes of the general public than at present. However, if the planning officer can work hand in glove with the Coal Board or ICI, he can also work hand in glove with Deadsville Community Action Group, Deadsville Civic Trust, Deadsville Women's Institute and Deadsville Community High School.

In one of his reports on the Liverpool Educational Priority Area project, Eric Midwinter referred to what he had called the planners' lip service to consultation and said, 'They may knock at the door of a client for rehabilitation or decantation and ask what sort of home and environment is required. What is the unfortunate interviewee to say in answer to this? What in too many cases he could say is something like this, "I was never educated to listen to that kind of question nor to articulate responses to it, whether technical or creative".'

In the world of environmental education at a school level, a minority of teachers are attempting, through involving their classes in real local issues and through the use of such invaluable techniques as gaming and simulation and role playing to prepare a generation, not an élite, *able* to participate. Two principles operate here. The first is that people, young or old, learn through involvement and not through being told. The second is that participation does not consist of having ready made decisions explained to you, it implies *making* decisions. In school this means that we are not educating for participation by pouring in information about planning legislation and procedures: we can only do it by involving the young in real issues and real controversies: they can look up the rules for themselves. In the adult world it embodies the very difficult art of convincing people that they can make effective choices and can organise themselves to put those choices into effect. The Skeffington Committee assumed that 'participation' would streamline the procedures of professional planning. It will not. In America it was assumed that environmental impact assessment would streamline the same process. Will it here? Only if we have a continual assessment – perhaps one could call it a social and environmental audit being carried out by the whole galaxy of community organisations. The apparently theoretical exercise proposed in Newcastle by Robert Allen was in fact intensely practical for several reasons, not the least of them being, as Mr Allen said: 'Everyday decisions by local government are taken with a number of limited futures in mind, and sometimes with none at all. This is why they betray so little imagination or insight. If you want to change the decisions, big or small, you've got to change the framework in which they're taken.' In school a strategic plan for the region can be tackled through a range of subject areas as a continuing and developing theme, linked with local inquiry and local publicity. In the adult world it can provide a yardstick against which to assess actual plans and to formulate alternatives, to decide what to support, what to oppose, and what to advocate.

Education for environmental impact assessment should seek for nothing less than a change in the meaning of the word 'planning' from an esoteric activity associated with parternalistic government to one of the normal attributes of citizenship.

Notes

[1]   J. Tinker, 'Britain's environment: nanny knows best', *New Scientist*, 9 March 1972, p.530.

[2]   Ibid.

[3]   See Self's lengthy critique of economic accounting methods in P. Self, *Econocrats and the Policy Process: The Politics and Philosophy of Cost Benefit Analysis*, Macmillan, London 1975.

[4]   J. Catlow and C. G. Thirlwell, 'Environmental impact assessment', paper presented to the DoE symposium on environmental evaluation, Canterbury Kent, 26 September 1975.

[5]   I. Illich, *Deschooling Society*, Calder and Boyers, London 1971.

[6]   W. R. D. Sewell, 'The role of perceptions of professionals in environmental decision-making', in J. P. Coppock and C. B. Wilson (eds), *Environmental Quality*, Scottish Academic Press, Edinburgh 1974, pp.109–31.

14 Implications for interest groups: the need for planning aid

D. LOCK

The Town and Country Planning Association (which, though its name may not make it clear, is one of the oldest pressure groups in the world that is exclusively concerned with environmental matters) did not respond to the DoE's invitation to comment on the EIA study. Its reasons were threefold: first, as a small voluntary body it has become weary of the burden placed upon it by the government who have inundated it with planning issues of one kind or another, seeking its comment before legislation or regulations are drafted. As the Association had sought this participation, it may appear irrational now to spurn the extended arm of government, but the burden of consultation has turned it from creative thinking and initiative taking into a markedly unpaid think tank so wedded to the processes of government that to the outsider it has often been mistaken for a government department or, much worse, a research body. With its small resources of both money and manpower it has turned to concentrate on new thinking on planning matters: to set its own pace in planning rather than be led by the nose by the civil service.

Second, there is some cynicism of the technologies of environmental management, which makes the members of the Association sceptical of the EIA study from the start. Too many lives have already been ruined, and future generations already damned, by the men of science operating through the planning field: the economists and technicians who gave us high rise housing; the statisticians and engineers who have brought us the noise of urban motorways and wholesale clearance of city housing; the chemists who have polluted our rivers; and the supremely naïve nuclear physicists who are stacking the land with waste that needs guarding for a period longer than that of recorded past history. These simply expressed views are not a pretence that all this could have been avoided. They are rather an honest reaction to what has passed and are given here to explain the care with which the Association approaches those who seek to quantify values patently unquantifiable.

The third reason for not responding to the EIA questionnaire is that the Association felt that the planning system already had the latent ability to cope with the problems for which the EIA study seeks an answer, and that there was no critical need for new systems and procedures of the complex and expensive kind apparently envisaged.

Planning aid

The Association runs a Planning Aid Service, the only one of its kind, which is now in its third year of operation. The term 'planning aid' was first coined by the Town and Country Planning Association in 1969 and was taken up by F. J. Amos when he was president of the Royal Town Planning Institute in 1972. Writing for the Presidents' Committee for the Urban Development, he said:

> the implications of planning decisions for the lives of individuals and communities are coming under increasingly critical scrutiny. This is a response to two important (and connected) trends:
>
> (a) a growing realisation that planning decisions can have momentous effects on people's lives, and that not all groups of individuals affected are equally able to defend themselves. Better off people or communities are usually more aware of what is happening and can afford to pay for professional advice. In any case, they are less often affected by large-scale planning decisions. It is, on the whole, the poorer communities near city centres that are decimated by slum clearance, sliced in half by urban motorways, and rehoused on new estates. It is these communities which lack knowledge, resources, and political power. Unless they are given active assistance, the effect of planning decisions can be highly regressive.
>
> (b) the growth of residents' groups, community councils and action groups. The provisions for 'public participation' in recent planning and housing acts are a recognition of these trends, and of the inability of traditional central and local government processes to cope with all the issues involved. Thoughts about planning aid are a small part of a large and complex area of concern, involving questions about the distribution of resources, the inadequacies of representative democracy, participation in public policy decisions, citizens' rights, and so on.

Following this, David Hall, the director of the TCPA, established a planning aid service. 'Planning aid' has since been defined as 'the giving of information or expert advice free, or at low cost, once or over a longer period, to groups or individuals concerned with a planning issue.' [1]

In brief, the service provides free information on planning law, procedures, techniques, and practices; it offers advice on how to use such information effectively, and occasionally helps with the presentation of arguments and points of view in connection with a particular planning proposal. It has not taken sides, and has sometimes helped more than one opposing group in a dispute: it believes in the educational benefits of such a service for the recipient groups, and in the importance of the full presentation of all points of view if the resultant decision is to be a better one. It has been involved with almost 1,000 cases, although only with a minority of these in any full or influential manner. The work was recognised by Mr George Dobry, QC, in his *Review of Development Control* [2] as being of the greatest value, and as a result some of the costs for the current year are being met by the DoE. [3]

The need for planning aid in EIA

This section will consider first, the planning aid implications of the EIA study as it stands at present, and second, some implications in general terms of the study for interest groups in the environmental field.

The circumstances in which EIA may be required

It is stated in the DoE study team report [4] that structure plans 'should identify the circumstances in which an EIA would be required', involving 'the identification of types of development of particular environmental significance' etc. The structure plan process is already largely discredited: the reorganisation of local government has maintained the dangerously irrelevant boundaries of county councils and made a reasonable attempt at strategic planning most difficult. The issues which the public have shown themselves to be most interested in at structure plan level are proving to be issues outside the real control of the planning authorities: employment and the control of pollution being the most glaring examples. Planning techniques and skills have shown themselves to be inadequate even for the most identifiable strategic planning issues (e.g. population projection, transportation needs, housing demand and potential supply) and attempts to embrace the more vague, but politically more powerful, issues of employment, health and self fulfilment in structure plan reports have led either to complete omission or, at best, a general policy so bland that it does not need stating. In short, structure plans are prone to becoming declarations of false promises: not a satisfactory vehicle for identifying EIA principles.

More particularly, the structure plan has not proved a successful planning vehicle from the point of view of the public interest groups. They have been dismayed at the difficulty of grasping the issues presented to them on this scale, and they have found the examination in public (the follow up public enquiry) most difficult to grasp. The planning aid that has been needed in structure plans has been of the exhausting information dispensing kind, with much demand for help in articulating views at the examination stage. Experience leads to the view that to state terms that will trigger the EIA procedure in a structure plan would be to expose the procedure to all these traps and inadequacies. In any case, how *can* local groups identify and express in words the anxieties and concerns they might have in the future? How can they define in advance the areas and developments that will warrant an EIA procedure? 'Instead', say these groups 'leave it open. Build a system that will allow us room to organise and press for EIA procedure as and when we need it.'

The initiation of the EIA procedure

The study team suggests that the local planning authority (or in national or regional issues the Secretary of State if he wishes) should pay for and conduct the EIA; and that the key issues should be open to comment for one month before work begins. At this stage the only planning aid that would be needed would be a clear explanation of what was going on and of the steps involved in the whole process in the forthcoming weeks. Interest groups would not be reticent in stating issues which they felt to be the 'key' ones, but how would their ideas be handled? Would they be called in to justify their suggestion? If this is the case, they may feel they need some expert advice or even some representation and if so, who is to pay? Or are we to continue the present planning rule which is that each may participate according to his means? In addition would there be openings later in the process for key issues to be added if an omission was discovered? Would these key issues really be different from one case to another? How widely would their terms be couched? Beware the blandness of the structure plan.

Consultations

The study team also suggests that consultations would be necessary with bodies having an interest in environmental management. The point here is that there are very many voluntary bodies with an interest in a given locality that would claim the right to be heard. Would they all be admitted to such consultations? If they were, there would be planning aid implications if they have to prepare their own studies and reports as a contribution to the assessment of environmental impact.

After submission of the EIA to the local authority

It is this point in the procedure that raises doubts from the point of view of planning aid needs. The study team recommends that the analysis 'should be available to interested authorities and parties and to the general public, and that there should be a reasonable time to comment before any decision is made . . .'. Will the form of the presented EIA be suitable for its digestibility by interest groups?

Malcolm McEwan [5] notes that the USA experience with EIS has led to 'an enormous growth in professional consultation and litigation, much of it clearly parasitic' – factors which he feels contribute to the decline in the quality of the built environment. Planning aid work has proved just how participation in planning generally is frustrated by opportunities for litigation and the trend towards increased professional consultation. If the EIA procedure is going to increase the opportunities for litigation (and it is clear that it will) then the public both as individuals and groups are going to need planning aid – either cash or manpower to help them take part in the process.

Litigation apart, the way in which EIA procedure may lead to increased professional consultation has profound planning aid implications. The USA experience suggests that interest groups will need to employ experts drawn from many fields to help them digest the EIA statement and, if necessary, to challenge it in either its methods, assumptions or conclusions. If this is the likely consequence of the system proposed for the UK, then it raises the greatest doubts about the whole idea.

Interest groups concerned with environmental issues cannot afford to take part in this kind of exercise and, almost by definition, the EIA procedure will therefore exclude them from worthwhile participation. If this is the intention then to talk of opportunities for comment is wholly misleading.

Many interest groups avoid the expense of professional consultations by relying on their own professional members to act for them free, or on their own homegrown self educated (by experience) experts. McEwan's review suggests that matters raised by EIA are normally of the most technical kind, for which there are few friendly professionals and certainly no self educated experts.

If there was enough money to permit the professional consultations that would be necessary for concerned interest groups, are there enough professionals available for hire? This is the most serious question: the number of planning consultants is small, their range of skills and interests not matched to the latent demand that a flow of cash aid would liberate, and their geographical distribution over the country is most inconvenient. Is this a concern that should be applied to other professions that may be needed for EIA work?

General implications for interest groups

With regard to professional consultations, there is a widespread view amongst interest groups of all kinds that it is possible to employ an expert to say anything for you. Advice may be obtained both to construct and to demolish the same argument, and nowhere is this more true than in environment related issues where so many personal opinions, assessments, biases and obsessions can be dressed up in apparently respectable language. Although this is a criticism of the planning profession it would be most foolish to pretend that the view does not exist. The EIA superstructure appears to be built on foundations of professional skills, integrity and honesty: can we be sure that these foundations are strong? In the USA they are most certainly weak, and it is being argued that they are also weak in many areas of planning activity in the UK. Can we afford to run the risk of discrediting the EIA approach by encouraging the unscrupulous, and by exposing the deep divisions of opinion that exist on almost all matters within the professions with which we are concerned?

From the point of view of participating interest groups it is right that the EIA should be carried out at the direction of the local planning authorities, as they are subject to a degree of political influence which can be most important if the debate falls on planning grounds alone. From discussions within the TCPA it is clear that many local planning authorities (both officers and members) feel that the EIA procedure would make the final decision taking much harder. Councillors too, it seems, need a form of planning aid because they are too often overwhelmed by technical arguments.

Some constructive observations

In considering the work that has been undertaken by the DoE study team it would seem that the invocation of the planning inquiry commission (PIC) procedure has been far too lightly discarded. Section 47 of the 1971 Town and Country Planning Act provides for the referral of a development proposal to a planning inquiry commission. This author has already argued [6] that the commission procedure should be used for major development proposals for two reasons arising directly out of his planning aid work. First, the commission is composed of a panel with such *ad hoc* advisers as they may need; this detracts from the courtroom-like appearance of planning inquiries and may prevent the escalation of legal representation which has done so much to destroy the purpose of planning debates by making them expensive, overlong and frightening experiences. Second, and more important, the commission has power to set up studies either at its own or the applicant's expense to provide information on *any* aspect of the matter felt to be important.

The Town and Country Planning Association is wholly committed to the objective of the EIA debate: that is, to ensure that the widest environmental implications of a proposal are discovered and considered before planning approval is given. These are exactly the implications that a planning inquiry commission would pursue.

Why, therefore, has the planning inquiry commission not been used? Basically it was the traumatic experience of the Roskill enquiry into the third London airport which has frightened the government into never calling for a commission for fear of the cost and delay that can result when experts are given full reign over a major environmental proposal. The DoE study team are trying to find another way of conducting a Roskill type inquiry that would avoid such expense and delay. The commission would be an appropriate solution and would, at least in the interim, provide the equivalent of an EIA. The relevant sections of the 1971 Town and Country Planning Act which relate to the PIC procedure are considered below.

Matters that may be referred to a planning inquiry commission

(a) any application for planning permission which the Secretary of State has (under s. 35) directed to be referred to him instead of being dealt with by a local planning authority;

(b) any appeal under s. 36;

(c) any proposal where a government department must give an authorisation under s. 40 for planning permission;

(d)   any proposal that development should be carried out by or on behalf of a government department.

Any of the matters mentioned above may be referred to a commission if it appears expedient to the responsible minister or ministers that the question of whether the proposed development should be permitted should be the subject of a special inquiry on either or both of the following grounds:

(a)   if there are considerations of national or regional importance which are relevant to the determination of that question and require evaluation, but which cannot properly be made unless there is a special inquiry for the purpose; and

(b)   if the technical or scientific aspects of the proposed development are of so unfamiliar a character as to jeopardise a proper determination of that question unless there is a special inquiry for the purpose.

Alternative sites

Where a matter referred to a commission under this section relates to a proposal to carry out development for any purpose at a particular site, the responsible minister or ministers may also refer to the commission the question whether development for that purpose should instead be carried out at an alternative site.

How they go about it

A commission inquiring into a matter referred to them under this section shall:

(a)   identify and investigate the relevant considerations and the technical or scientific aspects of that matter which in their opinion are relevant to the question whether the proposed development should be permitted. The commission shall also assess the importance to be attached to those considerations or aspects;

(b)   grant the applicant and where relevant the local planning authority and legitimate appellants the opportunity of appearing before one or more of its members and being heard;

(c)   report to the responsible minister or ministers on the matter referred to them.

Any such commission may, with the approval of the Secretary of State and at his expense, arrange for the carrying out (whether by the commission themselves or by others) of research of any kind appearing to them to be relevant to a matter referred to them for inquiry and report.

Much of this book has covered the question of whether we have the skills and techniques presently at our disposal to undertake an EIA. If we decide that we can cope, then we must settle for a procedure that would invoke an EIA when necessary. The planning inquiry commission is an adequate procedure; moreover it can provide a method for interest groups to validate their participation. Therefore, from the planning aid vantage point the commission is the best procedure to accommodate EIA — a panel to ensure the interest group is heard, and a power to spend other people's money on research. Beyond this the politician will still have to make the decision as to what 'aid' *he* will need to handle the reports he is given, and to assess the risks of adopting, amending or refusing a given proposal.

Discussion

Ward's point (in Chapter 13) about the growing opacity of professional advice caused *Lord Zuckerman* to pinpoint the dilemma: that the increasing complexity of environmental issues is likely to obscure the picture even more so. As more and more citizens' groups enter the fray, guided by specialist advice, so the EIA review will become largely a gladiatorial contest among experts; and the more the evidence is indeterminate or problematical, the more chaotic the whole process becomes, and the more the national scientific establishments are viewed with suspicion. Hence the rise of pseudo science and the very real danger that proper scientific enquiry will forever be jeopardised. While he admitted it was right that political judgement should be the final arbiter, at least that judgement should be made on the basis of the best advice possible.

The problem for *Eversley* (Centre for Environmental Studies) was not so much controversial scientific debate as the priorities (and ethics) of the combatants. Any piece of evidence can be rebutted by countervailing argument; the important matter was for the specialist to decide which values were right and hence whether the needs of 'underdog groups' — the minorities who will not get houses, mobility, income or food — will be vindicated.

On a related point, *Shaw* (Norfolk County Council), as a practising planner, was concerned about the indigestibility of most planning reports. This was a problem which he felt would only be exacerbated by the introduction of EIA which, in turn, would make the life of the politician more difficult. Certainly this meant that disadvantaged groups of all kinds require expert assistance, but he was not so sure as Eversley that this should rest with the values of the specialist; surely the professional planner had a duty to serve the community directly and offer aid to particular groups as part of their professional responsibilities? The matter was not simply one of ethics, but of the freedom of interpretation granted to civil servants by their political masters. He could not be sure whether this would make the planner less suspect in the minds of the public.

Clark (Aberdeen) wanted to know at which point in the planning procedure planning aid would be most effective. If it was too soon the planning aid people might merely be responding to rumour, whereas if it was too late it might be difficult to play a useful role. *Lock* (Town and Country Planning Association) replied that if transparency of operation was a principal objective in planning, then planning aid should enter potentially at all stages, otherwise there was always the risk of political backlash. It was impossible to set any ground rules since each EIA procedure would have to be tailored to the particular issue and scale of public concern. Flexibility and careful monitoring ought to be the watchwords, but the keynote was that the citizens themselves were actively involved in the process of shaping their environments.

Notes

[1]   Further details of the association's programme are printed in the Royal Town Planning Institute's discussion paper *Planning Aid*, London 1974, and in various articles on the subject in *Town and Country Planning*.

[2]   G. Dobry, *Review of the Development Control System*, HMSO, London 1975, especially p.115.

[3]   In his response to the Dobry report, the Rt Hon. John Silkin MP stated that the DoE was giving serious consideration to the concept of planning aid, pending an upturn in national economic fortunes.

[4]   The interim report of the study team was published in confidence to those people who had responded to the request for views.

[5]   See McEwan's review of R. Burchell and T. Listokin's *The*

Environmental Impact Handbook, Rutgers University Press, New Brunswick NJ, 1975, in the *Architect's Journal,* 22 October 1975, p.852.

[6]   See D. Lock, 'Join the professionals', *Built Environment,* vol. 2, no. 12, December 1973, pp.682–4.

15 Beyond environmental impact assessment

T. O'RIORDAN

There is a great temptation to visualise environmental impact assessment somewhat naïvely as a rather more sophisticated form of cost—benefit accounting. Economists and policy makers now accept that even with all kinds of heroic assumptions and the application of novel measurement devices, many features associated with large scale development proposals cannot be properly quantified and translated into discounted cash flows. [1] So the EIA is seen as a device to collate these so called non-market effects in a systematic manner and attach (but not integrate) them to the cost—benefit balance sheet. This certainly seems to be the view of the Secretary of State for the Environment who in August 1974 approved the appointment of a two man study team 'to survey the techniques now being used or developed to measure the environmental impact of large scale proposals', and 'to consider the circumstances in which development proposals would give rise to the need for environmental impact analyses'. [2] The team thus have no remit to look at the wider implications of EIA, nor have they specifically asked for public comment on this aspect. Public debate on the matter therefore tends to be confined to the consideration of EIA as a predictive and measuring device to assist the determination of decisions that have already been made in principle, in the sense that the assumptions behind the decisions and the predominant pattern of thinking that has led up to the proposal have not been subject to comprehensive evaluation or public scrutiny. As a consequence, a very real merit of the EIA — namely to encourage interdepartmental and informed public discussion of strategic policy options relating to national, economic, social and environmental questions — is in danger of being dismissed or ignored.

Lessons from NEPA

We in Britain have the opportunity to review and appraise carefully the

American experience of the environmental impact statement and to consider how similar legislation could operate within the context of UK political and administrative institutions. This is a very valuable opportunity, for an analysis of the legislative history of the enabling US Act (the National Environmental Policy Act) reveals that neither the House nor the Senate of the American Congress ever properly discussed this crucial piece of legislation, and so had little idea of what it was letting itself in for. Indeed, if Congress had undertaken a 'political impact assessment' of the proposed statute it would never have been passed in its present form.

The EIS was the brainchild of two men, very different in temperament and motivation, but in combination a powerful political and intellectual duo. [3] The intellectual driving force was provided by Lynton Caldwell, an expert in environmental policy administration. In testimony before the Senate Committee on Interior and Insular Affairs, Caldwell called for a legislative guideline that would require federal licensing agencies to review the environmental implications of their activities. Caldwell had spotted a flaw in existing administrative procedures, and was merely asking that some kind of environmental assessment become routine. The chairman of the Senate Committee, Senator Henry Jackson, a politically powerful and ambitious man, saw in this modest proposal what he regarded as a necessary 'action forcing' provision that would require all federal agencies to take seriously the rhetorical (and potentially contradictory) proclamation in the preamble to the legislation:

> ... Congress declares ... that the Federal Government in cooperation with state and local governments and other concerned public and private organizations, use all practicable means and measures, including financial and technical assistance, in a manner calculated to foster and promote the general welfare, to create and maintain conditions under which man and nature can exist in productive harmony and fulfill the social, economic and other requirements of present and future generations of Americans.

Jackson wanted statutory guarantees to ensure effective federal response, for he was well aware that agencies would try to avoid the full import of the EIS. He modified Caldwell's modest suggestion to a 'general requirement that would be applicable to all agencies that have responsibilities that affect the environment'.

The Jackson version went over to the House during the summer of 1969 where it was steered away by Jackson's friends from two House Committees, the chairmen of which were both known to oppose the 'action forcing' sections of the Jackson bill. Consequently the bill was sent almost without discussion to Senate House Conference where the details were hammered out between three powerful politicians with conflicting political constituencies. These were Senator Jackson, Senator Muskie (who as chairman of the Air and Water Subcommittee of Jackson's Committee was anxious to see that pollution control procedures were not subject to full environmental impact assessment) and Congressman Aspinall, chairman of the House Committee on Interior and Insular Affairs, who was quite opposed to any 'upgrading' of existing agency responsibilities. Muskie and Jackson converted the notion of 'finding' — namely that the agencies cursorily review possible environmental consequences — to 'a detailed statement', a compromise which was later interpreted by the courts as meaning an exhaustive investigation subject to full public scrutiny. Jackson managed to persuade Aspinall that such 'statements' should be binding on agency deliberations 'to the fullest extent possible', [4] a phrase again subsequently interpreted judicially to mean that all federal agencies were required to show that they had taken environmental impact assessment into account before final commitment — in short, that the Act was substantive, not merely procedural.

Neither of these important phrases was given detailed congressional scrutiny since, by the time the conference report reached both Houses, it was mid-December and a quick vote was demanded before the expiry of the ninety-first Congress. In any case a Conference-approved bill is not subject to amendment, so the crucial five subsections to the famous s. 102(2)(C) of the Act essentially were accepted without formal deliberation and left dangerously vulnerable to a variety of subsequent interpretations. [5] Yet, as is now well known, this section set off political repercussions throughout the Western world.

Because we have the US experience behind us, it is useful to examine what can be learnt from the legislative experience described above. First, it is impossible to predict all the legal and political consequences of such a piece of legislation with any degree of accuracy. Even if Congress had devoted time to assessing s. 102(2)(C), it is doubtful whether it could have predicted what has happened in the succeeding five years. Nevertheless we in Britain should be in a better position to make some calculated guesses and consider seriously the possible legal, political and social ramifications of such a piece of legislation.

The second point is that the very reception of environmental impact assessment depends upon the responsiveness of what might be termed 'the political culture' — the framework of political institutions, laws, roles and responsibilities — that shapes policy formation and decision making. In the US the political culture encouraged a lively response to NEPA for three reasons:

1   The US courts are constitutionally far more independent of the White House and Congress than British courts are separate from Whitehall and Parliament. It is probably true to say that it was subsequent judicial interpretation that made NEPA the powerful Act that it is, not Congress. In the absence of this prodding by the courts, it is doubtful whether the political and administrative response to NEPA would have been so profound.

2   Partly because of the political role of the courts, NEPA launched an already active environmental lobby into a new role as a quasi public watchdog, protecting, it claimed, the nation from environmental abuse. After over 400 interpretative litigations, many of which have strengthened their political power, the lobby is still constantly poised to exploit the ambiguity of NEPA whenever a suitable occasion arises — and the agencies know it. Thus NEPA has 'politicised' environmentalism to the point where a powerful, non-elected coalition representing largely middle class minority interests has considerable influence over both policy formation and decision making.

3   NEPA has exploited the American dislike of secrecy and the control of information. The 1967 Freedom of Information Act in effect requires all governmental agencies to release information except where they can show that to do so would be prejudicial to the public interest. While many agencies have exploited this provision, [6] it remains true that all kinds of information leading up to decisions and policy analysis are generally more accessible to the public than is the case here in Britain where there are statutory guarantees for official secrecy and ministerial discretion. Indeed, not even Parliament has the power to extract information from its own civil service in the way that the US Congress can subpoena witnesses and force them to testify under oath. Consequently, Americans are almost overwhelmed by a plethora of detail, and even the most conscientious environmental pressure groups cannot handle the hundred or so EISs that are produced each month. However, if there has to be an extreme then overload is preferable to secrecy, for at least the premises underlying decision making are subject to public discussion before commitments are made.

The third lesson from the US experience concerns the role of specific personalities, rather than political institutions, in determining policy. This is an aspect of policy analysis that is little understood by those who remain outside the inner circles of influence. However, if the first instalment of the Crossman diaries is anything to go by (although this is merely one controversial man's view of a very complicated process), then this characteristic of decision making appears to be of even greater significance over here than across the Atlantic. By whatever means equivalent policy may be decided in this country, it is important that as many people as possible are aware of the wider implications of EIA and that their views are communicated to the few who will inevitably make the final judgement.

Major questions facing the UK

It is important to realise that the demand for EIA is not that the non-quantifiables are somehow accounted, but because many people honestly believe that our political culture is not adapted to deal with the modern environmental challenge. In particular there is a concern that our traditional decision making procedures and institutional arrangements do not enable us to review adequately the wider implications of policy formulation and strategic choice. What in fact are its weaknesses?

The 'honesty' of decision making procedures

Students of administrative theory tell us that organisations have a curious way of restricting breadth of vision and of diminishing a sense of direct responsibility. [7] Joseph Sax, a noted American lawyer and a strong advocate of the EIS, puts it this way:

> ... the special knowledge of the highly trained mind produces its own limitations, and it may be argued that expertise sacrifices the insight of common sense to the intensity of experience. It breeds an inability to accept new views from the very depths of its preoccupation with its own conclusions ... There is also a class spirit about it, so experts tend to neglect all evidence that does not come from their own ranks. Above all, where human problems are concerned, the expert fails to see that whatever judgments he makes which are not purely factual in nature bring with them a score of values which has no special validity about it. [8]

The point here is that even the most conscientious of administrators can fail to take wider considerations into account, given the pressures of time and interest group concern. This failure is all the more likely if the public is excluded from the crucial deliberations that precede the actual development proposal itself, for complicated decisions are made easier if key figures are shielded from coming directly into contact with real people and situations that will be affected by their judgements. Crossman [9] recounts an argument that he had with his civil servants who tried to dissuade him from going to see an 'actual situation' before making up his mind. They contended that if the Minister did so he would establish a serious precedent and in any case he might be exposed to evidence unavailable to the inspector who had prepared the official report. The function of ministerial 'shielding' is partly to establish consistency and partly to maintain the dominance of the senior administrative echelons in steering ministerial decisions. Crossman was basically happy with this state of affairs:

> Before I became a Minister I used to worry, wake up early in the morning in a panic about whether I had done something wrong. Now I have so many more things to worry about, so many big decisions to take, I find myself worrying much less . . . I find the job of a Minister relatively easy. When I sit at my desk at Prescote and pull out a mass of paper from the red box and see that I have to decide on the boundaries of Conventry or on where to let Birmingham have its new housing land, I find these decisions easy, pleasant, and take them in a fairly lighthearted way. [10]

One consequence of executive 'shielding' is that the present method of assessing environmental impact — namely the public inquiry convened either in response to an objection to refuse planning permission, or to appraise the consequences of very large scale proposals — is inadequate as an assessment device for it does not and cannot guarantee that all proper evidence will be heard, or, indeed, that what evidence is presented will be systematically appraised. The public inquiry relies upon the evidence of objectors and defendants — an *ad hoc* procedure that clearly depends upon the financial and data gathering resources of the organisations and individuals involved.

To be precise, the inquiry *could* provide a much wider review than it presently does, since an inspector has the powers to establish a planning inquiry commission, a panel of experts who would be able to collect and assess a wide range of information prior to the actual inquiry. In fact, in his analysis of the current arrangement for development control, Dobry [11] criticised the inquiry on the grounds that insufficient preparation of the evidence was undertaken during the pre-inquiry review period, and that all too often the nature of environmental impacts was not made public until the inquiry was actually being conducted. In his opinion, this gives the proponents the advantage of presenting the evidence in a biased way while denying the appellants the opportunity of preparing their case fully in advance of the inquiry proceedings.

There is currently some legal debate over whether some kind of EIA is statutory under the 1959 Highways Act. Paragraph 7 of the first schedule requires that official notices about a pending highway plan 'shall state the general effect of the proposed scheme'. Acting on behalf of the Conservation Society, Dobry believes that this is a *de facto* requirement for a wider appraisal, but DoE officials claim that this means merely a general statement about the location and visual appearance of the road. The matter is as yet unresolved, but is being keenly contested by environmental groups. [12]

However, in any case, the enquiry does not and cannot cope with the wider policy questions of, say, transportation planning, agricultural self sufficiency, nuclear power generation or the protection of urban and rural amenity. In fact, under commonly accepted rules of conduct, government employees may not publicly be permitted to question the policies of their departments or ministers, so a line of questioning that leads to the evaluation of the desirability of the proposal is usually quickly suppressed by the inquiry inspector. [13]

It is essential that proper procedures are devised to ensure that environmental implications of major policy areas are fully discussed prior to the preliminary decision to advance any particular proposal.

What form should these new procedures take? One suggestion is to widen the remit of the parliamentary standing committee to give it powers of information retrieval similar to those granted to US congressional committees. At present, backbench MPs are generally excluded from the deliberations of standing or special parliamentary committees, thus, when voting, they often have little idea of the wider implications of the policies Parliament is adopting. The Commons Public Accounts Committee has the best potential for policy review at present, but this is so overworked and understaffed that it cannot hope to do an adequate job. One or a number of permanent bipartisan committees backed by a strong independent research secretariat would provide a suitable focus for submissions by interested parties and an appropriate forum for medium range strategic appraisals of 'umbrella' policy questions which would then provide specific development proposals. This would have the double advantage of placing the determination of key policy matters where it properly belongs – with elected politicians – while freeing the development proposal inquiry to deal with what is often called environmental impact assessment.

There is no reason why such committees could not have a permanent review function, which would look at the effects of policies *a posteriori* as well as *a priori*. For example, the recent report of the Expenditure Committee on New Towns [14] argued that the Government should look again at the objectives of its new towns policy, since the wider implications of its present policies, particularly regarding discrimination against the urban poor and the elderly, have not been properly considered. But the committee has no time, nor remit, to consider the alternatives to new towns that would achieve a better degree of social fairness and improved opportunities for job training. This kind of task could be undertaken by the kind of policy review body as mentioned.

The second proposal is a complementary one but demands a smaller degree of political intervention. This is the notion of overlapping 'tiers' of EIAs, beginning with an initial assessment for all major proposals, including legislation and new departmental policies. This would incorporate the pros and cons of alternative proposals and even linked 'packages' of alternatives, a process that would stimulate imaginative interdepartmental consultation and public discussion. Subsequent EIAs would then be provided for successive steps in policy formation so that final project proposals need not contain (as they currently tend to do) the laborious evaluations of philosophy and policy that are inappropriate at the point of project development. This proposal differs from the earlier one in that major policy evaluation would be conducted by government departments rather than by Parliament, but both would improve upon the present practice of appointing special commissions of inquiry which invariably lack comprehensive terms of reference, and rarely encourage informed debate among interested parties who hold equally sincere but opposing points of view. It also differs from Dobry's suggestion [15] that a 'round table conference' of interested parties should review the evidence for and against a large scale development proposal during the pre-inquiry review. This is a necessary step but should come as a 'second or third tier' review, not a first order appraisal.

It is possible to combine the two proposals, as illustrated in Fig. 15.1. Properly constituted bipartisan parliamentary committees (at the national level) or local authority committees (at the regional level) could be established to review the strategic political, social and economic implications of various major options for such items as energy, transportation, housing and agriculture. They would be advised by a research secretariat which in turn would consult with interdepartmental working teams. Their deliberations, which would be made public, would

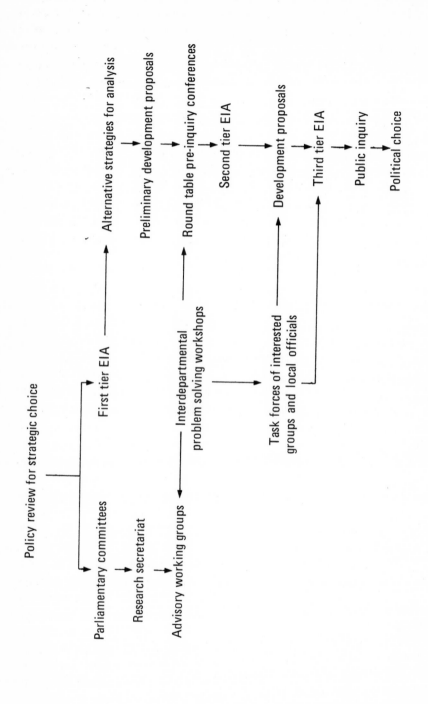

Fig. 15.1   Environmental impact assessment

result in first order policy assessment which would guide subsequent development proposals and plans. These in turn would be analysed through pre-inquiry conferences of interested officials and representatives of the public, or by hearings conducted by planning inquiry commissions (though the former would be preferable). This would produce a second order programme review which would then be used to judge specific proposals. These would be subject to a full EIA at the regional level (but at the national scale where appropriate) based on information supplied by the developer and scrutinised by task forces of local officials and interested citizens representing a variety of local interests. This third order review could form the basis of the present planning inquiry, the results of which would be presented to elected representatives for final political choice. If this kind of procedure were adopted, it is worth emphasising that EIA is probably the wrong phrase. This is about 'review' rather than 'assessment' where environmental implications are only one of a number of principal criteria that should be applied.

Citizens' environmental rights

In his Hamlyn lectures Sir Leslie Scarman [16] made the point that has long been discussed in North America, [17] namely that the ordinary citizen is not able to defend his rights for a minimum standard of environmental quality because legal standing to protect such rights does not exist under common law. 'Modern man', he noted, 'demands not only a safe and healthy but a pleasant and economically viable environment. He sees this as a human right independent of the ownership or possession of property'. What in effect seems to be required is some kind of 'environmental charter' which permits individuals to enjoy a certain level of environmental amenity (that may vary from region to region but has clearly defined absolute minima), and to prosecute anyone or any organisation which threatens such rights. While the protection of such rights is clearly a matter for the courts, the environmental quality standards themselves should be subject to an EIA and determined by national or local political forums.

At present there is little protection (either political or legal) for the ordinary citizen who is affected by second or third order repercussions from large scale development proposals, such as disruption of socially cohesive communities because of new motorway alignments or heightened psychological stress due to increased noise levels. A citizens' environmental charter would ensure that such effects were properly considered as a matter of law and would help to ensure that fair treatment was granted to all individuals.

This is a very important matter. There is strong evidence that many of the disagreeable environmental aspects of major planning proposals fall disproportionately upon the poorer and politically less organised members of society. There would appear to be no authoritative evidence for this in the UK context, but Table 15.1 reveals that the inner city poor of the US

Table 15.1

Environmental hazard by income class

Income class ($)	Suspended particulates ug/m^3	Sulphation $mg\ SO_3/100cm^2/day$
0–2,999	91·3	0·97
3,000–4,999	85·3	0·88
5,000–6,999	79·2	0·78
7,000–9,999	75·4	0·72
10,000–14,999	73·0	0·68
15,000–24,999	68·0	0·60
25,000 and over	64·9	0·52

	Poor		Middle income		Upper income	
			% affected			
	White	Non-white	White	Non-white	White	Non-white
Hypertension	23·5	35·5	11·1	19·7	11·8	26·6
Heart disease	16·6	29·7	6·0	17·2	7·9	26·0
Chronic illness	18·1	29·6	5·8	7·1	n.a.	n.a.

Sources: Council on Environment Quality, 1971, *2nd Annual Report*, p.195; Environmental Protection Agency, 1971, *Our Most Endangered Species*, p.19.

suffer from widespread and often quite severe environmental hazards which undoubtedly endanger their lives and make their living conditions distinctly unpleasant. In the absence of any legally guaranteed mechanism to protect everyone from such insidious environmental costs, it is difficult, if not impossible, for public officials to collect and analyse the distributional relationship between environmental benefits and losses.

Consequently those with the financial and technical resources to avoid the more distasteful spillovers of our industrialised society will continue to do so while those less fortunate will, with only ineffective protest, continue to suffer. Even the much heralded Land Compensation Act does not deal adequately with this problem, because by concentrating on property values, it avoids the whole question of protecting the more important psychological values associated with visual amenity and aural peacefulness, thus making it more rather than less likely that low density areas or low income areas (or both) will experience the worst blight. So without the necessary legal reform, EIAs could actually exacerbate the maldistribution of environmental disamenity since politically powerful groups would more readily exploit the EIA process to their advantage, leaving the less articulate groups further out in the cold.

Some kind of constitutionally guaranteed environmental bill of rights would ensure that every citizen had guarantees to an agreeable level of environmental quality and that public servants had a legal duty to ensure that such guarantees were met. In addition it would place the onus on a developer to prove that no unacceptable harm would be created by his proposal, rather than leaving the burden, as at present, upon the citizen plaintiff to show that he will suffer injury to a rather restricted bundle of rights. Contrary to widespread speculation, in the only case where such a charter has been legislated (the State of Michigan) citizen initiated action against defaulting developers or public officials has not proliferated or stalled the proper administrative machinery. On the contrary, the bureaucratic brokers are kept 'honest' and enjoy the new mood of public confidence that encourages them to act responsively in the wider public interest. [18]

Advocacy and the citizen planner

A US court has recently recommended that the fees of environmental lawyers clearly acting in the public interest be paid either by the losing defendant, or, in those cases 'where litigation serves as a catalyst to effect change and thereby achieves a valuable public service', payment should be by the state 'even where the suit never proceeds to a successful conclusion on the merits'. [19] In practice this principle of sovereign immunity forbids the state to pay the expenses of those prosecuting it, and in the particular case cited that part of the fees that should have been borne by the government was not assessed. But the principle remains. If the public interest is to be defended, it is not reasonable to assume that funds for the purpose will come from philanthropic foundations or individuals. A number of people believe that a certain proportion of the capital costs of a proposed development (say 1 per cent) should be made available to citizens' groups or their advocates to prosecute their interests unhindered by lack of financial resources. [20] If the kind of equity problem referred to in the previous section is to be avoided, then some form of planning aid becomes all the more necessary.

Sir Leslie Scarman is correct when he favours an extension of legal aid to include 'the financing of representative or test actions where a principle or policy of genuine importance arises', [21] but this should be extended also to more general cases if fundamental human rights are to be safeguarded. It is not simply a matter of vindicating rights, but of ensuring that this is done in a reasonable and authoritative manner.

If this idea is accepted then it may be possible to link the EIA to environmental education and planning design, especially for neighbourhood scale proposals which affect people's immediate living environments. Given the right kind of incentives, there is growing evidence that citizens' groups will work with planners in a responsive and responsible manner to create, as a team, pleasant and habitable communities. This not only produces beneficial results, but can lead to a much needed sense of trust in planning and policy machinery generally − a desirable state of affairs − which is sadly lacking at the local level. Whether the 'citizen as planner' concept can work effectively at the regional district or county level is more problematical, but there is evidence that a responsibly active citizenry can assist planners and policy makers on these larger scales, given proper mechanisms for consultation and problem solving.

Environmental education

The nature of public response to EIAs and to participation in planning will depend upon innovations in education at all levels of learning. In its purest form, environmental education is simply 'consciousness raising' − the opening up of the mind to new levels of awareness and experience. This should encourage a greater sense of responsibility to and understanding of the interests of others, while improving personal knowledge of what is practically possible (and impossible). Properly speaking, an environmentally aware citizenry is a prerequisite of environmental impact assessment, since such people should be able to cope more effectively with the processes of social change and hence come to grips with the deepseated inconsistencies that infiltrate our values and question our actions.

One of the many consequences of NEPA in the US has been to

214

encourage government agencies to devise new procedures for interdepartmental consultation and problem solving. Two of the more successful
outcomes are the problem solving workshop (where professionals with a
variety of skills meet regularly to identify, analyse, and solve particular
problems) and the study leave sabbatical (where agency officials leave
their offices for short, intensive study periods and refresher courses). It is
possible to combine the two: for example, to offer a postgraduate degree
in environmental studies where individuals from both the public and
private sectors meet for short, intensive seminar courses, and then
cooperate as study teams over much longer periods while remaining in
their jobs. They thus lose no salary, yet are able to cope much more
effectively with the management issues they have to face. Needless to say,
the universities which might provide such 'courses' would benefit
immeasurably from such an arrangement, for the educational process
would work both ways.

Taking decisions

At the present time most planning decisions are taken by senior civil
servants, not by politicians. This is a matter of expediency, not
impropriety. It has been estimated that in theory the Environment
Secretary has only 13 seconds on average to consider each of the planning
cases that requires his attention. Thus it is quite impossible for him to be
aware of all the facts of a case, let alone to be able to weigh these in all
fairness to the various publics concerned. If the EIA is properly done, it
should indicate who gets what, who loses what, how, when and why. This
is the stuff of politics and it is entirely appropriate that this kind of
evidence be placed on the minister's desk or on the tables of local
authority councillors. The business of weighing this information is
properly the responsibility of the elected official, so it is essential that the
EIA be prepared in such a manner as to make his job possible and just.
Given this to be the case, then it is reasonable to assume that society will
endeavour to choose individuals whom they believe are capable of
executing this difficult job in their interest; and if we also assume that
their interests are made manifest by means of the legal, educational and
political innovations discussed above, then the EIA can and should
become a valuable instrument for improving the political process. After
all, the EIA is not an end in itself, but a guide to better political
judgement and performance. This is the ultimate focus for our attention.

215

Conclusion

The demand for environmental impact assessment is part of a more general anxiety about the functioning of our political and legal institutions, particularly in the arena of what might loosely be described as 'environmental justice' — the protection of the rights of all living things to an acceptable minimum quality of existence. This concern also extends to procedures for decision taking so that the interests of all affected publics (both present and unborn) are fairly and adequately represented. If these anxieties are to be mollified then the EIA must be considered as one element in a package of reform. For if we can assume that the public is mobilised by a system of environmental rights, by planning aid, and by improved educational curricula to take the EIA seriously and to elect its representatives with the knowledge that they will be ultimately responsible for determining the proper course of action, then the EIA should enhance the status of the politician, place public participation in its proper perspective and generally safeguard the proper functioning of democracy. However, if the EIA is merely to be tacked on to the present institutional pattern of policy making and decision taking, then its function might prove to be detrimental to the future of democracy — and, paradoxically, to our environmental wellbeing.

Discussion

O'Riordan made a number of specific suggestions which became the focus of considerable, albeit inconclusive, debate. Turning first to the matter of parliamentary review of strategic policy questions, *Warren* (Cabinet Office) remarked that in view of the long parliamentary traditions and the enormous demands upon the time and expertise of MPs it would be very difficult to reform the existing committee system with any measure of success. The unsatisfactory outcome following Richard Crossman's proposals for a Ministry of Science and Technology and a Standing Committee on Science and Technology illustrated this point all too well. *Woolf* (Lawyers' Ecology Group) pointed out that Parliament did have powers to undertake this kind of reform if it so wished; indeed, it could improve the existing procedures of policy review without substantial change to its committee structure. *Brooks* (Liverpool) stressed that existing committees, particularly the Public Accounts Committee and its various subcommittees, already had the power to obtain relevant information on all matters under its remit. For example, after receiving a lot of evidence the Select Committee on Science and Technology advised against the construction of light water reactors largely, but not exclusively, on the matter of cost. He admitted, however, that the Public Accounts Committee generally looked at well established programmes, such as Concorde, where the major policy decisions had already been made, and was not suitably designed to review the wider implications of incipient policies or even ongoing projects.

Despite Brooks' optimism over the powers of parliamentary committees to obtain information, both he and *Lord Zuckerman* agreed that the extent to which any committee could extend its enquiries would be subject to parliamentary approval, and in practice it would be most unlikely that senior civil servants or their ministers would be required to discuss publicly the various issues underlying their policy prescriptions. A number of participants observed that British parliamentary committees did not have the powers to subpoena evidence, but in any case, ministers and their senior advisers were well known for their ability to sidetrack specific questions. In addition, it was common for MPs on committees to use their question period as a forum to make various (and quite frequently irrelevant) political points.

There was definitely a consensus of informed opinion that parliamentary committees were neither suitable nor properly staffed to undertake the kind of detailed policy investigation suggested by O'Riordan and found with congressional committees in the United States. Certainly the kind of work undertaken by the Central Policy Review Staff or the new Agricultural Policy Unit at the University of Reading were not viewed as desirable models, since these tended to be introvert think tanks whose deliberations were not subject to informed debate or political assessment.

By way of summary of this matter of strategic policy review, *Brooks* remarked that where a proposed Bill has passed its second reading and was subject to final committee appraisal, there could be an opportunity for the committee to call upon expert advice. Thus the legislative committee could become a specialist inquiry body of the standard of a Royal Commission, with a remit to look at the wider impact of a proposed statute. In addition it was possible for parliamentary committees to conduct *ad hoc* and/or special inquiries to look at specific matters of policy, subject, as always, to parliamentary approval and its setting of the relevant terms of reference.

Turning to the second and third tier assessment, *Lyddon* (Scottish Development Department) commented that the structure plan review procedures, though not adequate, did provide some opportunity for second tier assessment. *Shaw* (Norfolk County Council) disagreed: neither regional strategies not structure plans adequately took into account the social and economic changes that they ultimately created. He noted, however, that the new Parliamentary Committee on Regional Affairs did provide a forum for looking at some of the implications of regional strategies. This could provide a promising arena for second tier review on a case by case basis.

As for the third tier review, *Lyddon* repeated his plea for a change of name; it was not a narrowly focused environmental impact assessment that was required, but a broad based development impact statement. This should look at a proposal, define what it was trying to do, state how it proposed to do it, and show who would gain and lose as a consequence. This would help everyone concerned to identify the issues and pinpoint the areas of complaint and the opportunities for compromise and conciliation. This would also help those who wished to object to appear before a public enquiry that had already debated the wider issues of policy and need. Given this, the third tier review should confine itself to the specifics of a particular development proposal. It was possible therefore to envisage two levels of inquiry, one dealing with the wider questions of regional strategy and policy options at the structure plan scale, the other limited to the merits of a given proposal.

As for coordinative procedures, *Warren* observed that despite the restrictions of ministerial responsibility and departmental financial accountancy, departments did talk to each other at various levels. Interdepartmental workshops may not be formalised, but they did exist. He was also concerned whether the cost of these three levels of review could be justified in terms of the value of the final product. *Lyddon* responded that since existing resources were not deployed very well, reviews could be made with existing manpower. But what might be the cost, he asked, of not undertaking these reviews? Delay, antagonism and possibly a deep seated lack of trust in the system. *Woolf* agreed: unless the system was seen to be responding openly and credibly to the new demands made on it, then there would always be deep suspicion of the speedy solution. Nevertheless he recognised that there should be clearly defined limits to the review procedures.

O'Riordan's second proposal, that of some form of mid-career professional workshop centred on real life regional issues, prompted the remark from *Lyddon* that some mechanism which brought together practising professionals, academics, and possibly on occasion politicians, in an ongoing seminar arrangement appeared most attractive. Public officials would have the opportunity to learn new techniques and provide a sensible, realistic criticism of academic research but, above all, everyone would benefit from the experience of having to work as part of a team. The opportunity to cross departments and disciplines would be invaluable. In addition the outcome of the programme should provide practical and beneficial results for the community as a whole. *Clark* (Aberdeen) remarked that something of this sort already existed: an environmental liaison committee made up of university faculty and local authority staff was activated whenever a major development proposal was advanced in the Aberdeen area. The committee's advice was certainly respected precisely because it reflected the views of a cross section of informed opinion. He also suggested that elected members would welcome and benefit from participation in some kind of multidisciplinary seminar, a point with which both *Lyddon* and *Hookway* (Countryside Commission) concurred. But the university need not be the venue for such a programme, merely the catalyst; certainly there was no suggestion that either the university or these multidisciplinary task forces would determine public policy.

Notes

[1]   Although the Roskill Commission tried to quantify everything it could, it could not predict the kind of political reaction that greeted its recommendation that Cublington be the approved site. It should be stressed, however, that the Commission dug its own grave by noting that Cublington was superior as regards costs and the saving of travel time, while on the basis of environmental and planning considerations, Foulness was the preferable location. The two sites were simply not quantifiably comparable on the sole basis of cost-benefit accounting. See R. Kimber and J. J. Richardson, 'The Roskillers: Cublington fights the airport', in Kimber and Richardson, *Campaigning for the Environment*, London 1974, pp.165–211.

[2]   The team has published an interim report which has been circulated to interested parties. See J. Catlow and C. J. Thirlwell, 'Environmental impact analysis study: interim report', Department of the Environment, London 1975.

[3]   The legislative history of NEPA is more fully described by F. R. Anderson, *NEPA and the Courts*, Johns Hopkins Press, Baltimore 1974.

[4]   In the original compromise between Jackson, who wanted tough measures, and Aspinall, who wanted no change, Aspinall was led to believe that this was a sufficiently qualifying phrase to give the provision little

force. But a second document prepared by Aspinall's counsel gave a reading to the phrase that essentially adopted Jackson's view. Anderson, op. cit., p.9.

[5] The full wording of s. 102(2) (C) reads as follows:

Congress authorizes and directs that, to the fullest extent possible, all agencies of the Federal Government shall include in every recommendation or report on proposals for legislation and other major Federal actions significantly affecting the quality of the human environment, a detailed statement by the responsible official on —

(i) the environmental impact of the proposed action,
(ii) any adverse environmental effects which cannot be avoided should the proposal be implemented,
(iii) alternatives to the proposed action,
(iv) the relationship between local short-term uses of man's environment and the maintenance and enhancement of long-term productivity, and
(v) any irreversible and irretrievable commitments of resources which would be involved in the proposed action should it be implemented.

[6] See N. Wade, 'Freedom of information: officials thwart public right to know', *Science,* vol.175, 1975, pp.498–502.
[7] For American examples, see A. Downs, *Inside Bureaucracy,* Little, Brown, Boston 1967; and Y. Dror, *Public Policy Making Re-examined,* Chandler, New York 1968. For a British study see F. Brown, *The Administrative Process in Britain*, Methuen, London 1968.
[8] J. Sax, 'Environmental law; the US experience', in G. Morley (ed.) *Canada's Environment: The Law on Trial,* University of Manitoba Agassiz Centre for Water Studies, Winnipeg 1974, pp.164–93.
[9] Crossman Diaries, as published in the *Sunday Times,* 2 February 1975.
[10] Ibid.
[11] For a discussion of this and related issues, see J. Tyme, 'Motorway inquiries', *New Scientist,* 6 November 1975, pp.319–21.
[12] G. Dobry, *Review of the Development Control System. Final Report*, HMSO, London 1975, pp.81–3.
[13] Op. cit., p.319.
[14] 13th Report of the Expenditure Committee, *New Towns,* HMSO, London 1975.
[15] Dobry, op. cit., p.83.

[16]   Sir Leslie Scarman, *The English Law: New Dimensions*, Stewart, London 1974.

[17]   See J. Sax, *Defending the Environment*, Knopf, New York 1970; G. Morley (ed.) *Canada's Environment: The Law on Trial*, 1974, and G. Morley (ed.) *Ask the People*, 1973, both University of Manitoba Agassiz Centre for Water Studies, Winnipeg.

[18]   The Michigan statute is the 1971 Michigan Environmental Protection Act which grants citizens legal standing to sue regardless of whether they have specific economic or proprietory interests. In the three years following its enactment there were only 55 cases, only 20 of which went to full trial, and all were dealt with speedily. Surprisingly the chief plaintiffs have been the public agencies, especially the pollution control departments who now have statutory rights to prosecute when formerly they would often have to acquiesce to polluters' claims that pollution control standards were too strict. In addition, the Act has helped the agencies to get out of a politically 'hot' situation, since citizens' groups have sometimes forced them to act when otherwise they might have been indecisive in the face of powerful pressure groups. See Sax, op. cit. note [8], pp.101–85.

[19]   See the President's Council on Environmental Quality, *Fifth Annual Report,* US Government Printing Office, Washington 1974; p.394.

[20]   See J. Sax, op. cit. 1974; T. Aldous, *Battle for the Environment*, Faber, London 1972; J. Bugler, *Polluting Britain: A Report*, Penguin Books, London 1972.

[21]   Scarman, op. cit., p.37.

Epilogue

LORD ZUCKERMAN

Much ground has been covered in the work of this book and in the subsequent discussions, but while we have assumed that all of us are concerned with the same objectives, we have not defined them with any precision. Mr Meyers outlined the broad purposes of American environmental legislation. What he said in effect was that the environmental act is on the statute book because the Federal Government wants to do its best to protect the environment against misuse, not only in the interests of this generation, but for those of subsequent generations. He also said that because of general social demand, economic growth would have to continue, whatever the framework of environmental constraints.

It is from that point of view and not in isolation that we have been considering EIA. It would be a bad thing if EIAs were imposed on us through outside pressure, and this book has advocated that Whitehall should move slowly in this field. EIAs, either on the American or some other model, dare not be treated as a virtue in themselves. Unless we can assure ourselves that they will help us – and our political masters – to decide upon the right alternatives, where there are alternatives, they could prove a burdensome appendage to our existing planning laws.

The authors are a very mixed group of academics, professionals, and administrators. They share different kinds of experience. There are those who, from the beginning of their professional lives, have been working on the ground in order to ensure, for example, the wholesomeness of our water supplies, or the best use of land. Others are academics. Some have just recently started as environmental administrators in national and international organisations. This author has been involved in almost every phase of the political development of the environmental movement in this country and has also watched its growth abroad. All the authors differ greatly in their experience of the subjects under consideration.

Clients for whom professional environmentalists cater also differ widely in their concerns. Most of us wish to continue as members of a democratic society, but a large part of the public is totally apathetic about environmental matters. They are probably the majority. A few are utterly selfish. They do not want to see change because change will affect 'the view from their windows'. There are 'way out' environmental enthusiasts who often unrealistically stir up trouble for poor officials, and sometimes for industry. They may keep us on our toes, but they often go too far because they do not offer alternatives to action.

Have we the necessary skills and techniques to go in for a régime of EIAs? The problem of forecasting has been discussed and there was a reference to the International Institute for Systems Analysis in Vienna. This Institute is helped by the best consultants in the world, but it is still to be seen whether the work it does in analysing complicated social and political problems is going to help any politicians. There was a clear illustration of this difficulty when Dr. Hey said that at present even the analysis on a model basis of such apparently simple problems as water flow, river flow and sedimentation hardly provides a basis for prediction. It has been stated also that one cannot make a reliable impact statement about noise. There was a reminder of the Roskill report. The best thing about it was that it made people aware of its defects. Perhaps that is a useful function of impact statements. Hazard assessments, technological assessments, and environmental impact assessments are attempts to peer into a very capricious future. We try to peer into it by methods which themselves are frail, and into a future which is undergoing change as we search. There is nothing static about the material of our enquiries. Nor should we imagine that as members of the species *Homo sapiens* we, the enquirers, are going to continue unchanged over biological time. There will also be major changes in the ecosystems around us.

Environmental impact statements can at best be only partially scientific. Each case that we investigate is unique in some aspect or other, and once we do something about it, the problem itself changes. This is totally unlike what happens in proper scientific enquiry. If an experiment is carried out, or certain observations are made under specified conditions leading to specified conclusions, the whole area of enquiry can be verified or disproved by repetition. When this cannot be done, we are not dealing with practical science.

In the case of cost–benefit studies, unless one is fully aware of all the alternatives so that one is definitely comparing like with like, and comparing different approaches to the same goal, one merely risks being bemused with figures.

How then can environmental impact assessments, which deal both with risk–benefit and cost–benefit, help in the determination of policy? Mr Searle asked whether policy issues could be brought in at an early phase of the preparation of an environmental impact statement. If one did that one would soon be discussing something very different from the case under consideration. One might be discussing the background to all governmental policy. Think of the difficulties. The Permanent Secretary of the Department of the Environment might, for example, find himself arguing with his colleagues in the Treasury — before his master starts arguing with the Chancellor of the Exchequer — to determine what contribution to a cut in public expenditure would have to be made by his department's budget. Supposing that it had been decided that £100 million should come off defence, what basis would he then have for arguing that less should be trimmed from the environmental budget rather than from that of health or education?

Such matters belong to the very centre of the arena of politics. Several authors have admitted that, in effect, this is precisely what environmental impact statements do. Others have suggested that a true quantitative element can be introduced into the field of choice. But surely value judgements override? If we are not very careful impact statements may expose us to the danger of converting genuine political issues into bogus technical ones. Do we want politicians to shelter behind the backs of the scientists when dealing with issues like the relative value to society of, for example, a unit of expenditure in education, as against one devoted to the preservation of a particular landscape?

There are dangers in EIAs. Lord Ashby suggested that they could erode the democratic process. This author was challenged when considering changing modes of behaviour. If you were to go to Africa you would see environmentalists, usually white skinned, everywhere trying to change the modes of behaviour of the black indigenous people. People tell them not to burn down trees; that changes their normal way of life. Vast tracts of country are declared conservation areas and traditional hunting grounds then become closed. There must be more conservation areas in South Africa per head of white population than one would find in the rest of the world! When we deal with environmental issues we are interfering with ways of life. We must be careful lest, by developing a pseudo science, we hand over the process of democratic decision to vested interests.

Dr O'Riordan asked whether or not the institution of the system of EISs would call for the building up of a new professional class. Would it not divert people from more productive activities, from activities of greater social significance? The answer would be 'yes'. The budget of the EPA, after three years of existence, is already $7 billion! Central administration costs some $800 million. Mr Meyers has stated that, in addition, each Department of State in the US now has its own new band of impact statement writers, and that twenty-two states have got their 'micro-EPAs'. Who says that a system of EISs would not divert people's attention from more productive activities?

Of course there are environmental risks against which we have to guard. Toxic substances leak into the environment. There are risks about amenities, risks about the exhaustion of unrenewable resources, risks even in the misuse of the vegetative cover of this globe of ours. But we need to be careful. Rigid standards in any of these matters are totally unnecessary. We need to beware lest a minority of over enthusiastic environmentalists impose on all of us, on all who are concerned about the proper care of the environment, what would be the equivalent of the Delaney amendment to the food and drugs laws of America, and so transform all our planning regulations. That is a frightening prospect. Scientific administrators would have to waste time trying to prove negatives. That is something which no proper scientist ought to be prepared to do. Before any new drug or consumer product can be introduced to the market, the FDA has to give proof that it would not have any cancerous effect in any species of animal, apart from human beings. Obviously that cannot be proved. The Delaney clause has led to the concept of zero risk, or of no risk. The head of the FDA is slowly having to get accepted a new definition of zero risk. People have to be rational in their approach to problems of social risk.

This is where education comes in. What has to be conveyed is the understanding that we live in a world of risks. That is what is to be understood from Dr Brook's reference to 'the structure of informed confrontation'. People must accept that they are mortal, and that nothing which scientists or administrators can do -- and nothing that our religious leaders can do — will in the end save any of us from the grave.

There is some uncertainty as to what is meant by the term 'participation' in the present context, or by 'the principle of transparency of opposition'.

Will EIAs help us to a better future? In a qualified way 'yes', provided we do not rush the job, provided we do not allow ourselves to be pushed by our EEC partners into the acceptance of administrative measures which neither we nor they will in all honesty ever be able to implement.

Dr Hey observed that our knowledge is often less than perfect. This author would suggest that our knowledge is *always* less than perfect. Lord Ashby reminded us that environmental assessments were made even in the days of the Ark. Paul Valery, that great French poet, closer to our own generation, put it very nicely when he said that 'we move into the future backwards'. No number of environmental impact statements will stop us from doing so. We therefore need to be careful that we get our social and political priorities right. Let us not be judged ten years or so from now as a pack of enthusiasts who, like King Canute, had to embark on an extravagant experiment in order to prove the impossible.

List of participants

Professor Emeritus Lord Zuckerman, OM, KCB, FRS
Lord Ashby, FRS
C. T. Baldwin, University of East Anglia
Dr J. P. Barkham, University of East Anglia
C. G. Bentham, University of East Anglia
A. I. Biggs, Confederation of British Industries
Dr E. Brooks, University of Liverpool
M. Cassidy, Yorke Rosenberg Mardall
Dr B. Clark, University of Aberdeen
Professor K. M. Clayton, University of East Anglia
A. W. Davies, Anglian Water Authority
Dr D. E. C. Eversley, Centre for Environmental Studies
Dr M. George, Nature Conservancy Council
R. Goodier, Nature Conservancy Council
D. Hammer, Commission of the European Communities
Dr R. D. Hey, University of East Anglia
Professor T. P. Hill, University of East Anglia
R. J. S. Hookway, Countryside Commission
S. P. Johnson, Commission of the European Communities
G. H. Kinchin, UK Atomic Energy Authority
D. P. Lock, Town and Country Planning Association
W. D. C. Lyddon, Scottish Development Department
S. Meyers, US Environmental Protection Agency
Dr M. Moseley, University of East Anglia
Dr B. Moss, University of East Anglia
Dr T. O'Riordan, University of East Anglia
D. W. Pearce, University of Leicester
G. Searle, Earth Resources Research Ltd
J. M. Shaw, Norfolk County Council
Dr J. R. Tarrant, University of East Anglia
P. M. Townroe, University of East Anglia
Dr D. Train, Cremer and Warner
C. Ward, Town and Country Planning Association
Dr P. T. Warren, the Cabinet Office
A. D. Woolf, Lawyers' Ecology Group

Miss Z. Zuckerman, Docklands Development Team

Index

The editors

Timothy O'Riordan received his PhD from the University of Cambridge in 1967, then spent eight years teaching in Geography Departments in Canada, the United States and New Zealand before returning to his present post as Reader in the School of Environmental Sciences at the University of East Anglia. His book on *Environmentalism* has just been published (Pion, London 1976), and he is also the co-editor of *The American Environment: Perception and Policies* (with J. W. Watson, Wiley, Chichester, 1976) and *National Resource Decisions in a Democratic Society* (with W. R. D. Sewell, Westview Press, Boulder, Colorado, 1976).

Richard Hey graduated from the University of Bristol with a BSc degree and completed his doctorate at the University of Cambridge in 1972. Since 1968 he has been a Lecturer at the School of Environmental Sciences, University of East Anglia. He has previously been co-editor of *The Management of Water Resources in England & Wales* (with B. M. Funnell, Saxon House, Farnborough, 1974) and *Science, Technology and Environmental Management* (with T. D. Davies, Saxon House, Farnborough, 1975). He is also a consultant river engineer and hydrologist.

Other SAXON HOUSE publications